Dogs Are Better Than People:
Encountering Good and Evil in the Animal Rescue World

Lori Bradley-Millstein

Text and graphics copyright
© 2016 Lori Bradley-Millstein
All rights reserved. No part of this book may be reproduced in any form without written consent from the author or publisher: info@ianimalpress.com

ISBN: 0692776311
ISBN-13: 978-0692776315 (iAnimal Press)

DEDICATION

For Hawkins, the handsome, loving dog who introduced me to pit bulls and made me fall in love with the breed. Hawkins; you were by my side for so many years; I will always love and miss you.

CONTENTS

1 The Comfort of Dogs
2 Neighborhood Cat Lady
3 Flophouse for Dogs
4 Saddest Summer
5 Pain and Bliss
6 The Pornographic Hypnotist
7 Hawk in the Hood
8 Last Days in Asheville
9 Chopper Goes to Baltimore
10 A Dog With No Ears
11 Confronting the Beast
12 The Tightest Bond
13 Sable for Christmas
14 Bliss
15 Kindred Spirits
16 Ten Black Dogs
17 Worldwide Woof
18 Freewheeling Disease
19 Deadly Insects
20 Elvira
21 There is Evil
22 And There is Good
23 The Cat House
24 The Sadness of Southern Dogs

25 Just an Accident
26 I Am So Glad You Are Here
27 Moving On

ACKNOWLEDGMENTS

Thank you to my wonderful writing group members; Kathryn Kulpa, Mary Callahan, Kiersten Marek, Laura Stout-LaTour, and many others I've enjoyed meeting over the years. I never would have completed this book without your encouragement, editing expertise, sense of fun and joy, and lots of baked goods and coffee. Many thanks also to the dedicated faculty members of the Professional Writing Program at the University of Massachusetts Dartmouth for encouragement and feedback. Very special thanks to all the selfless, dedicated animal rescuers, shelter volunteers, shelter workers and animal control officers out there who work in the trenches every day helping animals. They will always inspire me, and through their heroic actions they make this world a bearable place in which to live.

 1. The Comfort of Dogs

Why am I sitting indoors typing away at a petition on a glorious late July day like today? I don't have to be doing this. I'm a teacher. I don't work during the summer – at least at a regularly scheduled job. I work at what I want to work at and that usually involves animals in some way. This petition does. Writing it scares me. I had to write it. Nobody else did and I waited two days to see if someone would. I'm writing it to help put an end to years of horrific cruelty to animals taking place, as I write, at a tenant farm in a little backward town that lies just outside of this city. It may not make any difference to write this, but I can't sit on my couch on this nice summer day with any peace-of-mind until this petition is out getting signed.

Town officials turned away and didn't take action after a similar first discovery because the landlord is a good old boy and a connected townie. That is why I'm writing this petition - putting my name to it and sending it out along all my social media channels – and, why doing it scares me. I can easily be identified and the petition may impact some very nasty people. But more than feeling fear, I'm feeling disgust at people who think they can continue to get away with abuses like this.

These tenant farmers breed farm animals that they torture for years then kill and eat at private parties and local festivals. This is horrific enough, but they also breed dogs, which are sold to dodgy people to be traded in drug deals or used in the underground dog-fighting rings that infest this little city. I'm nervous about confronting these nasty people – the lowest of the low. I worry about my own safety but more I worry about my hapless husband and my own pack of dogs, two of which were rescued from this very farm.

My dogs are the main reason I am putting the petition out to the public. They suffered in a hell created by ruthless, compassionless people and they survived. They love being alive. They deserve to live a decent life free of suffering before they die. All animals do.

Sable is over fourteen years old. She is a small brown pit bull with a big attitude, in spite of her several early years on the tenant farm. She was kept outdoors all year round, here in the volatile New England weather, even though a skin infection had rendered her hairless. A friend knew someone renting space at the farm and my friend witnessed the substandard living conditions of hundreds of animals.

Sable was being used as a breeding dog, inbreeding with her own pups which were given younger than three weeks of age to people who sold them on the street – popular thinking among dog fighters is that if puppies are removed from their mother and litter at a very young age they will not bond with other dogs and will fight more aggressively against their own kind in the ring.

My friend somehow was able to stash Sable in the trunk of her car and drive her out of the farm that day and that is how I came to be her foster mom. She was naked and she was wild. Her hair was lost to a body-wide skin infection caused by parasites in the skimpy pile of hay she was given as a bed to curl up in outdoors over the course of four winters. I don't know how she survived those years, but she certainly has a lust for life. The first day I brought her home, she ran into the living room and jumped up in the corner of the main sofa and looked at me and the other dogs with her golden eyes, daring any of us to move her. Her skin was peeling off in sheets because of the infection and I didn't want her in the living room, least of all on the sofa, but she lived there and grew old happily in that corner on that pile of pillows. Her skin healed quickly with antibiotics and she eventually grew a beautiful dark brown-orange coat.

Like all dogs, and especially pit bulls, Sable has a distinct and quirky personality that endears her to us. I can't bear to think of all the other Sables or any other animals still suffering away at that disgusting farm. So, I'm sitting indoors writing this petition.

So many people want to do something to help animals suffering in similar circumstances but they don't. Sometimes they, like me, are afraid. Perhaps if I had small children at home I might be more cautious and reluctant to expose my name on a petition like this, so I understand that people are afraid, but others are unwittingly cruel in their apathy. I learned this about people at a young age and it made me dislike them and distrust them.

I loved animals as a kid and bullies soon discovered they could have their best effect on me if they told me a horrible story involving animal cruelty. I'd cry. I'd scream in frustration that people could be so awful as to even think this stuff up, but it never did any good to react in this way.

Most people just didn't seem to care. As an adult, I found that I needed to make connections with like-minded people who shared my compassion for animals. Through my husband and other fellow animal-loving friends I found some humans I could trust and with whom I could communicate in ways that felt authentic. I didn't have to put on an act to get along with animal-people the way I always seemed to do with people who were indifferent to species other than human.

The truth is that I always preferred the company of dogs and most animals to people. Really, I preferred the company of just about any animal to that of humans. I say this with my tongue-in-cheek but I really do feel more at peace around animals; whether I'm snuggling with one of my dogs, watching the elephants rocking slowly back and forth together in the local zoo, or tossing corn to the squirrels in our little back yard. My husband accepts this about me, in fact, he is the same way and the mutual discomfort we feel when surrounded by groups of humans was one of our mutual first attractions. Even in art school we preferred spending the weekends camping in the lonely North Georgia woods to going to wild school parties.

Unlike my husband, I wanted badly to fit into society and when I was much younger I worked hard at it. But in spite of all my effort at obtaining social skills, jobs, friends, popularity - trying desperately to embrace the tricky intricacies of human communication - I'm very content at the end of a day to just lie down with my dogs and forget all about people.

My siblings were teenagers when I was born. I was the proverbial late-in-childbearing-life mistake. My brothers and sisters always generated a lot of drama. Our house was extremely noisy. My mother's capacity for affection and attention was spread pretty thin between us all, and often I'd be left lying on my back on a little blue and pink striped blanket - back down, face up - on a very scratchy brown couch in the living room. I remember it clearly, like it was yesterday, even though I wasn't yet old enough to crawl. I remember rolling myself over off the little blanket and face down into the crack of the cushions on the scratchy brown couch, my nose smashed into the unforgiving fabric and not being able to breathe. My brother saved me that time. I was what my mother called a whiny baby.

When I finally learned how to crawl I crept right off that couch and pushed my way into the nest of warm belly and fur provided by our family dog. Pepper was a big and very fat Springer Spaniel. She accepted me like her own puppy and from then on licked me and encouraged me to curl up with her on the floor. I stopped whining. My mother was so happy about my silence that she made Pepper my babysitter - plopping me down with the soft black and white dog when she was busy with housework and my attention-grabbing brothers and sisters. Pepper was more than a babysitter to me. She was my surrogate mother.

Pepper and I spent many pleasant afternoons in the backyard - sniffing at flowers in my mother's well-tended gardens, digging in the dirt, and lazing in the sun. I learned to walk by pulling myself up to stand holding on to Pepper's long velvety ears. I finally got my mother's full attention when I suddenly developed a rasping, dry cough. The cough became persistent, but I didn't have a fever or any other symptoms. After a couple of weeks my mother took me to the doctor.

He couldn't figure out what was going on. Much to my mother's dismay, I stopped coughing in the doctor's office every time and she was worried he thought she was just another neurotic mom.

   The doctor was a down-to-earth and kindly guy and he offered to drop by one afternoon on his way home from the office for a cup of coffee. That way he could observe me in the home environment and, hopefully, hear this mysterious coughing. He stopped by that week and this time I didn't disappoint. I was constantly making that disturbing hacking sound. The doctor was pretty wise and it didn't take him long to figure out that I was barking like the dog. I was barking when the dog barked and we both barked for the same reasons - when we were hungry, when we wanted attention, when we needed to poop.

   Barking made sense to me. It was simple. A simple language used to get basic, simple needs met. The language used by my siblings and parents was complex, confusing, and frequently angry in tone. The doctor laughed and laughed and said I'd bonded with the family dog to the extent that I preferred the company of dogs to humans, and in fact, thought I was a dog.

   The doctor's visit kicked up some guilt in my family and after that they started paying me more attention and reading to me a lot. They were worried

I'd never learn to speak like a human being. For a while I resisted. I preferred to bark. But, after some time, I came to recognize the beauty in human language - and its ability to tell stories. I started to love books and reading. But, I still preferred the stable, simple, unconditional love and company of a dog. Afterwards, the best days of my childhood were spent curled up with Pepper and a good book.

2. Neighborhood Cat Lady

By the time I was eight-years old I was already dividing people into two distinct groups by their capacity to either enjoy killing or loving animals. The first group I referred to (and still do) as Killer Apes. (Not that I think there are any apes nearly as dangerous as humans.) The second group was (is) Earth Angels. The Crazy Cat Lady was definitely an Earth Angel.

Now, I realize that I probably seem as eccentric to people now as the neighborhood Cat Lady once seemed to me long ago. Her externally attractive house was crammed with cats from corner to corner indoors - covering all the countertops and every available surface. My friends and I went over to her house every month or so to help her clean litter boxes – directed to do so by one Mom or another – and entering the small house, I was overwhelmed by the sheer amount of life swirling around me, rubbing against my legs, begging to be picked up, and crying for food or attention. The cats stared down at us from shelf tops and I knew from the look in their eyes that they were in control of the house. The Cat Lady wasn't in control of her life. It was no longer her house. It belonged to the cats. We were uninvited and rare visitors to a house not opened often to humans. My friends and I scooped poop while we elbowed each other and laughed behind the Cat Lady's back. We were out of our comfort zone. Unusual living situations, where someone dared step outside of what was accepted as normal bored living, were rare in our very ordinary suburban neighborhood. But secretly we all admired the Cat Lady's refusal to conform - her joyful crankiness, obsession, and utter refusal to be sucked in by either the pity or the scorn of her neighbors.

Two other defining childhood incidents helped to bring me to where I am now. The first occurred when I was seven or eight years old and just starting to wander beyond my proscribed neighborhood boundaries. I most enjoyed walking into an outlying area of new homes and unfinished foundations dug into a once flowery field. It was fun to feel I was putting one over on my mother by sneaking off on a hot sunny day, pretending the new foundation pits were forts and lobbing dirt balls at my neighborhood cronies.

One day I wandered into the former fields alone and happened upon a group of strange children huddled around a corner of an overgrown field, the only one left filled with flowers and wheat. The rest were all mowed and turned into a bright green outdoor carpet. A large group of new kids were swinging sticks in the air and I was curious about the frenzy of their activity. When I got close I was frozen with horror as I realized that the gleeful frenzy was centered on impaling and stabbing a nest of baby mice with their pointy sticks. I shouted at them to stop and being mostly boys I could tell that they glanced at me and quickly assessed my lack of importance, being a girl, and continued with their ghastly amusements.

    I ran all the way down the hill from the field of new modern homes to my own cozy home. I screamed for my mother who was busy making lunch in our peaceful, sunny kitchen. I blurted out the story of the killer kids, my tears flowing and my story garbled with hysteria. My mother quickly got the gist of it though, and she told me to sit and watch TV while she marched up the hill to confront the mother of the boys. My mother was naturally a very shy and subtle person, but when it came to animal abuse in any form, her everyday reserve was discarded like an ill-fitting apron.

    I sat waiting for her on the living room couch, curled up in the fetal position and pretending to watch a Perry Mason rerun. I was worried about future bullying from the new kids I'd just squealed on, but I didn't really care. The image I couldn't get out of my mind was the gleeful obsessive glitter in the boys' eyes as they tortured helpless tiny creatures. My younger mind couldn't accept that people could enjoy killing something I loved. I raised my own mice, rats, and hamsters and there was no difference between baby field mice and the tiny white baby mice growing in their cages in my bedroom. I felt a deep cold horror in my heart, as if those kids were murdering my pets.

Soon my mother walked into the living room and told me she'd spoken the boys' mother and told her how upset I was. She shook her head sadly and said the other mother explained that field mice were invading her new house and she had told her sons it was fine to go out and kill baby mice in their nests whenever they saw them. My mother explained she'd tried, with futility, to express concern that teaching kids to kill wasn't good for their future mental health. The mother of the new kids had been offended. My mother sighed with her usual sense of cynical resignation. I was familiar with that sigh and shake of the head. It didn't mean she was giving up or giving in, she was just tired of people in general. That made me sadder than anything else.

She said, "It's a terrible thing, to us, but something you've got to realize as you get older is that some people enjoy killing things. I don't understand it and

I'll never understand it. But, as you get older it's something you will have to get used to seeing from time to time. I hate hunters, I've always hated them, but some people think that killing is a sport."

I was an intense kid, and as with anything I couldn't change but couldn't accept, I turned my anger inwards and into a sort of deep self-punishing anxiety. I felt small and stupid and sad that I couldn't change things I knew I despised. And, I couldn't live with that unshakable image of the cruel and lustful gleam in the boys' eyes as they jabbed sticks into those tiny mice curled into a fetal position like pink shrimp on a stick.

All I could do for the rest of that awful day was cry on the couch and then get up and take my dog for a long, long walk until both of us were exhausted. That was the only activity that seemed to relieve my anxiety at living in a world I didn't like and couldn't change. It still is. Watching Pepper, my Springer Spaniel, get so much joy from sniffing plants and rocks, watching other dogs pass by, and pushing her head through the dense shrubbery woven throughout our neighborhood gave me joy too. I recognized possibilities in a dog's simple delights - living fully in the moment without premeditated prejudice and fear. Dog walking helped me survive my childhood. My friends sometimes made fun of me for my frequent dog walking, but unlike other situations, I never felt self-conscious or bothered by their teasing when it involved my love of animals.

My next memorable confrontation with the harsh reality of human nature came when I was fifteen years old. I was sitting listlessly on our front porch on a hot summer day, waiting for some friends to stop by, when a lanky black German Shepherd came wandering up and sat down right next to me as if he had always belonged in our household. He was too thin and his fur looked dry and brittle, but he didn't seem to be very old. He wore no collar or had any identification on him of any kind.

My Pepper dog loved meeting new dogs and I let the two of them romp around in the yard and tag along with my friends and I for the rest of the day. At dinner time the Shepherd, now called Black Star, was still hanging around and seemed determine to come into the house and just continue life as part of the family.

My father came home and put his hands to head saying, "No, no, no more animals. No more dogs. The animals already run this house. Why don't we just call this place the Bradley Farm?"

In addition to Pepper, my rodent family had grown exponentially and their cages completely filled my brother's bedroom as soon as he left for college. In addition, my mother had a soft heart for stray cats. Once people started to recognize my mother as a potential neighborhood Cat Lady Number Two, stray kittens started to miraculously appear on our front porch on a regular basis. My mother was never able to turn any cat over to an animal shelter, and our feline population was growing as rapidly as the rodents. And worse, it was becoming an ongoing and stressful battle to keep the two species safely separated.

My father, who was the town supervisor at the time, called his favorite animal control officer to come and pick up Black Star and asked him to take him to the local animal shelter. He explained to me that we had to give Black Star's true owners time to find him and that animal control would put a notice in the newspaper and try to find his family. In the meantime, Black Star would go out to the nice and clean Pleasant Valley Farm, an animal shelter several towns over, and rest in a nice, clean kennel until his loving family claimed him.

Pleasant Valley Farm was very familiar to me. In addition to a dog and cat shelter, the Farm had a collection of rescued farm animals including llamas, horses and goats. Since I was a baby, a favorite weekend activity was visiting the Farm and paying a dime for a handful of feed to give the pushy goats. My mother and I would bring chopped up carrots and apples for the grateful horses and laugh at the llamas as they lifted their puffy lips at us to reveal amazingly long yellow brown teeth. Even as a teenager increasingly concerned with establishing my popularity, I never lost interest in visiting the farm and I'd frequently drag carloads of friends out to feed the goats with me.

The evening we found Black Star, the animal control officer parked his white van in our front yard, and my father brought Black Star out to him on one of Pepper's old leashes. I was crying. Something didn't feel right. I told my father in front of the officer that things didn't feel right. My father was always helpless in the face of my tears and finally, with a sigh, he told the officer that if the dog wasn't claimed by his owners after the seven-day holding period, we'd take Black Star back to live back to live here.

I waited anxiously for the week to end. I had seven long days to wait for my new dog. I called the Farm a couple of times to find out if Black Star's owners had turned up to claim him. Each time the answer was negative and my anticipation of having a new pet increased. I loved watching Rin Tin Tin on TV with my brother when I was younger, and I was especially excited to have a German Shepherd.

On the seventh day I called the shelter as soon as I

returned from a fidgety day at school. The receptionist hesitated when I asked about the black German Shepherd. I had to give her a number, not a name that had been assigned to Black Star when my Dad dropped him off and I figured that was the reason for the delay in her response. She put me on hold and a male voice came back on the line.

    He didn't identify himself, or what his position was at the shelter. He just said abruptly, "I'm sorry, but we had to put to the dog down."

    I didn't understand what put down meant at first, but the stern yet tense tone in the man's voice told my heart what it needed to know. I felt a flash of cold horror seep all through my body and then managed to stammer out a meek "But, why?"

    "The dog had a hurt foot. It was hurt bad and we couldn't treat it, so he had to be put to sleep. It's kinder that way."

    Even then, I cringed at the "put to sleep" euphemism. I knew that death - dead, cold and curled up like those poor stabbed baby mice - was not warm sleep. Dead was forever. Then my temper flared, the temper my Mom hated and said I'd inherited from my father and Irish grandmother. I was furious. I was shaking and sweating with rage. Black Star, a beautiful, special German Shepherd was gone. Dead is forever.

And, there was nothing at all wrong with his foot. Even if there had been a hidden swelling there, or something happened at the shelter, it could have been fixed. I would have fixed it. My parents would have paid for the vet to fix it. I knew they would have helped him and by the time I made that awful phone call my mom and dad were as excited as I to welcome Black Star into our home. Dead is forever.

This was my introduction, at 15-years of age, to triage euthanasia in animal shelters. Incoming animals are slow to adopt out. Kenneling animals is expensive. Animal shelters always have to work to keep costs down. Keeping older, infirm, or unwanted breeds going until a good home is found is expensive. Stressed out volunteer and shelter employees don't have time to follow up leads to place dogs with breed rescues or foster homes. They don't have resources to transport animals to other shelters or rescues. So, the perfect are culled out – the adoptable: the meek, but not too meek, the outgoing, but not annoying, the healthy, those that don't require much veterinary expense on the part of the shelter. My head understood, but my heart screamed in agony. I just wanted Black Star to come back to me. But, dead is forever.

My mother tried to comfort me that night by saying, "There will be other dogs that come along that will need you."

But, I didn't buy that line. Of course there would be other dogs in needs of homes and kindness. But, there would never be another Black Star. Black Star was an individual. The way he shyly sniffed my hand to encourage me to pet him, his intelligent, world-wise eyes, the white spot right between his eyes - all that and more made him my Black Star. He was not some anonymous dog. No dog is just an anonymous dog. Every dog is an individual with a personality as clear and sovereign as a human being or any other sentient creature.

 3. Flophouse for Dogs

Now, several decades later, just as my father feared, my house is literally bursting with dogs, with their energy, their destructive tendencies when bored, their sometimes-overwhelming affection and hunger for love and snacks. Some are adopted from shelters, some are unwanted pets taken from my neighbors in this small-city packed with triple-decker, multi-family apartments and decaying single-family Victorian-era homes. Some are simply leftovers from shelters where I've volunteered.

Neighbors know, obvious from noise and general chaos, that our home is really a shelter, a guerilla set-up operating just underneath the radar of city officials. And, realizing this and accepting it, my neighbors put up with noise and the dog breeds, like pit bulls, that make them nervous. But, when people come to visit they are invariably amazed that the house is in good shape, even pretty, and it doesn't stink like the Cat Lady's house did.

All of our furnishings are by necessity shabby chic; no four thousand dollar tables, like the beauties my studio-mate creates, in this house. But, taken as a whole, the house looks nice, is clean and neat. It's an everyday uphill exhausting battle to keep it this way, between sloppy husband, and energetic dogs, but it's important to me. Order and cleanliness are my indicators that things have not gotten out of control. I've not crossed the thin line over to dog-hoarder. As long my health and energy holds (knock on wood) I can keep the dogs well exercised and the house in good shape.

After nearly fifteen years living in New Bedford, an old-fashioned neighborly city going through some hard times, locals see me walking my dogs and come out to chat. Some talk about their own pets and then bring their dogs to me when they can no longer keep them due to immanent foreclosure, or eviction, or illness, or death. Sometimes, owners move away and leave their dogs in their apartment like so much leftover furniture, tied to door handles, or left to break through screens when they are starving. Usually these owners are drug dealers and temporary squatters in the boarded up homes on the riverside of the neighborhood. Sometimes, a neighbor will hear a frantically barking dog and break into the filthy, abandoned, poop filled apartment and rescue the dog and bring the dog to me.

    On principle, my neighbors generally don't call police when things happen in this city. Animal control officers are police and not to be trusted. In reality, our animal control officers are kindly people who often go above and beyond the call of duty to help keep the animals safe from some of the humans living in this city, putting their own lives in danger in the process. Still, in this city snitching is taboo, police are feared, and the common thought is that the animal cops will just take the rescued dogs and kill them, which is sometimes, by necessity, true. Any suggestion that rescued dogs be taken to the city shelter is usually rejected with a statement like, "I'd rather drop the dog in the Freetown State Forest to fend for itself before I'd let a cop take it."

So, I take them. My husband helps sometimes but mostly he just sighs with resignation now and lets me deal with the dogs the best I can. I'm not a hoarder – someone who takes more dogs than they can handle and doesn't care for them, or give them necessary medical attention. Veterinary care for the dogs costs a small fortune and we justify spending it by saying that the expense balances what we don't have to spend on college since we don't have human children. So, my dogs, our dogs, live in relative doggy luxury. I've collected a bunch of cast off, fairly clean sofas, and those line my once shiny-floored dining room. Each is covered with a poly-fur blanket and two or three dogs splayed out, feet happily in the air.

My yard isn't large, being a city yard, but it's filled with trees and shrubs and digging places for dogs. The fence is high and solid – nobody can see in at street level, but my neighbors on top levels of triple-deckers can see into the yard and watch the daily dog drama play out. Some joke about it with me as I take my dogs on their daily walks around the neighborhood. The housebound older man next door enjoys watching the doggy antics and laughs and cheers them on as they chase each other around and around the yard, competing for a single stick or chewy toy.

    This neighbor once said to me, "Living next to you guys I feel like a live next to a park - like I don't live in the city anymore. Looking down into your yard makes me happy." That made my day.

4. Saddest Summer

    One autumn I was depressed, down further into the damp, listless depression of ninety-degree September days than I'd ever been, even though I knew by then that I suffered from seasonal affective disorder. My favorite dog, a beautiful, robust, speckled Cattle Dog named Cedric, died suddenly and unexpectedly on our usual joyous summer retreats to the Adirondack Mountains. His sudden, unexplained illness and death hit so hard and tainted the entire summer with grief and a horrible, unrelenting sense of guilt. And, this was the first year my parents were just too old and frail to meet up with us in the Adirondacks. This was the first year in my life we hadn't spent time together up there camping, hiking, eating Friday fish fry and drinking beer by the Moose River. This was our place; the place we forgave each other or at least realized that our enjoyment of one another trumped past troubles. That summer, I knew the end was lurking and not far away. I didn't know how the end would present itself. My parents (who in their 70's drove cross country from New York to California in their RV five times) couldn't muster the energy to drive from Asheville to the Adirondack. They too would know it was the end, both in their own way but both harshly, because mobility and stoic independence was everything to them.

That sticky summer, the feeling of loss was pushing me damply down into a depression and lethargy I didn't think I could escape. And, the guilt of losing Cedric and not being aware that he was ill was getting worse by the day. I had to do something to feel better, to pull myself out of this. I started to think that maybe I needed more of the dog that bit me, literally.

I'd volunteer at an animal shelter. When I'd walked into a bookstore to find something interesting enough to distract me from my sorrows the first book I saw was about volunteering as way to overcome life challenges. "Okay," I thought, "I need to do something absorbing, something to take me way out of myself and worrying about the future." Mark was back at teaching after Labor Day, and the thought of sliding alone from a hot autumn into a damp gray New England winter was enough to make me truly suicidal. I spoke to my friend Karen who I knew had volunteered at local animal shelters and asked her if she knew of one that wouldn't be too distressing to work at. She told me about a no-kill shelter in Fall River that she'd worked with a couple of years ago.

"You'll like the other volunteers," Karen said. "Watch out for the animal control officer that runs that place though. She is one tough cookie. But, she cares. She doesn't bump off the animals just because they don't get adopted right away or have issues."

That was a solid recommendation. I simply couldn't face becoming attached to animals that would have to be "put to sleep." That would surely be the worst thing I could do for my depression. But as Karen described this shelter it seemed like a hopeful place, a place where people came together to fight for animals they loved. And, this ACO was intriguing. She was disillusioned with people and cynical after so many years of dealing with animals hurt by people. I'd always been attracted to strong, bossy women so I wasn't put off by Karen's description. The ACO appealed to me as someone with a mission for which she was willing to fight. So, the next day I went to volunteer at the Hidden Falls Animal Shelter.

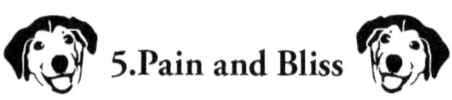
5. Pain and Bliss

On my very first day of becoming an animal shelter volunteer at Hidden Falls, I was shoveling up masses of dog poop with streams of sweat pouring down over my forehead into my eyes on a 90-degree day. Later, I took a slew of hyperactive barking dogs for walks around a garbage-strewn industrial park bordered by a polluted river. It was pretty to look at on the surface though. And, there was no relief in working indoors as the shelter was not air-conditioned. From time to time the smoke-hardened voice of Bliss, the notoriously cranky Fall River animal control officer cut through the raucous barking, "Hey, get your hand out of that cage if you're not wearing gloves! What's wrong with you? Why can't you listen?"

    I thanked her for reminding me not to put my hand in the cage of the new dog. She snapped, "I don't give a damn about your hand. I'm thinking about that dog. He's still in quarantine. If he bites, it means a bandage to you, but it will cost him his life. I'll have to have him tested for rabies and I think you know by now what that means."

    I've always believed, from the time I was a little kid, that people who liked animals are good people, people who don't like animals are going to be trouble for me in some way, and people who are mean to animals are to be avoided at all costs. I finally realized I owed a debt of gratitude to pay towards people who are kind, who care, who have made my life in this violent world better, easier, because I know they exist and are always out there helping the animals I love -

even when they are shouting in my face.

Of course, I had only to walk upstairs to the shelter storage shelves. They were packed with donated dog and cat food, blankets, toys, and at the top, a row of round Styrofoam boxes in varying sizes that looked oddly like old-fashioned hat boxes. They were very rarely needed at this shelter. They were lined with plastic and held the heads of animals that must be tested for rabies as they are sent securely up to the State Department of Health in Boston. If the quarantined dog had bitten me, his fate would be this very final form of testing.

Still, it was terribly hard not to reach into a cage to stroke the head of an animal that had just arrived at the shelter. The dogs, in particular, were hard to resist. They looked at us constantly as we rushed back and forth with food bowls and towels. Their eyes glittered with longing and showed a mixture of love and cynicism. They needed people. They wanted to bond with people. But most had seen the worst people could offer.

The job consisted of opening cages; lifting out the animals and grabbing a litter box, or poop-laden newspaper, and dirty bowls. We took the bowls into the tiny, cramped kitchen and added them to a greasy chest-high stack soaking in the sink. We emptied the filthy, overfilled litter boxes in an industrial-size garbage bag, adding to a mass of litter and old cat food. Then we scraped the rest of the poop out of the boxes and added it to the stack of stinky boxes in the kitchen. We repeated these tasks and then went to the kitchen to begin scrubbing the stacks of bowls and boxes.

I kept thinking, "Why am doing this?" I had a vague remembrance of doing penance in my father's Catholic church when I was a kid. I was doing penance. The idea was comforting. I found many of my fellow volunteers were doing penance here too.

Lillian, a robust 84-year-old woman was still saturated with grief and guilt at the death of her son in Vietnam over 30 years ago. She kept repeating, "I could have told him 'No.' He was underage and I could have stopped him. He wanted to go so bad, he thought it was the right thing to do, but I could have stopped him."

Many volunteers were Catholic. Several were nuns from nearby St. Anne's Parish. Others were prisoners on work release. A disproportionate number were nurses, or teachers. After long hours caring for humans, they came here and spent their few leisure hours caring for animals. These teachers worked nine-hour days teaching special education or gym or English as a second language in the Fall River Public School system and spent their weekends cleaning up poop at the shelter.

The paid shelter workers were mostly animal control officers and their assistants. They tolerated the volunteers as a necessary evil and the volunteers felt the same way about the paid workers. They had a policy of mutual avoidance, mental and physical, though physical avoidance could rarely be achieved in such cramped quarters.

One day as I worked side by side on the cat cages with Bliss I began to tell her about a painful incident in my life. I tried to communicate my feeling of guilt to Bliss, maybe looking for absolution. She just glanced over at me and summed things up in a few choice words, "Hey, shit happens."

A volunteer looked over, caught my glance and rolled her eyes at Bliss. "Shit happens." Exactly. In this microcosm of the world, Bliss saw the worst of human nature and saw it repeatedly directed towards the innocent. She knew better than to expect a perfect moral code from any human being.

The animal control officers had seen everything human beings can dish out and didn't have energy left over for politeness or social decorum. Everything they said was blunt and on-target. I sat outdoors with the shelter workers as they smoked cigarettes. Nearly everyone at the shelter smoked incessantly. I'd quit years ago but wasn't above enjoying the vicarious pleasure of second hand smoke.

 Volunteers and staff sat on a picnic table by the Taunton River, smoking and watching elderly fishermen go by in their rowboats. The table was in a large dusty yard surrounded by a chain link fence. Shelter dogs were allowed ten minute turns "out in the yard" to romp and play. We tossed balls to the dogs and they returned them eagerly back to the picnic table and dropped them on top, caked with drool and dirt. Across the river were rows and rows of abandoned red brick textile mills. A few scrubby locust trees arched up and leaned out over the shores of the river, the tips delicately waving in the sultry breeze and touching the water and the shiny reflections of the red mills.

 Each shelter worker had his or her own style of smoking. Bliss puffed at her cigarettes more and more rapidly as her break got shorter, finally quickening her breath to a rapid, staccato inhalation of smoke - puff, puff, puff - until she threw her cigarette to the ground, stomped on it, heaved a sigh and opened the door to the shelter.

 Tracy was a large, young woman with an illicit farm on her mother's suburban property where she kept a variety of rescued horses and German Shepherds. All her dogs had hip dysplasia and were scheduled to be killed in various shelters before she rescued them. She spent every extra penny she earned, and more, on her dog's vet bills. Her mother was pressuring her to move out and she was worried about her animals. She smoked her cigarette like a joint, inhaling a deep breath of smoke and holding it in a long time before exhaling and letting the smoke rise up over her face and sucking it back into her nose.

    Michelle was a tiny, nervous, young shelter worker and a student in the university biology department. She wanted to be a veterinary technician when she graduated but was having trouble with her advising professor. In spite of her delicate limbs and translucent skin, she had a deep, angry, argumentative voice and never shied away from a confrontation. She smoked her cigarette delicately and rapidly, filling each and every breath with a puff of smoke and lighting each new cigarette from the old.

    Tom held his cigarettes behind his back when he wasn't actively inhaling. He was a bulky, silent, middle-aged man whose elderly mother came to pick him up every day at the end of his shift. She didn't approve of his smoking. Tom's job was to empty the outdoor dog runs and dump the endless buckets of dog poop and water into the open septic system by the river. Every time Tom picked up the lid, an overwhelming cloud of sewage odor filled the shelter inside and out. Tom claimed that, finally, after two years of shelter work, he could no longer smell it. Rachel smoked heavily, but she was trying to quit. She was worried that smoking was giving her face premature wrinkles. She was an animal control officer, and a police officer, and always carried her weapon. Being an urban ACO is a risky business. Rachel thought her duties were more dangerous, by far, than the duties of a regular cop. Often the first indicator that a drug house existed was a call from a neighbor complaining about barking dogs in the basement. Then Rachel had to go in and confiscate the pit bulls. Some dealers claimed to love their dogs, and, even if they'd forgotten to feed them for a few weeks, they'd defend them to the death. Sometimes Rachel found a recently abandoned house filled with stacks of crates containing cramped, starving dogs.

    Pit bulls are often gentle creatures, although abused by their owners in an attempt to create a monster. Like many of the shelter workers and volunteers, Rachel had a mini-shelter in her house. She had five pit bulls, all taken from drug houses, or taken home from the shelter when a court case was over. Bliss usually immediately put criminal-owned dogs on death row, unless the owner is awaiting trial and the dog needs to be used as evidence. Dogs whose owners were awaiting a trial often remained at the shelter for months at a time. During their long stay Rachel became attached and couldn't bear to see the ordeal end in the death of the dog. Death row runs were at the back of shelter. At the end of each day, an elderly volunteer ran from cage to cage, run to run, with treats for all the dogs. She wanted to give them one bright spot in a day of anxiety and boredom. It was hardest to make the rounds of the death row dogs. They all showed a longing for love in their eyes. Many of them also exhibited distrust or fear and wouldn't take their treat until we left it on the concrete floor and walked away. Some had the telltale torn ears and long scars that indicated they were used as professional fighting dogs. Some were just old or ugly or otherwise deemed unadoptable.

    Volunteers didn't last long - soon feeling an inevitable creeping sense of burnout and hopelessness. Once in while something happened that renewed the shelter workers' emotional stores. On a sunny August morning, an Indian woman walked in the door wearing a shiny, rust-colored sari. She said she had a dream about a dog in our shelter. She'd never been to the shelter before but claimed the dream clearly indicated one of these dogs was the perfect soul mate she was destined to adopt. At first, the shelter workers rolled their eyes, quickly classifying the woman as a crazy, but it turned out she was a doctor at St. Anne's Hospital and was looking for a companion animal.

    Bliss shouted, "Will someone please get off their butt and show the doctor some of our dogs." We took her around to look at some of the smaller puppies and the "desirable" dogs in the outdoor runs, meaning the young, the small, the pure-breeds. "No, no, no.", she said, "I know what this dog looks like. I'll know the dog when I see him."   She wanted to be taken to the runs at the back of the kennel. I glanced nervously at her beautiful sari as she moved across the path of dust and poop. She stopped in front of a run holding an overweight ten-year old black Shepherd/Lab mix with a graying muzzle, sparse dander covered coat and stiff legs. Bliss knew which dogs would be adopted quickly and which would languish at the shelter month after month. She'd taken one look at this dog and promptly placed him on death row.

    The doctor bent down and the old dog plodded over to greet her through the cage with an air of hope mixed with cynicism and weariness. To my amazement the doctor said, "This is the one. This is the dog I saw in my dream. I want to take this dog home with me right now."

Bliss always went by the book and she didn't allow anyone to take a dog home until she did a complete background check. This process took a week and every day of that week the doctor came to the shelter to visit her dog, kneeling down by the cage and whispering, having a soft, secret conversation with her soul mate. At the end of the week, she took her new friend home. The old dog was shining from a bath and his expression had already been transformed by the attentions of the doctor.

In September, the terrorist strikes smashed New York City. Bliss had her old radio blasting the news from the top of the rusty refrigerator. Every time Lillian passed it to pick up a dirty dog bowl she made the sign of the cross. I glanced at Bliss as we passed the radio at the same time, and she gave me a sharp and weary look that said, "Don't say it. There's nothing to say. People are capable of any kind of bullshit. Nothing surprises me."

The night before, Bliss brought an emaciated, tick-covered pit bull into the shelter. She'd been making daily rounds of the dirt roads of the Freetown State Forest, a state-owned tract of sandy, piney forest bordering the city and close to a tenant farm where residents were suspected of breeding dogs for fighting. She suspected that this ring of dog fighters was holding bloody gambling events in the woods. She found the skinny pit bull tied to a tree in the middle of the forest with a bag of dog food placed just out of his reach. Was this an accident, a misjudgment in placement, or a deliberate form of torture to turn the animal mean? Or, was he a failure as a fighter and this was his final punishment? He had no access to water and was infested with ticks, fleas, and maggots.

    Bliss was investigating the forest with a group of police officers when she found the dog. She told us the story as we stood around the shelter with the radio blasting out news of the unspeakable crime in New York City behind us.

    "Imagine this; he was tied to a tree, couldn't even walk he was so weak and all these big men, these cops, are standing around him saying, "I ain't going over there. That's a pit bull. I'm not touching him." Well, I walked over and that dog just crawled over to me with his last bit of strength. He wanted to be held so bad. I just held him in my arms all the way over here. Normally, a dog like this would be going down right away, but I just can't do it. Look at his eyes. His eyes are so smart, so sharp, I decided to name him Hawk."

Hawk did have intelligent eyes. They sparkled softly as he gazed up at us and his heavy jowls curled up into a big smile every time someone spoke to him. We all sat on the floor, stroking Hawk and listening numbly to the radio. Bliss was picking engorged ticks off his back with a pair of big tweezers. She counted every tick as she picked, "One, two, three…64 freaking ticks. You know what? I can't believe people. I just can't believe people."

Watching Bliss and the dog, I was nearly overwhelmed by sadness. The incidents of the day made me aware again of how powerfully humans can hate and, while completely indifferent to the suffering of strangers, put both primitive and sophisticated technologies into action to annihilate their objects of hatred. I could see that without unending and exhaustive care and attention to individual lives, human and non-human, potential holocaust is always just around the corner. That day, Bliss and all the other shelter volunteers seemed to me the purest and most effective antidote to evil.

6. The Pornographic Hypnotist

The events of September 11 resulted in reduced donations to the shelter for about a month and then, suddenly, an influx of contributions. Volunteer fundraisers started making frequent shelter visits to plan events and publicity strategies to take best advantage of people's temporary generosity. The unexpected influx of contributions was energizing to the volunteers - an exhibition of public generosity and appreciation that was a small upbeat note in the murk and gloom of those autumn events.

The shelter was always in a constant, scraping search for funds. The costs of medicine and veterinarians were prohibitive, in spite of in-kind donations by local veterinarians. All animals were spayed or neutered prior to adoption. Bliss was adamant on that point. And no volunteer wanted to have an adopter return months later with a litter of unwanted puppies or kittens to add to the already overpopulated, crowded shelter. Bliss already had a large wire fenced arena set up in the middle of the shelter floor as a playpen for many abandoned puppies. They were happy just to have a warm place to sleep and eat and companions to curl up with at night and romp with all day.

Playing with the puppies were one of the pure joys of volunteering at the shelter - a joy not tainted with the knowledge one of them might not get adopted. All healthy puppies were adopted into comfortable homes. Giving attention and thereby getting attached to the older dogs was trickier. With most no-kill shelters, I discovered that there were clauses to that distinction. Older and infirm dogs, and others deemed potentially not adoptable, or those expected to sit on the adoption floor for a long time, were eventually transferred to other shelters and those were often high-kill shelters.

The high-kill shelters only kept dogs that were found on the street for the state-mandated 10-days, so an owner could be potentially located. The dogs transferred from other shelters, or turned in by their owners were often euthanized (killed) just minutes after arrival. So much for the myth of the unwanted and inconvenient family pet finding a brand new home at the hometown animal shelter. For the most part owner-turn-in dogs are killed quickly, unless somehow deemed especially desirable - a very young animal, often pure-bred, or very good or unusual looking.

A long building with open fenced dog runs extended out the back of Hidden Falls, stretching towards the river and with a view of the picnic area. Volunteers and shelter workers sit at the outdoor tables on nice days, unconsciously striving to avoid looking at the runs on the far side of the building.

These were the short-term dogs, or death row dogs as some called them - the ones that probably would be transferred to a large shelter, which wasn't a shelter in the homey sense of the word but large unwanted animal processing centers and crematoriums. After the first day of volunteering I knew that, we all knew that, and sadly tried to avoid too much contact with the sad dogs on the far side of the kennels.

We felt guilty ignoring those forsaken creatures, but it just hurt too much to fall in love then lose them. I knew if I spent too much time on the far side of the runs, I'd have to quit working at the shelter or risk sinking into a deeper clinical depression. And, even all with my avoidance tactics in place, I felt it coming on - a profound and continual sadness underlined by utter exhaustion.

Bliss knew how we felt about the doomed dogs and played on our sympathies to motivate us in the shelter's fundraising efforts. Fall is fundraising season and Bliss came out and sat with the group smoking at the picnic table and said, "Better start thinking about how we're going to make more money. We have a lot of good dogs that we need to bring over to the front runs." Once a dog entered the runs at the front of the building, Bliss generally kept the dog alive for however long it took to find a new home. In that sense, Hidden Falls was no-kill and always made good use of that term in fundraising efforts.

Cats were comparatively inexpensive to maintain and were arranged to take up as little floor space as possible. Cat cages were stacked four or five high nearly to the ceiling and we had to stand on chairs to lift the cats out and hold them while we cleaned their litter boxes. Because it was more convenient to keep cats, cats generally didn't wind up on kitty death row unless very ill, elderly or so nasty that we couldn't safely clean their cages or administer medications. The impossible cats were placed in cages in the attic storage area, in the middle of piles food and cat litterbags until they were transferred.

Through the autumn, I became familiar with the dynamics, classes, and personalities in the shelter community. There were meagerly paid employees with tough, dangerous, heartrending jobs - the shelter workers, the dog officers. There were the volunteers - the teachers, nurses, and nuns, the prisoners on work release, and others just doing penance. And there were the fundraisers - wealthy women who loved the animals, but didn't want to get dirty cleaning cages and had a knack for earning money. Every penny cajoled from sympathetic citizens, and pet loving local businesses owner was welcome. The pressure to constantly raise more money created an ongoing, endless nervous energy in both staff and volunteers.

There was increasing tension between the shelter classes, and the events of 9/11 made everyone edgier and angrier than usual. The volunteers and fundraisers were always irritated by the behavior of the kennel workers and animal control officers. "They are so crude," complained Edith, coordinator of the volunteers and a gym teacher at the city middle school.

I liked listening to the animal rescue stories of the shelter workers and took my breaks with them and listened as they smoked cigarettes outdoors, enjoying the pleasures of second hand smoke. Deirdre, a special education teacher asked me, "How can you stand to sit around with the staff? They're weird, and the smoke is disgusting." I declined to tell Deidre that I was an ex-smoker who got a vicarious thrill from both the smell of their cigarettes and their refreshing sense of misanthropy.

"Worse, they offend the visitors," added Pamela, lead fundraiser, and wife of a local real estate developer. Pamela drove a lavender Jaguar with silver leather seats.

This claim was based on an incident where Bliss confronted a man who had lost his Labrador Retriever, relocating him a week later at the shelter after Bliss found the dog wandering the city streets. The man was so happy to be reunited with his dog that he started bringing in weekly cash donations and dog food. On one of his visits Bliss became irate and said, "Why don't you just take better friggin' care of your dog instead of bringing us this shit. Get a fence for your yard. Get him neutered for God's sake. What is it with you guys that can't stand to see your dog loose it's balls? It's not like getting your own chopped off for Christ's sake."

We all froze, waiting for the man's angry response, but to everyone's surprise tears started to roll down his cheeks and he said, "You're right, you're right. I know I've been an asshole but I'm going to do better by him. He means everything to me. You just don't know him or me. I love him and I don't want to hurt him."

Bliss's response seemed brutal until I discovered that this man's dog had been picked up wandering the streets four times in the past two months. The big yellow Lab stalked all the unspayed females in the neighborhood and had no regard for territorial limitations, such as fences, when he was on the scent of a good time. Bliss repeatedly begged the owner to have the Lab neutered but he looked at her in disbelief and exclaimed, "I could never do that to him."

Bliss's special form of blunt honesty came as shock, reality check and absolution. I could see this man thinking for probably the first time ever about how his actions and apathy, directly impacted his dog. After that day, he continued bringing his weekly donations of food and added some toys and much needed flea medications to the mix. Bliss never again found his dog roaming the streets as the man finally found the courage to have him neutered.

Still, in the minds of the fundraisers, the incident added to the growing list of Bliss's sins. Bliss didn't communicate many of her shelter battle stories to the fundraisers. She didn't discuss her work as an animal control officer either. I thought the content might be too disturbing for the fundraising volunteers, as it was for me, but that wasn't always the case. Some of the fundraisers were tougher than they seemed. I'd judged them wrongly.

I discovered that many of them were once poop-scooping volunteers and some were kamikaze animal rescuers - entering dangerous neighborhoods after dark to save a freezing tied-out dog, or breaking into an abandoned apartment to save a litter of starving kittens. After years of shoveling poop, hosing dog pee out of the cracked concrete, scraping encrusted cat litter boxes, hearing sickening stories of cruelty, and facing desperate caged animals day after day they simply burned out cold. They still wanted to help. Fearing a little for their sanity, they needed to retreat to a calmer place of order, cleanliness, phones, computers and clean clothes.

Volunteers who were still in the trenches adopted a form of snobbery. "Look at how crispy clean her white cotton shirt is," a poop-scooping volunteer commented, as Pamela raced in and out of the shelter with paperwork and in high heels. We wore our filthy t-shirts and jeans as a badge of honor. Poop was penance.

The best part of the work, for me, was having direct contact with the animals, especially the dogs. I'd take them out each morning for their precious ten-minute walk around the truck yard and they'd roll on their backs with abandon as I stroked their bellies. I couldn't imagine myself avoiding the shelter or the animals. The fundraisers often raced in and out as quickly as possible without a glance at the inhabitants of the cages and runs. I didn't understand yet. My experiences at the shelter - gritty, sobering and disturbing - were just beginning to keep me awake nights.

Bliss was not concerned about justifying her personality or her decisions. She was fully invested in the animal shelter. It was hers and, being a misanthrope, all the peripheral people - the staff, fundraisers, and volunteers - were a necessary evil. After her parents died, Bliss spent her small inheritance on two things; the animal shelter and a log cabin on the northern fringes of the nearby Freetown State Forest. She bought enough land and trees with the cabin to provide a nice buffer on all sides, away from the sight of people. She lived with an understanding and patient husband, several rescued dogs and cats, a wildlife sanctuary, and an ever-growing family of foster children. "Cleaning up other people's messes. Yep, that's what my life is all about," Bliss declared loudly and often.

That year, autumn leaves turned especially brilliant and started to fall early after a brittle dry summer. Fundraising season began with energy fueled by tragedy. Late September was the time of the major annual fundraising event - The Italian Buffet. It funded most of the medications purchased throughout the year and the free spay/neuter program offered in conjunction with local vet clinics.

The Buffet was the original affair organized by

Bliss's friends and family, before the days of volunteers, the board of directors, and the official fundraising team – way back in the early days when the shelter was sanctuary for a few random stray dogs and cats. It wasn't the upscale charity event desired by the board of directors, but in a just a few years it had become a beloved and anticipated Fall River community social gathering.

"It's so tacky. It's just plain embarrassing," complained Deirdre, the reluctant principal organizer. "The entertainment is really not what we'd like it to be," groaned Pamela. Still, both participated in the affair with as much energy and good humor as they could muster.

The event was held at the American Legion Hall just around the corner from Hidden Falls. It consisted of an Italian buffet, silent auction, open bar and entertainment - featuring a pornographic hypnotist. Over seven years in existence, the event had reached near-legendary status in the city and attracted hundreds of people from Fall River and surrounding suburbs. Everyone was slightly embarrassed about being there and everyone had a great time. Everyone stayed late. A twenty-five-dollar tax-deductible admission fee enabled partiers to feel good about drinking and buying funky stuff at the auction - all proceeds went to the animals.

Businesses, artists and craftspeople donated items and services for the silent auction. The ballroom of the Legion Hall was packed ceiling-high with crocheted blankets, handcrafted jewelry and leftover holiday costume jewelry, huge themed baskets stuffed with pet care products, stuffed animals, chocolate, and wine and cheese gift sets.

Mark cut out some dog shapes out of plywood and I painted them to look like Labs, Poodles and Spaniels - favorite breeds I hoped would bring big bids at the silent auction. It felt good to create something crafty, silly and fun, without the usual self-consciousness I felt making artwork to show at a gallery. I felt like a kid back in Girls Scouts again, before they became uncool in middle-school. For a little bit, I forgot my oppressive guilt and depression over Cedric's death. For the first time since the horrible events of the summer, and then 9/11, I began to glimpse moments of contentment and delight.

The parking lot outside the Legion Hall was jammed with people before the official six o'clock opening hour. The Legion had donated the massive hot buffet consisting of Italian pasta dishes with huge chunks of Portuguese sausage. A local liquor store supplied the generous open bar. By eight o'clock some of the attendees were already drunk and raucous. Scratchy rock oldies and disco blasted from huge, 1970's-style speakers. Revelers of all ages stumbled between tables as they danced in an odd mixture of styles. People were impatient but politely quiet for a short round of speeches by local politicians, followed by a moment of sincere silence, tears and bowed heads for those lost in the sabotage of the World Trade Center.

Next, humorous awards for shelter volunteers were given out, including Best Pooper Scooper, of which I was the proud recipient. Finally, the most anxiously awaited event was about to occur and the pornographic hypnotist took the stage. A group of elderly men and women, lining the walls in wheel chairs, made respectful way as a white-haired man in a tight, shiny, three-piece suit ceremoniously paraded towards the small stage. Children ran around the tables with cupcakes and shiny, Mylar balloons while their parents drank and laughed, anticipating the fun of witnessing the hypnotist torturing his willing victims.

The hypnotist's routine consisted of selecting a group of audience members to come on stage and be abused by a routine inspired by memories of summer sleep-over camp. The subjects were mostly shelter employees and volunteers. Their long-anticipated annual encounter with the hypnotist had been a frequent topic of conversation at the shelter for weeks.

I was surprised that many of the soberest fundraisers, Dena, Audrey, and Lisa, got into the act. They were wild beyond their element, and I suspected some of their exuberant antics had been rehearsed. The hypnotist put on an act fit for film as he worked his best tricks to lull the group into a trance. As their heads slumped heavily against their chests, he asked them to conform to a variety of embarrassing situations and perform the most socially unacceptable acts on stage for all to see - farting, throwing up, and imagining they are dancing naked and groping an irresistibly sexy partner. It was a silly form of semi-family-friendly pornography, and the audience responded with a combination of raucous laughter and self-conscious glances at their neighbors.

I'd never been hypnotized before and I told myself that the man-in-white was just an amusing fraud. Still, I was afraid of the hypnotist as he urged the audience to participate in a practice session. I clasped my hands together as he instructed, then listened as he repeatedly suggested that my hands were stuck together with Superglue. During his mind-numbing repetition of the same statement I felt myself becoming more and more relaxed, with a tingling feeling growing at the back of my neck. Suddenly, the hypnotist commanded the audience to pull their hands apart. I tugged and pulled, but I couldn't break my grasp.

    I started to feel a prickling of panic on the back of my neck until the hypnotist clapped his hands and commanded us to wake up and separate our hands. It worked. I was amazed how suddenly it became easy to part my hands. I glanced over at Bliss who was sitting alone at a table near the stage. She was looking and me and laughing smugly. She had her hands crossed firmly across her chest as a firm indicator of her resistance to the group hypnosis session.

    The culminating episode of the fundraiser was the Parade of Dogs. The Legion Hall speakers started blasting the raucous Baha Men song "Who Let the Dog's Out." The chorus to this song was a series of human dog barks and the kids in the crowd shouted at the top of their lungs with each repetition of woofs.

    Stacy led a group of nearly twenty volunteers in walking the cutest, friendliest and most malleable shelter dogs around through the audience so people could pat and hug them. The dogs were joyfully delirious with all the attention they were getting after days and weeks spent in caged boredom. Adoption rates soared for a week or so after the Parade of Dogs.

    At the last minute, Bliss decided to add Hawk to

the parade. He was gaining weight rapidly and the bald patches on his fur where the ticks were feasting were healing over nicely. He was still very weak. On his morning outings he would reluctantly walk a few feet and then roll lazily over on his back smiling and waiting for a belly rub.

Still, Bliss didn't want to pass up an opportunity to get Hawk adopted. So in spite of his weakness and Lisa's protests of "We don't want to feature pit bulls in the parade. We don't want people to think we are a pit bull shelter," Hawk walked proudly among the audience at the fundraiser. Bliss put him in line at the end of the Parade of Dogs. He rolled over on his back after only a few steps, to the great delight of the children, who ran up in a pack and gathered round to rub his belly.

Hawk was in pure doggy heaven with all those little hands on his chest and stomach. He smiled up with a huge grin, his hefty jowls drooping away and exposing a set of teeth that reminded me of the Hound of the Baskervilles. I suddenly felt such an appreciation for this group of animal-lovers. How caring, tolerant and trusting they were to let their children roll about on the floor with a dog whose face was literally the face of fear to so many.

Hawk finally stood up and made the rounds of the

audience. He leaned with his full weight against the legs of anyone who stooped down to pat him. He sat on the feet of people at tables, and rested himself against wheel chairs as their occupants stretched their hands over to rub his big boney head. He loved everyone and anyone, and was soaking up the attention with a goofy, beatific expression on his face.

I was standing next to Bliss as she oversaw the parade and said to her, "He'll surely find a family tonight. Everyone loves him I know he'll go home." Bliss responded, with the flat, nasal, cynical tone she always adopted when discussing shelter animals, "He's got three strikes against him; he's big, he's black, and he's a pit bull. Big, black dogs are always the last to get adopted out of shelters, even the Labs, and nobody wants pit bulls. Most insurance companies won't even issue you a policy if you have one. Like it or not, they have a bad rep."

Hawk was descending into a state of attention-overloaded delirium, walking around giddily and butting his huge head against legs for pats. "He's actually got four strikes against him," continued Bliss, "he's got health issues." She pointed at his leg joints that were swollen to the size of human fists. "That's an autoimmune disorder that causes that. You know what that means? A lifetime of regular vet visits. Most people can't even find the time to take their dogs to the doctor once a year. Who's going to want a dog that needs ongoing health care? I should have put him down when I had the chance, right at the beginning. Now I'm attached, he's costing the shelter big money, and he's going to be here forever, or worse."

I started to feel exhausted and depressed after my conversation with Bliss. I located Mark at the bar and we headed out into the crispy, cool fall air coming in off the ocean. After the early laughter of the evening, I couldn't shake the feeling of unease, and the sadness of the summer months was sweeping back into my mood. I couldn't stop thinking of how disappointed Hawk was going to be when a volunteer closed the gate on his lonely crate later that night.

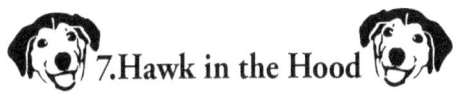

7. Hawk in the Hood

The day after the big fundraising event, I decided that Hawk would be coming home with me. Mark would be annoyed and possibly very upset, but it would pass. I decided not to tell him that I planned to bring Hawk home. We'd just argue about it, I'd get a headache, and I'd bring him home anyway. Hawk would just be sitting there one day when Mark came home tired and crabby from teaching all day. Then we'd eat dinner and Hawk would just blend into the evening and into our lives.

That fall, when everything in the country changed, the reality of not having kids and, at the same time, seeing the elders in my family fade away hit me really hard. I envied my friends who were busy building big, loud families, packing their lives with frenetic activity surrounding kids, schools, and shopping. No time to think about life, about being alone. I still envy that sometimes, but not as much now with a house full of demanding dogs.

Mark came from one of those boisterous homes, along with loving, pushy parents. That was his perception of them. I thought they were great and that Mark was immensely lucky to have parents who phoned him every Sunday at exactly 11:00 am, never failing. They were eager to listen to Mark recite the most mundane details of his daily life and cheered his accomplishments with vigor.

My parents would sometimes ask me questions about my life as an afterthought. I'd call them after I hadn't heard from them in a couple of weeks, and then usually spend an hour trying to help iron out some difficult detail of their lives. Before we'd hang up, my Mom or Dad would say, "Oh, and how have you been doing?" Throughout childhood, and beyond, I felt like a useful, yet mostly invisible sidekick for them. An odd aspect of my relationship with Mark was that his need for solitude seemed to equal his aversion to the same frenetic attention and affection I'd always longed for and envied.

During the ten days I had to wait to bring Hawk home, according to shelter protocol, I decided it was a good time to visit my parents in North Carolina. My father had physically recovered from his aneurysm surgery but his mind was deteriorating. He was beginning to wander around the neighborhood, knocking on doors in search of friends and family from his youth, and it was driving my mother to distraction. I hired personal care assistants long-distance, over the phone, and one after the other, my mother fired all of them, telling them she couldn't imagine why I called them in the first place, she was doing just fine on her own.

Then she'd phone me and tell me she could no longer manage without help. She wanted my full-time help. I was beginning to think I'd have to move to Asheville for a while. I'd run out of agencies to call and my brothers and I needed to do something resolve the situation but they would never consider moving in with my parents, not in a million years. I dreaded flying as much as I hated facing the situation, but it was time for me to head down to North Carolina and start researching nursing homes for my father.

I spent much of my visit walking with my father around his flowery suburban neighborhood, and the lush garden he'd spent so many years laboring over. We strolled slowly, much in the same way I walked my dog Maggie - keeping him from walking too far in front of me, letting him stop and investigate the things he enjoyed the best - flowers, ducks, the pond - and bringing him safely home for a contented snooze on the sofa.

My mother was in a flurry of anxiety and frustration. After sixty years of marriage she could see the inevitable separation enfolding before her. I'd tried to engage her in conversations in years past about how she would cope with things when this day came. She simply refused to talk about it, as if not speaking of the future would prevent it coming. If I persisted, she'd cover her ears and stomp her feet, just as I did at Hidden Falls when I didn't want to hear about animals being euthanized.

I had to find fresh, new home health care workers

that hadn't heard about my mother. They were getting harder to find. This time I decided to warn them that my mother would fire them, but I pleaded with them not to listen to her and to stay on anyway. My mother just couldn't help being combative about every decision I made. This was unlike her, and I knew she was losing her grip on reality.

This trip helped me realize that I desperately didn't want to move in with my parents. But, I felt my mother relentlessly pulling me away from my home, Mark, Maggie, my entire little life in Massachusetts. If I left home to live with her again I didn't feel I would survive the experience, or afterwards someone would find me out wandering in the street - homeless, depressed, crazy and muttering to myself.

To dispel my frustration and guilt, and to feel I was doing something upbeat, I went to Home Depot and bought supplies to build railings on all the staircases, inside and out, to prevent my tipsy father from falling. They didn't look very good, and weren't terribly solid, but they did the job for a while and my Dad loved them. Prior to his brain injury he would have remade the stairs I built. Now, the critical part of his brain seemed to be entirely missing. He'd become a more loving and affectionate person in his illness. But, he couldn't protect me from my mother.

My normally mild-natured mother was angry and frustrated with her situation, and she began to take it out on the nearest able family member - myself - in subtle ways. She started to compare me to my siblings, other relatives and friends. So, as I hammered away at my awkward railings, my mother told me how handy my sister-in-law was and how much better she would perform the same task, and she could cook better, too!

On the sixth day, I was trying to be patient, worrying that my mother was showing signs of dementia, but I starting to become short-tempered. I hired a day nurse to come and sit with my parents for a couple of hours so I could get away from them and do something fun. I found a craft show in Asheville. I always find comfort in craft shows. There is something calming about artists in casual clothes, working on soul-felt objects, doing business without any great promise of monetary gain but still feeling happy.

On the way back to my parent's house, I passed a large pet shop in a strip mall and stopped in to buy Hawk a new collar to wear when I returned. The anticipation of bringing Hawk home filled me with happiness, excitement and a renewed energy. Holding the green collar made my current situation seem less bleak.

I missed old Maggie too, but she and I hadn't

developed the bond I had with Cedric. She was a smarter dog and more aloof. Dog/human friendships need that same mysterious chemistry, that little spark, that fuels any great marriage. Maggie and Mark had that. They'd bonded thoroughly. She followed him around the house and stared mournfully at the door when he went to work. She slept on our bed curled up tightly at Mark's feet, and I was sure she was happily sleeping on my pillow, snoring happily on my side of the bed, every night I was away.

I decided to have a little silver tag engraved for Hawk's collar at an automated machine in the pet shop. As I typed in his name I decided to change it. Bliss gave Hawk his name but it reminded me of the names the dog fighters gave their dogs - always some predatory wild animal. But, I didn't want to confuse the poor dog by giving him a name he couldn't recognize, so I decide to call him Hawkins - a nice genteel, English Staffordshire Terrier name.

One evening toward the end of my stay in Asheville, I asked the neighbors next door if I could take their two bored Golden Retrievers for a walk. For just a few minutes, I wanted to walk happily with uncritical dogs and enjoy the magical bloom of azaleas in the South. I was feeling lonely and lost without a canine companion. I seemed to lose my sense of balance; the road seemed wavy and unsure when I didn't have a dog trotting happily along on a leash in front of me.

I'd clung onto my childhood dog Pepper as if I was a drowning kid. Pepper gave love without bounds. She didn't criticize. My mother worked hard for her children but needed to have us around, while at the same time she was annoyed by our incessant neediness as kids. She was quite happy to plop me down on the floor with Pepper as a babysitter for the day. Pepper became a great surrogate mom. I pulled myself up on her thick fur to take my first steps. I curled up cozily into her warm, fuzzy belly for my naps. She went everywhere I went and stood still and silent as my friends and I dressed her up in our old clothes.

Sometimes we'd take vacations to destinations where dogs were not welcomed and Pepper would go to the boarding kennel. Alone with my parents, without a canine companion to grasp, I felt indescribably alone and lost, as if I were floating without any roots or guides through the universe. I guess I was feeling something similar when I went over to the neighbor's gate to leash up their happily bouncing Golden Retrievers for a walk. Afterwards I felt grounded and ready to board the plane back to Massachusetts.

In two days, my brother was coming to North Carolina to take over the nursing home search. While waiting for him to arrive, I kept Hawkins' collar close to me at all times, in my pocket where I could reach in and touch the shiny new tag with his name etched into it and feel a happy anticipation at the thought of bringing our new dog home.

The very next day after I returned, I put Maggie in the van and drove to the shelter to get Hawkins. We had to introduce Maggie to her new buddy with the help and protection of the shelter staff. I was confident she'd accept him into in her home.

I wondered if Hawkins had missed our morning walks or would remember who I was after my short absence. As I approached his crate he was all wags and smiles, no more or less than he is when anyone approaches. Hawkins seemed to love everyone and all, equally. I put his collar on, but Bliss came up behind me and said he needed to be taken out of the cage in his official collar before he could be transferred over to me. Bliss never sacrificed shelter protocol for a minute.

As I pulled Hawkins' new collar from his neck he became visibly agitated. He seemed to know that the collar meant a new home, and a new life, and he wanted to keep it on. He bit at the collar and tried to keep me from taking it out of the crate. Bliss reached in and deftly slipped a choker leash over his head and pulled him out to the yard for introductions to Maggie.

All the volunteers were out in the yard to watch. Nobody could believe that someone was interested in adopting Hawkins. He'd been lying in the crate by the front desk for so long that he'd become a fixture at the shelter. He was the first dog to rise and stretch and whine for his walk in the morning. He was the eager repository for leftover McDonalds sandwiches, and stale Dunkin' Donuts baked goods. He'd grown large and stocky, with a drooping belly and huge rear end.

Everyone seemed very nervous about Hawkins meeting Maggie. I wasn't nervous. I'd never seen any sign of dog aggression in Hawkins, but I was nervous because the other shelter workers had more experience with pit bulls. Sadly, pit bulls are victims of bad breeding and bad treatment by humans and have been bred for hundreds of years to fight with other dogs. The shelter workers were always cautious when introducing "the pits" to new dogs. Contrary to popular myth, pit bulls don't have locking jaws, but their muscular mouth can be terribly difficult to pry off a bite victim.

On top of Hawkin's crate sat a smaller one that usually housed tiny dogs. The crates in this crowded shelter were sometimes stacked three high. Dogs were stacked up in order from the floor - large, medium, small. A little, elderly white Poodle-mix named Cody was currently residing on top of Hawkins. When Cody began to bark, Hawkins jumped up and down, snapping at the thin plastic barrier that separated the two. Every time his head hit the barrier Cody popped up in the air. The two could continue on hopping and popping for a half an hour. I never viewed this as aggressive behavior, but as a game that helped alleviate the oppressive boredom of shelter life.

Mark brought Maggie out of the car and into the yard. Berta was hanging over the fence and squealing, "Ooooh, Hawkins, be a good boy, please be a good boy. I want you to have a home so bad. Please be nice to Maggie. Ooooh, I'm so worried." Bliss asked Berta to go back inside the shelter during the introduction.

Maggie and Hawkins sniffed at each other for a second. Maggie's hackles were way up on her back and she looked more like a huge hedgehog than a dog. Hawkins tried to go around the back of her and mount her in a show of macho domination. Maggie would have none of it. She spun around and in true Cattle Dog style nipped him firmly on the heels. Everyone drew in their breath loudly, but Hawkins didn't retaliate. He interpreted the nips as an invitation to play and tucked his legs under his butt and started to spin in circles scooting his butt on the ground.

Maggie took Hawkins up on his invitation and the two chased each other around and around, under the picnic table, through the riverweeds, and between our legs. Hawkins was still relatively weak from being crated for so many months, and on this hot day he and Maggie quickly stopped to rest in the shade of the old tractor-trailer that sat disabled in the yard.

"Wow", Bliss said, "Just look at them. They look as if they've been together forever. I can't believe Hawk put up with that crap from Maggie. Just goes to show, every man needs a good woman to put him in his place."

I pulled Hawkins' new collar out of my pocket and he ran over and stood between Mark and me as I attached it around his neck. Bliss walked over, and in an unusually affectionate gesture, put an arm around both our backs.

She said, "Thank you guys. You don't know what it means…I mean it's always hard you know - the inevitable - if a dog doesn't get adopted for too long. But, this one, man, I've put so much work into him, I just couldn't face it. But he couldn't sit around in that crate forever, just being bored and getting fatter and fatter. Well, thanks, thanks so much."

I started to say to Bliss, "Thank you for giving him

a chance..." but, Bliss shook her head and said, "Let's get him into the van."

As we walked to the van, Tom laughed and called out to me, "You're the last, absolutely the last person I'd expect to see walking a dog like that." His mocking tone suggested that he means a somewhat prissy-looking white woman with a large, black and white pit bull. In this city, pit bulls are generally seen sporting heavy pinch collars or chains while walking by macho-looking guys, or just chained up in concrete side yards. Sometimes the puppies are sold on street corners for twenty-five dollars or less, maybe as an incentive to close a drug deal.

Maggie quickly showed Hawkins where his territory in the van would be from then on which was firmly in the back seat. Maggie rode proudly between the two front seats. Hawkins was right at home in the van, and didn't seem to mind Maggie acting as queen of the vehicle. This was probably because of the frequent car trips to Dunkin Donuts that Berta had been taking him on. He plopped his big paws over the back of the seat and rode backwards, all smiles, tongue lolling, looking out at his new world rolling out behind the rear window. The shelter workers all came out into the parking lot to wave goodbye as we drove away, as if we were going away forever, and not coming back to the shelter tomorrow to clean cages and walk dogs.

Hawkins became my new shelter-trip companion. On cool days he sat in the car, jealously watching and barking raucously at the dogs taking their daily walks. On hot days, he was invited indoors and was happy to rest inside his old crate by the desk, which Bliss left empty for his visits.

"He's the only dog who likes to come back here," she said. "Most of them pull to get out that door and never look back." But Hawkins' first allegiance was to Bliss, the woman who pulled his ticks, shoved pills down his throat, and bathed his rashes and swollen joints when he couldn't walk without extreme pain.

Then, I started to feel a dark depression descending over me when we got home with Hawkins. After all the excitement of adopting him, I again felt guilty about Cedric's death, and was emotionally drained from the frustration and sadness of seeing my parents fading away in North Carolina. I went upstairs and lay down in bed with the air conditioner blasting and curled up, exhausted under the comforters like I was sleeping away a deep winter day. Hawkins wandered about the house, investigating every corner, with Maggie fiercely showing him the boundaries of her territory.

After an hour, I felt a bump at the side of the bed

and lifted the covers to see Hawkins standing there staring at me with his golden eyes. He kept bumping the side of the bed with his huge head and I wasn't sure what he was trying to tell me. I lifted the covers higher and quickly Hawkins jumped up into the bed and dove under the comforter, pressing his warm body up against mine as if he'd always done this, always been here. He lay down, curled warmly into my belly and gave out a great satisfied sigh. It was so comforting. I fell asleep with my arms around him under the covers. Napping with Hawkins became the best part of each day. Hawkins read my emotions and pressed in close when I felt sad, especially when it was chilly outside. It was an equally beneficial exchange of affection and warmth.

    I started taking Hawkins and Maggie for walks around the neighborhood together every day. I wanted to build up Hawkins' strength and help him to shed some of the pounds he put on from eating so many donuts at the shelter. After renting little cottages by the sea for years, when it came time to buy a home, we'd chosen to restore a big very old house in the city. It was a money pit, and aggravating in many ways, but it suited us and the dogs. We enjoyed meandering around the streets watching neighbors restoring their own homes, looking at the crumbling historic architecture and greeting the other neighborhood dogs, which are plentiful. I learned many more names of dogs than human neighbors.

Some of my suburban friends commented, "How can you live in that city? I mean, the old buildings are nice, but you know, the people…" When people ask this question they never finish it and just let it trail off at the end, maybe hoping I'll finish for them and are embarrassed at not appearing to be politically correct. I guessed this comment referred to the many groups of teenage boys that hang about the neighborhood during the summer looking bored, while sitting in clusters on street corners and stoops or the many very young women pushing baby strollers, or the many macho guys walking their own pit bulls, or all of these people combined.

Our little city-by-the-sea was troubled in many ways, and notorious for a thriving drug trade, resulting in nights peppered with the sound of gunshots from frequent gang shootings. These gang shootings were usually over petty arguments perpetrated by hopeless, bored middle-school drug dealers shooting each other in short-lived shows of desperate machismo. As Hawkins, Maggie and I passed street corners, groups of sweatshirt-hooded and bandana-wearing young men clustered, ignoring the sweltering late-spring heat.

Hawkins could walk about six blocks in the heat. Then he'd find a grassy spot and collapse onto it, rolling over on his back, kicking his feet in the air for a minute then heaving a big sigh before stretching out on his side to sleep right there for the rest of the afternoon. I'd let him roll and rest for a couple of minutes before pulling him up and dragging him home.

What I noticed most when walking Hawkins anywhere was the abject fear in the eyes and faces of most people walking near us. It made me sad. Hawk was so enthusiastically friendly and goofy about people. He was the first dog I'd ever had that I trusted fully with strangers, anybody, any age. This was unlike Cedric, who would emit a low growl when someone approached us and, in order to avoid having him bite someone, I'd quickly cross the street.

In contrast, Hawkins loved everyone and delighted in meeting new people, leaning on their legs, and soaking up their pats and strokes. Hawk would stand and stare in confusion at the people who veered away from us when he longed to greet them and offer them all his love.

Still, like many pit bulls, Hawkins did seem to have an uncanny sense for people who really meant trouble. If he saw someone walking towards us a little too quickly or erratically, he stood in front of my legs with his head down sniffing the ground near the person as if their odor was communicating something to him about their personality. He'd give a frozen stare from lowered lids at the person in question until they passed by without incident. I had no fear when I was walking Hawkins. Maybe that was the appeal of the pit bulls for the macho guys - a dog who is secretly sweet and lovable, but has a tough look and demeanor, and would mean business in a confrontation.

Because of the fear I saw in the eyes of so many people, I start avoiding them on our walks. When I saw someone approaching, I'd cross to the other side of the street to avoid them as I did with Cedric, sometimes crossing back and forth many times in a few blocks. One morning I saw a group of hooded boys approaching and shifted the dogs quickly across the street.

This time, when I had crossed the road, one of the boys mumbled, "That's right, run away, get as far away as you can." He sounded hurt. I glanced back and the three boys were walking down the sidewalk hunched over in their heavy jackets on another hot day. I feel guilty. I was trying to spare them from the fear of passing Hawkins, but they thought I was afraid of them.

I was determined to walk Hawkins right past the

next group of boys I encountered on the sidewalks. The next day I took the dogs for a longer walk to Clasky Common, a pleasant little city park about a mile away from our house. About half way there, a group of four young men in their mid-twenties approached us on the same side of the street. This time I didn't rush the dogs away but just moved a little over to the side, holding tightly to Maggie's leash, since she was the dog most likely to take a nip.

The young men walked towards us and their eyes looked nervous when we didn't move. They passed by, giving wide berth to Hawkins. When they were safely past, one of them turned around and asked shyly, "Is that a Pit?" When I said "Yes," he said, "I see a lot of them around here, and not always being treated so good. Is he friendly?" I responded, "Very friendly." To the great joy of Hawkins, the young man and his friends all walked over to pat him gingerly on the head. They laughed as Hawkins immediately rolled over on his back for some more serious belly rubs. I held Maggie's leash in one hand with my arm extended keeping her away from the group. Finally, Hawkins popped up and seemed ready to move on. We all said our goodbyes but every time I met this group, and others, Hawkins was ready to meet and greet. Eventually he became very popular in our neighborhood. Everyone knew his name, though few knew mine.

Sadly, many of the children and young adults we met had stories to share about dog fights they'd witnessed or heard about in neighborhood gossip sessions. They seemed genuinely disturbed by these incidents and wanted to talk about the traumatic fights with someone who would sympathize. I didn't believe them at first, but their stories rang true and sounded similar to many similar stories told by shelter volunteers, animal control officers, and by Bliss.

At first, I thought the dog-fight stories sounded like urban myths, and as such, they didn't bother me much. I was wrong. The neighborhood stories were consistent and started to ring true. I found them terribly disturbing. I tried not to hear and to tune out the details, but at the same time I wanted to gather facts that I could report back to the Bliss and the animal control officers at the shelter.

Some of the children telling these devastating stories were very young - just eight or nine years old. I also witnessed animal cruelty at a young age, not to the extent of dog-fighting, but what I did see shocked me and stayed with me. I remembered an incident with a riding instructor when I was a kid, where he yanked so violently on an unruly horse's bit that foamy blood and spit poured from the animal's mouth. I was so upset, I ran home and told my parents who promptly called the stables to complain. The best aspect of my parents was that they always stepped up to advocate against animal abuse.

    I couldn't even look at Hawkins while the children talked about dog fighting. Hawkins came close to being sacrificed to this cruel street sport. Bliss thought he'd been bred for fighting at a rural tenant farm, just outside of our city, then been abandoned in the Freetown State Forest because he was a fighting failure, or perhaps he was tied to a tree to await a future fight. She wasn't sure exactly, but I was sure that if she hadn't been persistent in patrolling that forest, Hawkins would have met with a horrible end.

    I couldn't bear picturing my gentle giant in such a horrific situation. I hoped that encountering a nice, happy, friendly pit bull would someday prompt some of these young people to speak out when they were confronted with cruelty, and report dog fights perpetrated by neighborhood bullies, their friends, or even their relatives.

    As the children spoke, I kept hearing Bliss's voice reverberating on that awful day of September 11 saying, "I just can't believe people. I just can't believe people." I was beginning to understand the roots of

Bliss's deep dislike and distrust of people.

I collected and filed neighborhood animal abuse horror stories away in my mind for later use. They were anecdotal evidence I'd find useful for activism someday. I was going to do something to help pit bulls and help stop the cruelty perpetrated on these loving dogs; somehow, some way. I was determined to do that.

8. Last Days in Asheville

The approaching holidays season brought an increasing dread and anticipation of the winter trek back down south to check on my parents again. As they grew older, we'd started visiting them in the spring, summer, and then again during the winter holiday break. As soon as the semester was fully over and the last student had been graded, we'd pack our van with clothes and dogs and head down the icy northeastern highways south to Asheville.

Because Mark was now chair of his department and had to tie up a lot of loose administrative ends before leaving for the winter break, we were stuck traveling on the twenty-third of December. The grueling trip down I-95 across Connecticut to I-81 gave us some exquisitely beautiful moments as compensation. Icicles punctuated the dark green slate slopes and tunnels near the Danbury River. The thick water was shifted and shook underneath it's oily surface as if a restless creature were living underneath.

 I loved the heavy gray clouds of winter. They reminded me of my childhood near Lake Ontario. Riding south, I'd become hypnotized by the spurts of white snow circling on the black pavement in front of us. Mark drove on steadily, a task he took on with mechanistic determination, never responding to my offers to drive so he could lay his head back on the seat and take a nap. He drove for ten hours straight, silent, eyes fixed on the road, unless we needed to stop for a bathroom break. I wondered what he could be thinking about so mutely for so many hours, but he was a master of self-containment. I envied his ability. Never bored and seemingly lost in thought he'd grunt out an "Unnngh" sound when I made a futile attempt to start a conversation. I brought along a lot of books for the ride.

 But, a transformative element in the ride this year was having Hawkins with us. He'd fattened up quickly once out of the shelter and I had an eighty-five-pound pit bull sitting on my lap for the duration of the trip. Hawkins seemed to think he was the size of a Pug. Hawkins had eventually worked his way into the front seat position and now I couldn't get him to shift his position and ride in the back with Maggie. I'd shove him into the back seat and he'd barrel his way back up into my lap, relentlessly, hour after hour.

We'd piled up comforters and fuzzy blankets for the dogs to help make the twenty-hour drive somewhat comfortable. Maggie was completely buried for most of the trip, snoring in a nest of fabric with only the tip of her black nose sticking out for air. Hawkins, on the other hand, was balanced precariously on my aching knees. After a couple of hours, I gave up trying to shift his weight and let my legs go completely numb.

Finally, when I began to worry about the long-term loss of feeling in my legs, I moved to the back seat to snuggle up with Maggie. Hawkins took his place proudly on the front seat as if this was what he'd wanted all along. He rode face forward, just glancing at me for a moment with a look in eyes that clearly said he wondered what had taken me long to figure out my rightful place in the car. He and Mark were in control. Mark slipped a seatbelt around Hawkins and that made him feel even prouder. He puffed his big chest out and stared at the highway with Mark.

Exhausted, we stayed that night at a Best Western in Virginia, just off the roaring truck highway. The road ice had quickly turned black and treacherous. A jackknifed tractor-trailer resulted in a two-hour back up on that dark, lonely stretch of highway and we'd finally had enough. We were drained and punchy, happy to be bringing a limp pizza and warm six-pack back to the motel to share with Hawkins and Maggie.

I'd requested two double beds, anticipating that the dogs would stretch out on one of them and leave the other for us humans. But, as soon as Mark lay down on one of the slippery pink polyester comforters to eat and flip through the television channels Hawkins hopped up and stretched out beside him. He seemed to be making his thick body as long as he could so he'd cover every inch of the remaining bed space. He was the king of his domain.

No room was left for me so I moved over to the second bed with Maggie.

Mark said, "So, is this how it's going to be from now on with this dog?"

I replied with a lie, "No, no, just tonight when I'm too tired to struggle with Hawkins. We'll train it out of him soon. Let's just let him be for tonight."

The next morning was a splendor of rosy sky, and shining ice crystals coating the trees along the roadways. The beauty of the day erased the fearful dark drive of the night before. And, the final ride over the Blue Ridge Mountains and into Asheville on Christmas Eve was always a glorious one, no matter the weather.

Mark woke up from his stupor as soon as we saw the foothills off in the distance and begin to groan, "It's going to be icy up there. I'm really very afraid of driving up there in this thing."

I was nervous to be forcing the old clunker to make that climb too, but I was also filled with a lively, dangerous anticipation. I just couldn't visualize the violence of the van sliding off the road and into the rocks of those beautiful, friendly mountains.

These trips were made before the days an Interstate extension tore a hole in the mountains and linked the southern past of tiny white churches and rusty abandoned cars with the strip malls surrounding I-81. So, our van crawled up a narrow, dark, curvy country road, up over the highest point where, in the darkening evening, we could glance off to the side and see waves of jagged mountains, light with snow against the dark sky, icy puffs of mist and cabin chimney smoke rising up in the distance. The scene was magical and enthralling. It reminded me of childhood late-fall camping trips with my parents to the Adirondack

Mountains in New York State. We usually shivered through those weekends and warmed ourselves by setting big campfires. Those were our best times together. I gripped the dashboard tightly for the slippery descent into the tiny rural villages surrounding Asheville. Mark pumped the brakes of our rickety van with abandon and as soon as we hit the flats we glided safely to our destination.

My parents built their small retirement dream home a few miles outside of Asheville in a plowed-under farm turned suburban community of one-story homes, accommodating the increasing numbers of old and arthritic northern retirees seeking southern warmth and comfort. I missed my hardier parents of the fall camping days. A lighted sign sporting a jumping metal fish indicated we had finally reached the entrance to our holiday destination.

We arrived very late. I knew my mother would be nearly frantic with worry, in spite of years and years of my late evening arrivals. What made things worse for my mother that year was that my father couldn't participate in her anxiety, nor scold her for it. His mind was in a perpetually peaceful daze.

As usual, he was sitting in front of the television watching David Letterman, but he was oddly silent. His usual pattern would be to wait for us to come in the door, remove our shoes, use the restroom and then release a tirade on us about how much he hated David Letterman, even though he watched him every night.

Our greeting was always something like, "How can you young people watch that arrogant, bumbling, wise-ass fool. I'd like to wipe that smirk right off his face. Smirking, smirking, he's always smirking."

That year his greeting was very different. My father was watching but he was just staring at the TV with a vague smile on his face. He looked up at us standing there, at our suitcases, and at the jumping dogs, and said, "Oh, back from your walk already are you?"

He seemed to be losing brain matter quickly since the last time I'd seen him in the spring. Even immediately after emergency surgery his memory was stronger than it seemed now. He remembered that he had eaten dry chipped beef the night before at the hospital and said he sure didn't want that again. The doctors had high hopes for his memory recovery when he complained about the dry chipped beef but it didn't improve.

During our holiday visit Dad couldn't remember what he'd eaten the night before, and certainly did not have any urge to complain about it. He was docile and ate was he was given, remotely, and unenthusiastically.

He was nothing like the pre-surgery father who my mother always admonished for bolting down second and third helpings of dinner and dessert. My father was in a sort of remote and seemingly pleasant stupor. All his cranky, rusty, fiercely independent and sharp edges were worn down to smooth nubs. He was now a vague, kind, and needy father who was also a stranger.

One evening, when we were lying in bed watching TV with Hawkins between us, Mark said, "I hope you don't take this the wrong way, but it seems to me like your father has been kind of lobotomized. I feel like I'm watching the end of One Flew Over the Cuckoo's Nest over and over again. How much longer do you think we have to stay here?"

I'd been thinking the same thing myself but I knew we needed to stay in Asheville for as long as possible that winter. My mother was still refusing assistance from strangers in her home and I didn't know what to do next. I had to figure something out before we left.

So, we all went through the motions of having a happy holiday but it was mixed with horrible anxiety on my part. My father seemed to watching us and imitating our actions, trying hard to follow the established routine, like a child in a brand new school. While he seemed to know what holiday we were celebrating, he couldn't remember or understand the logic behind all the activities he'd developed over the years with my mother. Christmas breakfast, opening of the presents, lighting the tree and fireplace, and hanging stockings were all new to him.

What my Dad did still love to do was to take long slow walks. Hawkins and Maggie were more than happy to keep us company on as many we could take. The four of walked through his neighborhood and people came out of their houses and waved at us sadly and wished us a Merry Christmas. My Dad waved back with enthusiasm. Before his stroke, he was always helping anyone who would allow him to trim their trees or clean their garage. As always, he was a much-loved asset to his community. I could tell that his neighbors would miss him greatly.

We meandered out to the little muddy pond so he could feed the winter ducks and strolled up through the fields to the falling down little cupola partially hidden on the ragged, weedy island. The mountains rose gently blue and misty behind. The island was supposed to become the centerpiece of a golf course that never happened and now it was slowly slipping into the muddy river but I liked it this way and so did my father. It reminded him of his childhood home in northern New York State where he seemed to be spending more time in his mind every time we visited.

When we could get away for an hour or two, Mark and I took the dogs up to the Blue Ridge Parkway that was pure-magic in the winter. A slight snowfall always resulted in a total closure of the Parkway to cars. We parked our van near a Parkway barricade and walked out onto the slippery surface of the road in our boots. I remembered summer camping trips with my Mom and Dad, traversing this twisty dangerous, beautiful road, often sitting in bumper-to-bumper tourist traffic with my father swearing and hollering.

Now, we were isolated with the sounds of rattling brown leaves in the encompassing sloping forest. Great sheets of crystal white ice clung to the dark rock walls bounding the roadway. The road itself was an endless winding rink of smooth black ice. We slid our way up and down the hills of the road for hours with Hawkins and Maggie, unleashed and skittering and slipping joyfully behind us.

The woods and trees were a new world for a city dog like Hawkins. He no longer looked like a ragged city pit bull but like a fat Labrador Retriever in an outdoorsy photo on the cover of the L.L.Bean catalog with his shiny black fur and thick neck covered tightly in the red winter coat we bought him for Christmas. Hawkins didn't have hair on his feet like Maggie to protect his pads from the ice but he ran for hours -

from the ice into the woods and back to the ice, sometimes flopping down and using his wide butt as a sled to skid across the surface and into our legs.

Our flexible teaching schedules enabled us to stay in Asheville for a full month. We cooked dinner for my parents, took my Dad and dogs for long walks and skated on the Parkway while I made numerous calls to elder care professionals in the area. I desperately wanted to keep my parents in their house together for as long as possible. I was hoping someone would have a new solution. I wanted them to have a protector and caregiver in their house full-time but I didn't want it to be me.

But I felt horribly guilty about that because I knew that if and when they left this place they would be separated - my father into a nursing home and my mother into an assisted-living apartment or something similar. They'd be deprived of their beloved garden, cats and mountains.

Finally, I had a plan. I managed to find a nice adult day care facility that wasn't too far away for my mother drive to. She could drop my father off for a day of activities and have some time for herself where she didn't have to constantly watch to make sure my Dad wasn't escaping the house. I arranged for an emergency call system for nights, and finally found a nurse that my mother agreed to tolerate coming in for a wellness check a few times per week.

For a break, Mark and I visited the studios of the area's traditional southern potters. We loved them because they seemed to be sacred protectors of a rapidly vanishing way of life. Sadly, I felt their grip on this place slipping just as I felt our own connection unraveling. The suburbs would grow and make the place increasingly generic, but my parents would not be there to witness the changes.

On the last day of our visit my mother asked me if we'd like to have their motor-home. This was my parents' most beloved object in the world. That clunky twenty-four-foot box attached to a Chevy truck front had driven them across the country three times, up through the Canadian Rockies, into Alaska, into the Arizona desert where they were stuck in a dry river bed for a week and were lucky to be discovered, dehydrated and frantic, by a passing fisherman. They always loved treacherous adventures.

This was truly the end then. In offering the gift of the motorhome I knew my mother was acknowledging the end of her way of life as she knew it and her sense of freedom and adventure. My Dad was her abler companion in her schemes and endeavors and she needed him beside her to indulge her restlessness and wanderlust. She wouldn't do it alone.

    Still, I hesitated in accepting her offer. In a fanciful way, I felt I'd be driving away any possibility of my father's recovery. But, he wasn't going to recover. He was losing ground steadily. We decided to accept the gift. Mark didn't want us to drive two vehicles back up over the mountains and onto the Interstate. But, my mother said, "If you don't take it I'll just have to sell it to some strangers..." I couldn't let that happen.

    I knew she wanted us to keep it and maybe somehow keep her own memories alive by knowing we were seeing the world through its windows. I agreed to drive it home. I told Mark it was a done deal and he groaned and said, "You've got to be kidding. One of us has to drive that beast all the way home, over the mountains in the winter, that gas guzzling box-on-wheels. Oh, my god..."

    I drove my mother's motor-home north. Mark refused to drive it. He followed close behind me in the van with Maggie snuggled happily in the back seat. Hawkins rode with me, sitting proudly riding shotgun. Luckily, the snow and ice was fully melted on the steep, curvy climb to the Viewing Spot. The motor-home lurched and ground its gears but made it to the top of the highest rise in the road, while I kept glancing at the scene off to the left - a vast expanse of rippling mountains, orange and purple in the cold morning air, smoke rising mysteriously in thin spirals from dark spots here and there.

    I had a sudden lurch in my stomach at the thought that I'd never be driving down this curvy section of road again, at least not with the joyful anticipation of seeing my parents. The countryside landscape was changing. Our lives were changing. I'd never see this same scene again. I glanced often in the rear-view mirror to check that Mark was still driving behind me. I looked over at Hawkins in his seat - oblivious to any sadness or nostalgia - he had both paws on the dashboard and was gazing joyfully out the front window, immersed in the movement of the pavement under our wheels.

    And, we never did drive back that way again. The following summer the relentless Interstate connector drove a massive hole through the mountains near the Viewing Spot. It was too much stress for my mother to manage my father as his dementia progressed relentlessly. He began walking out to the island every day believing it was his childhood cabin home. He decided he wanted to sleep on the island. Finally, my older brother swept down from Michigan and gathered my parents up and brought them to live in his home. I didn't see my father again for several years. I never saw my mother again, except in my dreams.

9. Chopper Goes to Baltimore

When I was still a rescue innocent, I never considered living with dogs that had to be separated from one another in the house and yard. Volunteers at Hidden Falls animal shelter sometimes talked about their separate packs of dogs that just couldn't get along and had to live securely in separate parts of the house to keep horrific fights from breaking out. Whenever someone told me they lived that way I thought they were a little crazy. Now we too live in a pack-oriented house with dogs tenaciously separated by baby gates and locked doors.

It turned out that Hawkins didn't like any dogs other than his little Cattle Dog buddy, Maggie, his first and only canine companion. Hawkins was, after all, bred and trained as a fighting dog. We were learning all about the baggage that comes with that. Hawkins would just flip out, a raging, foaming display of aggression, at the site of another pit bull. I don't know what the telltale physical sign was for him but he could always pick another dog of his own breed out of a group and go right for it. So, any newly rescued foster pit bulls had to be kept on a floor to themselves and behind a solid, locking door. Hawkins was sneaky and determined in seeking out his arch rivals.

Many of my fellow rescue friends felt that it was unethical and much too risky to have any other dogs in the house with Hawkins. And, it was very risky. But the pit bulls that came here were the ones that were scheduled for euthanasia at the shelter. Even at Hidden Falls, where everyone made a great effort to adopt out the pit bulls, many remained for months, waiting for a home long after the state mandatory ten-day holding period for strays ran out. But, Hidden Falls advocated hard. At many other shelters, the pit bulls were put down on the eleventh day.

Sadly, all the negative media - breed bans, Internet rumors, sensationalized and lurid news stories, and insurance dangerous breed policies - had taken a toll on this once valued and noble breed of dog. Most shelters just refused to spend time and energy on them, saw them as a liability and didn't want to adopt them out. Small rescue operations were often their only hope and I wasn't about to turn a friendly pit bull away if its time was up on death row.

So, we went over and over various strategies with Hector, the dog trainer at Hidden Falls. But, no training seemed to curb Hawkins's animosity for dogs other than Maggie. Maggie was his woman and he was willing to fight to the death for what was his. So, at some point, rather than risk any potential violence, we resigned ourselves to having Hawkins living peacefully on his favorite sofa in the living room with Maggie and any new dogs were relegated to upstairs bedrooms after a quarantine period in the finished basement.

In November, as the politics and bickering at Hidden Falls became irritating I began to distance myself from Bliss and the crew a bit by spending more time volunteering for other local animal rescue organizations, in addition to transitioning our house into a safe sanctuary for misfit dogs.

Often, these new volunteer duties didn't occur on-site but required long-distance driving. The Internet was just starting to invigorate the shelter and rescue industry. New rescue sites like Petfinder.com were popping up all over the Web and interstate rescue transport trips brought scores of dogs from overcrowded and miserable southern shelters to the northeast. Also, adopters were now able to pick out the perfect dog from a photo and description and a shelter representative could drive a dog anywhere in the continent to a new home.

On a dank early December afternoon, I found myself on one of these transports for the first time. I had an art education conference my boss wanted me to attend in Baltimore, but I balked at flying in with her. I didn't want her to see how panicky I get on airplanes. So I told her I wanted to drive down and visit my nonexistent cousin in Philadelphia on the way.

I mentioned my trip to a fellow volunteer and she cried, "What a coincidence!" She just happened to have a large Old English Bulldog that needed a transport to a breed-specific rescuer just outside of Philly. At first I thought this coincidence was a payback for lying to my boss. But, after thinking it over, I welcomed the opportunity to drive long hours with a canine companion. I was still feeling very sad after the holiday weeks spent in Asheville. I was fighting another depression that threatened to exhaust me to the point where I just retreated to bed. Maybe transporting this misplaced dog across the northeastern seaboard would be just what I needed to wake me up and make me feel a little less desolate.

Therefore, in the bleakest of mid-Januarys, I passed the smokestacks and stench of northern New Jersey with a massive dog named Chopper stretched out across the back seat of our rickety minivan. Chopper snored rhythmically and soothingly as he pulled me into a slowly nodding trance. I desperately needed to make a coffee stop but didn't want to get off the interstate and officially enter the murky maze of industrial buildings.

I was thinking that this drive may have been a mistake. There were so many other pleasant ways to spend a late winter afternoon, like curling up beside our phony electric fireplace for the third reading of an Agatha Christie mystery with Hawkins and Maggie. Why was I so neurotic about airplanes that I was wasting two days driving back and forth on icy highways in the midst of a smog-heavy, grey-orange New Jersey day?

Still, I was looking forward to meeting Joyce, my destination rescuer in Bucks County, Pennsylvania. A couple days after our online introduction through Chopper's shelter, I answered the phone to hear the shouting voice of Joyce, of Old English Bulldog Rescue, Inc. "Hey, how ya doing?" Joyce asked, in a cheerleader's outdoor voice. I liked her right away. She sounded so outgoing and different than me.

Joyce said, "Chopper is a great, I mean a really great dog, not aggressive at all. I want to get him down here for a while to get him healthy. He's pretty skinny. Can you pull him and hold him for a few days until I can get a transport lined up?"

I hesitated. Pulling and holding a dog meant removing the animal from the shelter, taking official responsibility for it, and bringing it home until the transport could be arranged to depart. But then I thought it would only be for a few days. I could get to know Chopper better before driving alone for eight hours in the van with him. It would be good practice in keeping the dogs in our house separate and happy in case we needed to do it again in the future. And all I had to do for the next few days was pack my things for Baltimore.

The whole plan was a good way - a great excuse - to avoid the plane flight! I'd be saving Chopper's life, my own dignity and my nervous system at the same time. Obviously, things were meant to line up this way, with Joyce and the shelter calling just days before the trip!

For a sufferer of mid-air panic attacks, the idea of a ten-hour minivan drive down the eastern seaboard in the middle of winter was much more inviting than a two-hour plane flight. And, it turned out that I didn't need to bring Chopper to my house after all. The shelter agreed to hold on to him and I could just pick him up on my way out of town.

Joyce was enthusiastic. "Wow, that's so great," she shouted. "It's all meant to be. I'll get to meet you in person, and Chopper won't have to go through the stress of dealing with multiple transport connections on his way down."

Mark was less enthusiastic. "That old van is having electrical problems and it will probably be snowing somewhere along the route. That thing is terrible in the snow," he said with heavy futility in his voice. He knew nothing would change my mind once I was set on doing something.

So, I picked up Chopper at seven in the morning on the day of the trip. The Swan Shelter in Fall River agreed to have a volunteer open up early for me. I'd never been to this shelter before, even though it was in

Fall River just a mile or so from Hidden Falls. I'd heard rumors among the shelter volunteer network that Swan didn't keep animals for long and euthanized many more than necessary, considering the amount of donations it received.

I now doubted the rumors. After all, the shelter had cared for the aging Chopper for several months and was willing to contact a rescue organization to help him find a home. Those were signs of a good compassionate shelter. My visit that morning confirmed this assumption. The shelter was clean, well-organized and spacious. A kindly volunteer met me at the front door and guided me through the white halls with obvious pride, pointing out the new low-cost veterinary clinic and warm, wide runs where a variety of dogs were snoozing.

"Let's meet Chopper outside so we don't wake up the whole crew," she said, as she led me out to a small fenced yard at the back of the shelter. I stood out in the cold as a few snow flurries started to fall while the volunteer went to fetch Chopper. I'd never actually met an Old English Bulldog before. I'd seen many in photos sent to me by Joyce but I had no idea of their size. I pictured a fat, short little dog, like a regular English Bulldog.

What came out of the door had no relationship to

those floppy short Bulldogs. Chopper was huge and very bony, yet muscular, weighing at least a hundred and twenty pounds. He had a huge round blocky head with drooping lips and a pushed-in Bulldog face that looked like a sad clown with painted-on black lips. He had a widely overshot jaw and his bottom row of teeth perpetually protruded up and over his top lip, hence his name.

His fur was white but his facial fur had the typical rusty orange tearstains many white dogs get and they made him look even more droopy and sad. I shouted, "Hi, Chopper!" and he plodded over to me and leaned against my legs with the demeanor of an old sway-backed horse. "You know," the volunteer said, "Chopper is really not a full Old English Bulldog. He's got some Mastiff in him and maybe even some Dane. That's why he's so big and has such a goofy face. I've discussed that with Joyce of course," she added quickly. Joyce was willing to rescue a mixed breed if something about a particular dog pulled at her heartstrings.

I'd never been afraid of dogs, but I did feel a little anxious at the thought of handling such a large and powerful one alone. "So, Chopper, we need to hit the road," I said as we tried to entice him into the large metal dog crate I'd placed in the back of the van. I hated to see him cramped up in a crate after all the months he'd spent in the shelter, but I was worried that if he tried to climb into my lap while I was driving I wouldn't be able to shift him. I headed onto the interstate with Chopper whimpering softly and staring at the back of my head the whole time. I could feel him in the rear view mirror gazing longingly at me. After his months of isolation, he was dying for some affection.

We drove through Rhode Island and into Connecticut before we stopped at the welcome center to take a bathroom and coffee break. At first, I was worried that Chopper might become overexcited by an unfamiliar situation and try to pull away from me as I guided him out of the crate; but his demeanor was much the same as it was at the shelter. He leaned against my legs as we slowly meandered over to an area thickly wooded with pines. He did his business quickly, heaved a big satisfied sigh and wandered back over to prop himself against my legs.

I just couldn't bring myself to push mellow Chopper back into his crate for the rest of the ride. I opened the side door and he happily heaved himself up onto the blanketed back seat and promptly stretched out right across it. We sat in heavy traffic on I-95. Normally the stress of dealing with weaving drivers and tailgaters would leave me exhausted and edgy. But

Chopper's non-stop, rhythmic snoring sent me into a relaxed, trance-like state that lasted all through the New Jersey Turnpike.

The sky was steely gray and cold and the web of industrial scaffolding and detritus filling the distant landscape, combined with my depression, could have left me feeling the more than the oppressive loneliness I sometimes feel on lone road trips. I reached behind at intervals to stroke Chopper's massive head and he'd emit a slow groan of pleasure between snores.

I stopped at a rest area outside of Philadelphia and got an extra-large coffee for myself and a plain cheeseburger for Chopper. He swallowed the burger in one gulp and reluctantly slid off the seat and out the door to urinate in the cold. It was becoming sharply cold as we headed south. Light snow flurries were swirling around like miniature tornados on the asphalt. I reached down to hug Chopper before returning to the car and I could feel the boniness of his ribcage and I wondered what his former life had been like and hoped his future life would be much better.

We drove another half hour on the Philadelphia bypass and took an exit that led through a series of recently industrialized farmlands that were quickly becoming encrusted with a layer of icy snow. The road meandered through industrial parks until it came out into a contrasting antiquated village street. It was not yet five o'clock but the day was fading fast into twilight and the rows of quaint shops were closed early in anticipation of a snowstorm. I felt a twinge of nervousness about the weather. I could possibly stay over at Joyce's and drive the last two hours to Baltimore in the morning and still make my presentation in time.

But, I wanted to press on. The long ride was beginning to wear on me and I was visualizing a warm room with a fluffy bed and a hot bath. Also, I was beginning to feel the animal rescuer's melancholy - that horrible feeling of loss and concern when faced with giving up an animal to a new and uncertain future. In just this one afternoon I had become very attached to Chopper. His calm, appreciative demeanor, his hypnotic snoring, the way he leaned against my legs while walking - as if he didn't want to lose physical contact for even a second endeared him to me.

I almost bypassed Joyce's house altogether. I had a wild thought about sneaking massive Chopper up to my room on the tenth floor of the luxury hotel my boss had arranged for us and hiding him until after I'd finished my presentation in the morning. Maybe I could just leave him at Joyce's place and swing by on my way home to pick him up and bring him home. Or,

I could call Katherine and tell her I'd run into car problems on the road and wouldn't be able to get to Baltimore. I could turn right around and take Chopper home. My presentation seemed trivial in comparison to Chopper's plight.

Yet, though I was slowly turning the house into a sanctuary and temporary rescue shelter, the idea of keeping three dogs in my house long-term seemed crazy, and besides Chopper needed a real, permanent, loving home. The dogs we had were a challenge, and Mark and I were just learning to cope with the complexities of inter-dog relationships. I knew I had to let Chopper go like all the rest of the shelter dogs - hopefully to good people with a lot of space in their home and hearts for his huge body and neediness. I hoped they had plenty of time to lavish him with the attention he craved.

I pulled up in a circular driveway in front of a small white antique colonial house with a red door. It was surrounded by dark droopy pine trees and set into a hill of gray rock. It looked to me like a perfect, old fashioned Christmas card. Chopper seemed reluctant to leave the van so I left him in the backseat and went to the door and rapped on the knocker. A few minutes passed with no response and I had a flash of fear that I would actually have to find a way to keep Chopper for the night. Then the door opened suddenly and I was confronted with a short wiry woman with long blond hair and a tough yet elfin face. This was exactly how I had imagined Joyce from her voice on the phone.

"Well, hello there," Joyce piped in her boisterous voice. "I was getting worried about you two. We're supposed to get a big snowstorm tonight; do you believe it? We've had practically nothing at all this year and it comes on the night you're driving through." All the time Joyce was speaking she had me in a tight bear hug. I was so much taller than her that her arms reached around my shoulders and her head was practically on my chest. I marveled again at what a tight and immediate family animal-people can become.

In my entire life I have no memory of any member of my own family giving me an extended bear hug. Most of the time we tip-toed around each other nervously with averted eyes, afraid to show affection or enthusiasm for the other's presence, except for rare handshakes. As alien as it felt, I welcomed Joyce's warm hug at the end of the long ride just like I would welcome a warm fireplace at the end of a hike in the snow.

"Well, where's Mr. Chopper?" said Joyce as she walked over to the van and opened the side door. Chopper still seemed reluctant to leave the warm van but he slipped off his seat dutifully and came over to lean against Joyce's legs. "Oh, he's a big sweetheart," she squealed as she knelt down in the snow and gave him a great bear hug, too.

"And we've got to name him something besides Chopper. Why do people call these dogs names like Chopper? I can't find him a decent home with a name like Chopper. We'll attract every macho nut in the world. Anyway, come in, come on in and have a cup of coffee. I think he looks like a Bluto maybe, don't you?"

I nodded in exhausted agreement and followed Joyce into the house. I was anxious to get back on the road but I did want to see where Chopper was going to be staying. I only had a couple more hours to drive. If I could leave in the next few minutes I could probably get to Baltimore before the snow had time to accumulate on the thruway. I needed some closure with Chopper though. I couldn't simply hand over his leash to Joyce and climb back in the van and drive away.

As we walked through the front door into the living room I was dismayed to see a row of crates lined up against the wall. Five crates held Bulldogs of various shapes, sizes and breed mixes. A sixth empty crate sat at the end of the row. All the dogs started barking as soon as Chopper entered the room and he cowered behind my legs. Joyce saw the look on my face and said quickly, "Don't worry about Chopper. These guys don't stay in the crates all day. I check to see which dogs get along good with each other and they go out and play in the fenced yard in back. My boyfriend comes over and we walk all the dogs every day. If Chopper gets along with Bella, he can hang around with us loose in the house."

Joyce nodded to a large white pit bull stretched out territorially on the couch. Bella had soulful eyes and gazed longingly at us but she didn't make a move to come over until Chopper was placed safely in his crate. He looked sadly at me from behind the bars as Bella came running over with her butt and stumpy tail wiggling enthusiastically.

I noticed that Bella's tongue was perpetually hanging out of the left side of her mouth. Joyce said, "Bella's jaw was broken when we found her. It had started to heal the wrong way so the vet had to break and reset it. Then we had to have some teeth removed so now her tongue hangs out all the time and that's what makes her so damn beautiful!" Bella wagged and wiggled more vigorously in response as Jodi went into the kitchen to get a bowl of food for Chopper.

I started to relax when I saw that Chopper was not so distressed by his situation that he refused a bowl of food. He was snarfling happily away in the big bowl as Joyce showed me around her house. The exterior was traditional in a cute touristy way with gingerbread trim on most surfaces but the inside was a cave. The kitchen was built right into the rock wall, and damp gray rocks pushed through the wall forming the entire back end of the room. A large picture window looked out on a ravine filled with more dark pines and twisted ivy - a deep black and green vista punctuated by white drifting specks of snow. It was a fairytale house, a Hobbit house right out of my imagination.

"It's a pretty cool house isn't it?" said Joyce. "I got it really cheap. Want to know why? Come on upstairs." We climbed up an extremely narrow, twisting stairway that opened out on to a small landing and a large bedroom, the back wall partially ripped away to reveal more of the damp rock wall.

"The lady that owned this house was an artist too, and obviously, she wanted to be close to nature," laughed Joyce. "She died in this bedroom. She lay dead here for a really long time. She lived alone and didn't have any family close by so nobody knew she was gone. I don't really know how anyone would have found out at all if weren't for the mailman. It's always the mailman finding them isn't it? Anyway, an article about her was in the paper and after that nobody wanted to buy the house, except for me."

"People were worried about the artist's ghost haunting this place but I don't care if she wants to live here with me!" Joyce continued breathlessly. "In fact she's welcome to share this room with me and my dogs. My boyfriend can't make up his mind whether he wants to move in here or not but I don't need him if he doesn't. I've got my dogs, my ghost artist, and my rocks. Come on downstairs and have some coffee before you hit the road."

We snuggled into the plump couch with our coffee, Bella curled tightly between us, and a crackling fire going in a stone fireplace. Joyce kept talking in her rapid, chirpy breathless way. Chopper was snoozing soundly across the room, his snores and the chorus of snores from the other Bulldogs providing a relaxing backdrop to our conversation. Before I knew it a couple of hours had passed and I was reluctant to pull myself out of that snuggly warm den and back into the cold, lonely minivan.

When I started for the door I pulled my keys out of my bag and Chopper jumped up in his crate looking at me as if he was ready to climb into his backseat and continue the journey. Once again, I felt overwhelmingly sad about leaving him behind. I was starting to get teary-eyed when Joyce said, "You're doing the right thing for him. You got him out of that shelter and probably saved his life. His time was almost up. You drove him all the way down here and now I'll find him the very best home, the very goddamned best. Don't you worry about Mr. Chopper Man. Just get to your hotel safely."

We hugged goodbye and I started the van, noticing a little hesitation as it rattled to dubious life in the bitter cold. I remembered Mark's warning about the electrical system but pulled away from Joyce's cozy house anyway. I wanted to get to a place where I could relax alone. I felt depressed and exhausted again and, despite Joyce's assurances, kept seeing images in my head of Chopper looking forlornly at me from his crate.

Twenty miles outside of Baltimore the van started to hesitate and jerk pretty seriously and I thought for the first time that maybe this trip had been too reckless an undertaking. The snow was falling heavily enough to make a scrunching sound under my wheels that told me I was riding on only snow and not on solid road any longer. As consolation, my constant attention to the health of the van helped me avoid that horrible existential feeling of road trip aloneness. I missed Chopper terribly.

I used to drive up I-95 several times a year

between Georgia and New York to visit home when I was in school before the panic attacks became more frequent. My sister-in-law used to marvel at my driving saying, "How can you ride for days alone like that? I can't drive over an hour by myself. There's nowhere to go to get away from yourself." Now, I understood where she was coming from.

There were not very many other cars on the road and no salt trucks anywhere in sight. Finally, after what seemed like dozens of hours, I passed through the Fort McHenry Tunnel and took the exit leading to the waterfront. The Baltimore streets looked beautiful in comparison to the thruway. The fresh snow covering the red brick row houses, and the flakes swirling in front of my headlights all seemed festive and welcoming. Where the thruway had been deserted, Baltimore was bustling in the midst of the snowstorm. People were walking in clusters and laughing in the streets as they exited cozy-looking restaurants and bars and breathed white puffs of steam into the air.

The van scrunched, slid and faltered over the snow into the parking garage. I slammed the door gratefully and got out with my night bag not knowing whether it would start in the morning or not. At that point it didn't matter. I was so tired I'd have welcomed the opportunity to spend a couple of days in a comfortable hotel bed. I could arrange an alternate way to get home in the morning. The waterfront and streets around the hotel were filled with people tossing snowballs at one another. I felt a surge of energy and would have liked to take a walk, especially if I had had Chopper with me. But I went down the massive marble halls of the hotel and up the elevator to my room.

As soon as I put my bag down I reached for my phone to call Mark and hoped he hadn't heard anything on the news about the storm. Before I did, there was a knock on the door and I was a little dismayed to see my boss Katherine standing there with another woman next to her. Both had wet hair and red runny noses. I was bone tired and afraid she'd want to give our presentation a trial run.

"Welcome to Baltimore," Katherine said. "This is my sister Diane. We were just having drinks and dinner. She's the reason you get this lovely room to yourself tonight. I'm not going to be staying with you. I'm heading to Diane's place down the street. We just thought we'd stop in and make sure that you made it here okay."

Katherine and Diane seemed to be very tipsy and some of Katherine's professional veneer had melted away with the dripping snow. "Well, as long as we're here let's order another round of drinks and have a toast to your long successful drive." Both women laughed good-naturedly and room service quickly delivered a bottle of wine and glasses.

We all sat on the huge bed that was situated just a foot away from an immense floor to ceiling window offering a breathtaking view out over the whitening city and dark frozen Chesapeake Bay. Katherine, whom I now heard referred to as Kathy for the first time, and her sister wanted to reminisce about their childhood. It turned out that Katherine grew up in Baltimore. I'd worked with her for years and never knew where she had lived her childhood.

It was fun to have a drink with the sisters and listen to them chatter and laugh away the rest of the night as I sat back in an exhausted, drunken and comfortable stupor. Finally, Katherine stood up and said, "Well, we really need to get some sleep if we're going to do a decent presentation so early in the morning. It will be fine; I know it will be just fine. I'm not even worried. Back out into the storm, Diane."

After they left, I had just enough energy left to call Mark, change my clothes, and lie back on the massive billowy bed. Nothing in my life had ever felt so comfortable as that bed. Still, I had a sudden longing for the calming Chopper and his snoring and I wished he were stretched right out next to me. I had a second of pain thinking about him in that crate, but knowing Joyce a little better now, I guessed he was probably snoring away with her in her rocky bedroom along with Bella and the artist's ghost. The thought made me smile as I thought about Joyce's tight hugs and Chopper's warm regular breathing.

As I turned out the lights, the vista of the sparkling city, shimmering icy water and eddying snowdrifts seemed to come alive. The combination of wine, snow and exhaustion gave me a feeling that the bed was slowly tilting over onto the enormous window and suddenly I was floating on top of the panorama stretching out far below. A flood of well-being came over me, without any of the uncomfortable memories that sometimes plague me before sleep. I was alone and suspended above the dark streets and bay. It was a blissful night. And, I remembered that night again even more fondly three weeks later when Joyce sent me photos of Chopper (now Bluto) sprawled out happily and luxuriously on a fuzzy blanket-covered sofa in his new home.

10. A Dog With No Ears

Safely home from the Baltimore trip and relaxing and reviewing my emails with a cup of coffee and pile of dogs on the sofa, I encountered an agonizing plea. The very long subject line was "PLEASE, please look at these photos. Dog in desperate need. One-day left. Never seen injuries like this. Look at his eyes. They are saying that he wants to live." In my short time in animal rescue, I'd learned to avoid emails like this – to delete them immediately – and never ever look at the attached photos.

As soon as I began posting photos of the Hidden Falls shelter dogs on the wide-reaching rescue website, Petfinder.com, I became increasingly inundated by emails from strangers. Many were pleading for help for a particular dog or cat. These were the hardest to cope with as they began to flood my inbox. Animal rescue people were zealous in expanding their email lists and my address quickly spread out to hundreds of organizations. I was receiving rescue pleas from all over the country and Mexico, Canada, Indonesia and Romania.

I was still exhausted from the long drive and my

inclination was to ignore the newest email. But something about the wording made me curious to look at the attached photo of this dog. I didn't really want to see horrendous injuries. And, what could I do to help? Hidden Falls was completely filled with dogs coming in from the city animal control team. Bliss would be furious if I brought a new and injured dog to the shelter. And, I couldn't keep a strange dog here. Two dogs were enough work and Hawkins would not like it one bit.

But, it was the comment about the look in the dog's eyes showing that he wanted to live that made me move my finger and click on the email. I did it. Two photos popped up right away, before the text and I saw a very beautiful orange and white pit bull with closely cropped, pointy little ears that were barely ears at all. This was probably the result of a home clip job. Basement and backyard breeders like to make pit bull puppies look tougher by clipping their ears into devilish little points. Not being able to afford plastic puppy surgery at a veterinarian's office, the cropping was done at home, with scissors. Fight-cropped ears were what Bliss called them.

The ears were the worst thing I noticed about the orange dog. I was relieved that the horrendous injuries were not as bad as I had anticipated. At least his legs and body were intact. The other problem was a nasty gash circling the dog's entire neck. The rest of his body looked sleek and healthy though thin. Further photos showed close-ups of the neck area, and it did look like the dog had suffered a horrible wound. The dog's entire neck was gaping open and red, with some rough black stitches poking out here and there through the mess. From one angle, the stitches seemed to be the only thing holding the head to the body.

I could clearly see why the email writer was so passionate about saving this dog. His eyes were an odd color, bright gold, and he was looking suspiciously but longingly at the photographer. His head was lowered and defensive but his eyes were looking directly up at the camera. I felt my heart twist and tighten until it was hard to breathe.

I recognized that look from other animals coming in to Hidden Paws. I'd seen it in some children too sometimes as they were being dragged through the store by an impatient parent. I'd felt emotions creating that look in myself. Confusion, a plea, the naïve thought, "I'm here, I'm alive, I don't know why I'm here or why life is like this or why people are the way they are. But, I'm here, I'm frightened, and I want to live. Please take care of me, so I can live."

I'd opened the email and it was only one of

hundreds. But, I strongly felt that this dog needed me. I resolved to do whatever it took to get the dog out of whatever high-kill shelter the email said he was in. I'd bring him back to health and find him a good home. He'd have to stay at our house for a few weeks but somehow we'd make it work.

I adopted several dogs from shelters over the years but didn't have any experience in pulling a dog from a shelter for a rescue organization and that's what I'd have to do here. The woman who posted the email asked me to be an agent of her rescue organization because animal control would only release an injured dog to a rescue group. And, according to the email, this dog was at the same awful, sad high-kill shelter from which we'd adopted Maggie. My stomach lurched again. I dreaded, absolutely dreaded, returning to that place.

I replied to Jennifer, the email writer, asking for more information about the dog. She turned out to be a vet-tech from a local animal hospital and volunteer for an organization called Pitty Love Rescue. She was the technician that stitched up the dog's neck when New Bedford animal control brought him for emergency surgery for his wounds.

Jennifer and I spoke over the phone. She said, "I wanted to do better for that dog for sure. I hated the way those stitches looked. But when it's a pit bull, and from Animal Control, and going on to the city shelter, we just don't spend much time on them. The state says we have to fix them - it's the humane thing - but it's just quick and dirty, you know? My boss wouldn't let me spend more time on his neck. It's really sad. We see a lot of them like this, but this one got to me, you know? Pitty Love is backlogged with rescue requests so he can't go there. But, I decided I'm going to send out emails to everyone on my rescue lists and someone will come through."

I asked hopefully, "Has anyone else responded to you?"

"Nope", she answered, "You're the only one."

So, it was meant to be. I justified this new trouble coming in to our house by thinking that I was tapped by destiny to save this dog. I was the only person who responded to that excruciatingly painful email. I worried that I was starting to think like some other long-term rescuers I'd met - the ones with houses or barns filled with dogs. Every animal they saved had appealed to them especially. There were little indicators; a look in the eyes, a rekindled memory of a family pet, a sign, or an omen like seeing a similar-looking dog walking down the street or on television - these were the ways rescue decisions were made.

Jennifer explained that pit bulls were never adopted out to the public from this dank, sad shelter. They had a firm policy of not adopting out pit bulls - written in stone. If a licensed shelter or rescue organization did not step forward to help pull a dog from the shelter it would not be released. Every pit bull coming through the sad shelter was killed unless a rescue organization came forward to help.

I supposed the shelter felt they were performing a service to the public by keeping potentially dangerous animals off the streets of the city, but the policy seemed terribly misguided. I thought how awful it was that people devised policies for animals that they would never apply to themselves - or would they in the right circumstances? Well, of course, history proved this to be so. There is still unrelenting racism. There are still human genocides. People can be unspeakably immoral if they think their god is on their side. And, these eugenic policies are applied to animals all the time without much thought. The rationale might be that a breed is rumored to be dangerous, or perhaps that breed animal stock needs improvement, or maybe an owner of dog show champions wants to have staunch unrealistic breed standards despite resulting health problems, and so on. And factory farming is another story altogether. Human treatment of other animals can be shockingly, disgracefully, evil.

I felt very angry and more determined than ever to get this earless pit bull out of that awful shelter. I'd started referring to the dog as No Ears. I hadn't let Mark in on any details of the No Ears drama. He'd be exceedingly worried that I was going to bring another dog into our home. Mark relished calm, quiet and control. Hawkins and Maggie upset his peaceful days by merely barking at pedestrians passing by our front gate.

I hadn't fully fleshed out a plan of what to do with No Ears once I'd had him released from the shelter. I didn't do any long-term planning for No Ears because I knew how difficult it was to find a foster or permanent home for the thousands of homeless pit bulls in need every day. Many people, even those who supported the breed, did not want to foster them because it took so long to adopt them out.

Still, I just knew I had to get No Ears out of that shelter. I'd really started to adopt the rescuer's mode of magical thinking - "If I rescue him there will be a place for him because if I rescue him it will mean that he was meant to live and therefore a home will come because it was meant to be..."

On my volunteer days at Hidden Falls I talked with the shelter's resident dog trainer about No Ears.

Hector was a kind and gentle man and I was hoping he would use his connection with Hidden Falls to support me in using them as a back-up shelter situation if No Ears didn't work out at home. Hector looked at me in disbelief and said, "No way. I just can't do that. You know how many pit bulls are looking for homes here already and we are full up. Just look in the back runs. They are full of Pits. Why don't you foster one from here? Why are you fixated on this dog? Just because of the neck injuries? There are many out there with worse. I just can't do it for you, even though I'd really like to…If you foster that dog you will end up keeping him - plan on that - and you know nothing about him, nothing at all. You could get badly hurt."

Hector was right, of course. I knew nothing about No Ears' personality, behavior, or health. Like Jennifer, I was just thinking about the look in his eyes that said he was lonely and confused and longing to live. I was "thinking with my heart and not my head" as Bliss was fond of saying. "You'll never, never, never last in rescue if you keep doing that," she'd say. But, my heart would always win out over my head. I'd already changed No Ears' name to Ricky. I thought he looked like the Little Ricky character with the rusty red hair on the Lucille Ball Show.

11. Confronting the Beast

Jennifer agreed to meet me at the shelter the following afternoon. She reminded me again that her Pitty Love organization was totally swamped with dogs needing foster homes and couldn't shelter Little Ricky if things didn't work out. I'd have to keep him or foster him until an adoptive home could be found. If he turned out to be a mean dog, I'd have to make the ultimate decision on whether he would live or die and I'd have to be the one to take him to a vet to be euthanized if he turned out to be a dog that was resistant to rehabilitation.

"Are you willing to do all this for the long-term?" Jennifer asked?

I agreed hesitantly but was filled with awful feelings of guilt. I still hadn't told Mark about any of this. I had to figure out how to break the news with tact, but, however I told him it was going to happen. Little Ricky was coming home with me. I rationalized, "Little Ricky is a good looking dog. Once his neck heals, it won't take any time at all to find him a nice home. Once Mark sees how horrible his neck looks now he won't be able to kick him out of the house. Once I have time to work with this dog he'll be a quick adoption. I recited all the rescue platitudes; " Just take it one day at a time…It's a lot of trouble but it's a life saved…I can't save the world all but I can make it a good world for this one dog…"

I'd absorbed many rescue rationalization clichés from the people I'd met through Hidden Falls. They all recited them, especially when briefing their families on the entrance of another animal to the pack. Yes. No matter a lack of space, angry spouses, mounting veterinarian bills, animal behavioral incompatibilities, dirt, hair, dust, stress, injuries, lack of time, it will all work out in the end if we just take it one day at a time.

I drove into the parking lot of the sad shelter on a gray March morning. The air was damp and cold. The shelter was a block away from the waterfront wharves and fish processing factories. The excess dead fish were processed into cat food and the air was heavy with the smell. I wondered if it permeated the concrete walls of the shelter to further torment all the cats and dogs in their crates. My childhood dog's favorite days involved rolling in the dead fish along the shores of Lake Ontario. There would be no such joys for these shelter dogs. The animals facing impending doom in this shelter didn't seem much interested in food.

Maggie was ravenous the day we brought her home. We were told that she didn't eat at all during her ten days in the shelter, and since she was starving I fed her repeated small portions of food. She gulped them down in a second and looked at me pleadingly for more. I spent hours feeding her teaspoons of canned dog food.

I remembered how Maggie looked at us when we looked through the gate and was finally sure she was getting into our car. She seemed to be so aware of her fate in that place and overwhelmed with frantic relief when we sprung her out of there. She started to blow her entire coat of fur as soon as we brought her into the adoption room. I had to throw out my favorite dark green wool coat after that day, so much white fur had been embedded in it.

Jennifer arrived at the shelter before me and was leaning against her car smoking a cigarette in the fish-laden air. She stomped it out on the ground and shook my hand. She was young, maybe in her mid-twenties. She had a reassuring crisp, efficient manner and was well-dressed with well-controlled and elegant thick black hair, so unlike the volunteers and staff at Hidden Falls.

Jennifer introduced herself and said she was not only a full-time vet tech but a graduate student in biology and volunteering for Pitty Love Rescue in her spare time. She'd fallen hopelessly in love with the Bulldog breeds after encountering them in school labs.

I found Jenny's confidence and professional demeanor reassuring as I faced the doors of that depressing gray concrete building. I was starting to feel somewhat panicky, sweaty and slightly faint. I wondered for the first time, but not the last, if shelter volunteers suffered from post-traumatic stress disorder. Little specks of spring snow were dropping on us and I could hear the barks and wails of the dogs in the runs behind us. Jenny looked at me and sighed, "Are you ready for this?"

I was not ready, nor would I ever be ready, to enter that avenue of misery again. I could feel my heart racing and the heat and sweat of increasing anxiety creeping up my body from feet to head. I said, "I'm ready. If I wait another minute, I won't be able to go in there."

"I know! This place has a horrible reputation," said Jenny. "I volunteered to come down here for you, in part, because I'd heard so many horror stories and I'm curious to see this place for myself."

I tried to calm my nerves with slow, deep breaths and more rationalizations then started to walk towards the double metal doors when Jenny grabbed my sleeve.

"Wait," she said. "I forgot to tell you that we can't let these people know you'll be fostering the dog. The only way I could convince them to release him was for me to agree that he'd go to our rescue shelter. We don't really have a shelter though, just a network of foster homes, but they don't need to know that. It's funny, but I don't want to get fired from my volunteer job."

Jennifer informed me that we'd pull the dog and she'd hand him over to me when we got back out to the parking lot. She asked me to pretend that I was her assistant until we get out of there. She assured me her organization didn't usually pull dogs like this - ones without prior behavior testing. This dog also had never had a rabies shot that we knew of but he'd been quarantined for ten days now so was probably safe to handle. I cringed. I had a deadly fear of contracting rabies and always refused to touch the street cats when they first came in to Hidden Falls.

Jennifer stepped in front of me and pulled the metal doors open. A security guard stood by the front desk cleaning his fingernails and didn't pay much attention to us at all. I wondered briefly why this shelter needed a security guard. The sound of howling and wailing had increased ten-fold when the dogs caught the scent of new visitors. It was deafening and echoed and rolled off the concrete walls. The odor of dog feces and death was more intense than I remembered. Jennifer walked over to a glass case that held a depressing display of tacky pet cremation urns and resin graveyard souvenirs. I couldn't imagine why anyone would want to purchase a keepsake from this place.

The display case doubled as the main desk and was covered with a wide gray linoleum board. Behind it was a set of metal shelves holding rows holding tattered files and paperwork. Next to that was an old-fashioned employee punch clock and a small rack of forlorn time cards. A small silver bell sat on the makeshift linoleum desk with written instructions for visitors to ring for assistance. The guard still didn't look up from nails to greet us or to acknowledge our presence.

Jennifer rang the bell several times, banging on it hard to make it audible above the animal sounds. The barking changed rhythm from a monotonous repetitive sort of wail and became staccato - hopeful and frantic - when the dogs heard us enter. I felt panic again as I had the thought that they were all trying to communicate with us, pleading for a sympathetic ear, howling their anxiety and fear that this place was the last place they'd ever know.

I didn't think I could stand their cries any longer when a door banged open in a distant hallway and we heard heels clicking towards us. A tall dark-haired woman appeared in the doorway behind the linoleum counter.

"Can I help you?" she asked coldly.

I felt dismay mix with my sweaty panic. I remembered this woman from when we'd adopted Maggie. She'd been officious and abrupt, with an undercurrent of something else – indistinct, but very repelling. I'd grabbed up Maggie and ran with her out the front door, leaving Mark behind with the adoption paperwork. The woman's manner this time around seemed similar and I was shocked by how very congruous her appearance was with the horror of this grim shelter. She had dark hair and black, hard depthless eyes. Perhaps it was an intentional effect of her face powder, dark lipstick and eyeliner, but she had skin that didn't seem to have any color to it all, like a grayscale painting.

The woman was probably in her twenties but had the telltale wrinkles surrounding her eyes and lips of the hard, chronic smoker. The first time around she'd had an aura about her of a bad horror movie vampire. This time I saw her as a dark angel of death. I didn't really care to know her real name so I named her Elvira.

Elvira's outfit would have been more appropriate in a backstreet Goth club than in this crusty, dark, dirty shelter. She wore a tight black mini-skirt, black net stockings and absurdly high-heeled gladiator shoes. I couldn't imagine how she trotted so briskly around the shelter without snagging them in the cracks in the concrete floors. To complete her unnerving appearance as a deathly disco diva, she wore a tight sweater that exposed a lot of cleavage.

"Can I help you?" Elvira repeated. I glanced over at Jennifer and she seemed to be struggling to suppress a smile. She produced her shelter license and explained that we were here to pick up the injured dog that had been brought in by Animal Control last week. She told Elvira that she'd called the shelter before she left home, to confirm that everything was in order for her to pull the dog.

Still, Elvira hesitated and lazily thumbed through a messy notebook. "Hmmm, I don't see anything here about that", she said and then stared at us silently.

"Weeeellll," drawled Jenny sarcastically, "I spoke with several folks, yesterday to a man name Carl, and this morning to a woman whose name I didn't get. She sounded a lot like you though."

"Nope, wasn't me," replied Elvira. She continued to stare at us with a crooked smirk curling her wrinkled lips. Only had she been snapping a wad of chewing gum could her manner have been more mocking and unconcerned.

Jennifer was done sparring with Elvira. "Okay, okay," she said. "I just drove up here all the way from Providence on the basis of the agreement that Carl made with me on the phone yesterday. He said I'd be able to pull that dog today. I don't have time to come back another day, and as I understand it, this dog will be put down tomorrow. This is his tenth day. So it has to be today or no day, and I'm not going to let you waste my one day off."

"Well," said Elvira again with an exaggerated sigh, "hold on and I'll see. Okay?"

She turned her back on us with a snap of her black hair and clicked her way back down the hallway of howling dogs. We could hear her screaming for Carl above the pandemonium. All through this conversation the security guard stood by the desk looking down at his nails and his phone and skillfully avoiding our glances. I was beginning to understand why the shelter might have hired him.

Finally, a muscular man appeared in the doorway behind the linoleum. I was relieved to see that he had a kindly look on his face. He wore a greasy blue bomber jacket and had an official-looking badge pinned to his collar. He was the animal control officer who had brought No Ears to the shelter.

"You just got here in time," he said. "I'm not usually here on Wednesdays, I just had to stop in for a few minutes. I left a note on the desk this morning about you guys, I don't know what happened to it."

Jennifer said, "It's fine, forget it, but I really don't have much time left today. I need to get this dog and get back on the road. Can we take a look at him now, please?"

Jennifer pulled a large dog halter out of her coat pocket.

"I thought we'd put this on him," she said, "seeing as his neck is so terribly injured. I don't want to rip the stitches off that wound with a collar."

Jennifer tried to hand the halter to Carl. We thought we'd be waiting up front with Elvira while Carl went back into the runs and got No Ears for us.

"Oh, no," said Carl and pushed the collar back towards Jenny. "I can't touch the dog now he's been at the shelter, you understand? He's not officially ours anymore. This is all pretty much under the table. It's the only way I can get this dog out to you, okay? No paperwork, no records, absolutely no contact with the animal. He's all yours if you want him but on these terms, okay? No records. It's the only way it can be done and, really, it's for your own protection and mine, if anything were to happen to you with the dog in the future..."

I started to panic again. Now that I was actually standing inside the doors of this sad shelter again, I wanted nothing more than to get Ricky out of here, on any terms. I didn't care about the consequences of Mark's anger or any of the future difficulties in caring for another dog. I just wanted to get him out of there safely.

I glanced over at Jenny and I could see she felt the same way.

She said to me, "We don't normally do this. No records, no shots, no behavior test, no anything. It's bad, really bad, but now that we're here let's just do it."

"OK," said Carl, "Let me just go get Paula to help you out. I've got to get back on the road too. Good luck!"

Carl shouted for Paula, who turned out to be Elvira. Carl left with a smile and a wave and we were left with the dark angel Elvira. Jennifer started to hand her the halter but Elvira pushed it back at her.

"I'm not going near that animal," she said. "You want that dog so much, you go in and get it."

My heart skipped a couple of beats. I was hoping not to have to see the death row of the shelter again, ever in my lifetime. I couldn't bear the pleading looks on the eyes of the dogs trapped there. I felt a new cold sweat starting to cover my body and looked at Jennifer. She had been so kind to drive to New Bedford to do this. Now, she was accepting a legal risk for her organization by pulling a dog without paperwork. I couldn't let her go into those runs alone.

"Let's go get him out of there together," I said to Jenny.

Six or seven long, narrow runs sat along the far corner of the shelter building. A stockade fence topped with razor wire surrounded the runs. "Why the wire?" I wondered. The dogs wouldn't be able to scale the eight-foot fence if they escaped from their runs. Maybe the wire was there to keep out people who wanted to steal the dogs or maybe drug-dealers who'd had their guard dogs confiscated by animal control officers. I was relieved to see that Little Ricky was the only dog in the outdoor death row runs that day.

He was walking around the perimeter of the run like a restless jungle cat trapped in a zoo cage. I was struck by his catlike appearance in the email photograph. Now his rhythmic pacing, tiny pointy ears and light golden eyes all combined to give him the appearance of a golden tiger. He was stunningly beautiful, in spite of his injuries. He was sleek and muscular and very, very large for a pit bull. Most of the

Pits that came to Hidden Falls were of the smaller, stockier English variety. Little Ricky was of the longer legged American breed, closer to the size and shape of a Mastiff.

"There he is," said Elvira with a tight little laugh. "Have at him."

She took a tiny silver key from a chain hanging around her neck and put it in the padlock outside of the run. Little Ricky never stopped pacing as we stood near his run. He never slowed down. He had the desperate shelter dog look in his eyes - pure animal panic - condensed down into one obsessive, repetitive motion back and forth. His eyes were fixed and staring but not really looking at his surroundings. Every few seconds he'd snap a nervous sideways glance at us.

"I'm going to slowly open the run door a little bit," said Elvira. "You slide in through the opening and get the halter and leash on him."

"Are you fucking kidding me?" shouted Jennifer. "This dog could rip us to shreds."

Elvira responded that since Jennifer had been the vet tech that had stitched up Little Ricky's neck, she should know that he was a friendly dog. Otherwise, why would she be rescuing him? Jennifer tried to explain that, yes, he hadn't tried to snap at her while she was stitching up his sore neck without anesthesia but animals act very differently when they are trapped in shelters.

"Dogs can behave very differently at the vet's than in the shelter," said Jenny to me. "But, we're here now and if you still want to I feel like we should follow through. Do you mind going in and putting this halter on him though? I'm not good with doing it myself. I don't want the dog to feel unsafe in this situation with too many people in there."

I hesitated but took the halter from her. I wasn't really afraid of Little Ricky. For better or worse, I'd never been afraid of dogs. I might feel panic in almost any other situation, but not in meeting a new dog. Even a menacing dog could have a calming effect on me.

My mother liked to tell a story about when she took me to a yard sale when I was about eight years old. The house in the distance was guarded by a lunging, barking Doberman Pincher. While my mother was sorting through used dishes and glassware, I wandered across the yard to the dog. I heard the owner shouting at me but my mind didn't register the warning. I walked right up to the barking dog and started rubbing his neck and back. The big dog calmed right down and licked my face. I had my arms around him when my mother and the dog's owner came running up.

"What on earth are you doing?" gasped my mother.

"Aw, don't yell at her. All's well that ends well, right? Hey, brave kid you got there!" said the dog's owner while wiping away some sweat dripping down his forehead.

My mother just glared at me. She didn't like it when my rebelliousness earned compliments from strangers.

I took the halter and entered the run with Jennifer behind me. As soon as we were beyond the threshold, we heard Elvira slam the metal gate shut behind us with a loud clang and walk away fast in her spiky heels.

"Shit, she just locked us in here with this injured fucking dog!" said Jenny breathlessly. Little Ricky was still pacing. We stood in the middle of the run and he circled us, around and around, glancing and circling, glancing and circling.

"How are we going to stop him from circling so we can get them damn halter on him?" asked Jenny.

Ricky had short, smooth fur and didn't have a collar on or anything to grab onto except his tail. I remember Bliss saying if there was nothing to grab on a dog put your thumb in the ear and grab on to the ear flap with your fingers but this dog had no ears. I walked towards Little Ricky and tried to block his path to see how he'd react. He started to circle around my legs only, closer and closer, but gently, not with any discernable aggression.

I gripped Ricky gently by the shoulders keeping my face as clear from his as I could in that position. I could sense that Jenny was holding her breath. I held Ricky still, very lightly, for a minute or two and then started rubbing his neck and back as I had done so long ago with the barking Doberman.

After a few minutes Little Ricky seemed to relax. I could feel the tension leaving his back and his neck becoming less rigid. Then his tail went between his legs as a sign of fear and submission. I was careful not to touch his torn and bloody neck while slipping the halter over it and onto his chest. I let it sit on him for a minute, unbuckled, and then reached around his large barrel chest to snap the buckle along the side.

All the time I was maneuvering the halter Ricky stood very still. I couldn't see his eyes to check his expression. I wanted to see if they were still fixed and staring, indicating that he might decide to bite me. I snapped a leash to the halter and slowly stepped back away from Little Ricky. His eyes were looking straight into mine.

"He looks okay. He looks good," said Jennifer with

relief sounding in her voice. She was breathing heavily and fast. She shouted for Elvira. "Okay! Come and get us out of here now! The gate latch doesn't release from the inside. Slimy, fucking bitch," she muttered under her breath.

Five or maybe ten minutes later we heard Elvira's heels clicking down the walkway towards us.

"How did it go?" she smirked, looking at Little Ricky standing stock still in his new leash and halter.

"Oh just fine. We're still alive aren't we?" said Jenny sarcastically.

Elvira opened the run gate and Ricky suddenly sprang into motion jerking my arm roughly forward. He pushed in front of our legs and out of the gate, pulling at top force down the hallway, his entire sleek, feline-like back and tail wagging back and forth with exuberance. It was a joyous motion that I would see every time we'd take a walk together.

Little Ricky led us into the foyer and collapsed exhausted by the linoleum display case. He was panting heavily and his legs were spread out frog-like on the cold concrete floor. Relief seemed to overtake him as soon as we'd snapped the leash onto his collar.

"Do we need to do anything further?" asked Jenny of Elvira, who was now behind the counter with the apathetic security guard, filing her black polished nails over the computer keyboard.

"Nope, sure don't" said Elvira. "Just please get that damn dog out of here so we can get on with our day."

I nudged Little Ricky to his feet and we all walked out into the parking lot, inhaling the fishy air with relief, as if it were the freshest spring air we'd ever breathed.

"That bitch just threw us to the wolves, literally!" laughed Jenny. "What if things hadn't gone so well? No fucking rabies vaccine on record and she locked us in that cage with him. What if he'd attacked us? What then? She just left us alone there. And what gives with that loser standing like a stature behind her desk? They'd never have heard us yelling if something happened, or maybe they wouldn't have cared if they did. Unbelievable! That fucking bitch! That place certainly earned its negative reputation!"

We both glanced over at Little Ricky again spread out in his favorite position, on his belly and frog-legged, next to my van. He heard my keys rattle in my hand and looked up at us with pure joy and relief in his golden eyes.

"Oh God, but it was totally worth it though!" cried Jennifer. "Just look at his eyes! And I'm so glad I got to see this fucking dump for myself. Unbelievable.

I'm going to report these fuckers to the MSPCA. Somebody really needs to shut this place down. They must be violating every code in the book."

I thanked Jennifer for coming to Little Ricky's rescue and we apologized to each other for the stress and risks we'd put each other through in getting him out of there.

"Well, I've got to hit the road," said Jenny finally. "I'm giving two obedience-training classes tonight, then it's back to the vet's office tomorrow morning. Hey, good luck with Ricky; and, if there's ever anything I can do for you in the future let me know."

We hugged in the parking lot and parted ways. I opened the van door for Little Ricky and he jumped in without any urging from me. He curled right up in a tight ball on the front seat and went to sleep, as if he'd always belonged right in that spot. Hawkins was not going to like that at all.

I glanced back at the bunker-like shelter. It looked sad and desolate in the misty, fishy air. I was angrier with Elvira than I ever had been with anyone in my life. I remembered my childish division of people into Earth Angels and Evil Apes. I didn't want to insult any apes by equating them with Elvira, ast she seemed purely demonic and inhuman. I was angry with the that system brought that horrible shelter into being.

How were these places of death and misery being called shelters?

I was sorry for the people of this small city who were duped into thinking that this shelter was a public resource and there to help them with their pets. I was angry and sorry for the people who donated money to this place thinking that they were caring people who were helping animals.

Like Jenny, I wanted to do something change this sorry situation and the sad, unnecessary waste of beautiful lives at the hands of apathetic and abusive people. The idea that Elvira was the last person most of these animals would know just sickened me. I felt a vague dread that I was going to come into contact Elvira again in the future.

When I drove off with Little Ricky curled comfortably in the front seat of my van I found that I didn't want to go home just yet. I wanted to keep driving around. I was sure Mark wouldn't be home from work but I knew that Hawkins wasn't going to accept Little Ricky without a fuss and I didn't want to face the chaos right away. I needed to calm down after our encounter with Elvira.

On closer inspection of the neck injuries I found that they didn't look so horrible. They weren't so terribly deep, though there was plenty of dried and crusted blood tangled up in the rough stitches. Little Ricky looked like a stuffed dog I'd once had as a kid. The memory made me smile and Ricky seemed to smile back at me. And, there was a regular pattern to the circle of his cuts that reminded me of an injury I'd seen on a dog at Hidden Falls and I realized the neck wound was probably caused by a choke chain that had been allowed to grow into Ricky's neck. The thought gave me some relief. Surely it was better to have a chain grow passively into your neck than be violently choked and cut with it. The behavioral aftermath of a passive injury from neglect might be easier to deal with in training than direct injury from cruel aggression.

    I had already set up an appointment for Little Ricky with my own vet and planned to bring him over there the following day. I could ask Dr. Williams more about the origin of the injuries then, not that the history mattered that much. I'd never know anything about his former owners other than making guesses based on his behavior. Animal control would never be able to successfully prosecute them for cruelty. Little Ricky was just one of countless neglected dogs who walked the streets of this city, and others across the country and across the world.

    Every dog wanted a safe place, a warm bed, companionship, and a purpose. All dogs long for the sweet comfort shared with their mother dog and litter of siblings sleeping cuddled and piled on top of each other around her warm soft body. They can't articulate that longing for a safe place but some are determined to find it - those that haven't given up hope and become too exhausted and bitter to try any longer.

I thought Little Ricky probably needed some fresh air after ten days in that fetid shelter. I decided to take him to Buttonwood Park, a homey city park with a little duck pond. Little Ricky still showed no signs of aggression towards me in any circumstance. He slid reluctantly off the car seat as I opened the door, but put his white-stocking feet on the ground, yawned and stretched luxuriously. I was amazed by the brilliance of his orange coat and white markings. He was angular and thin but seemed in good health in spite of his injury. I had one of Hawkins' bandanas in the back seat of the van and I tied a blue one gently around Little Ricky's neck to conceal his injury. I didn't want anyone staring at him and asking me how the injury happened.

Also, I wasn't sure how Ricky would react to other people, or towards other dogs, so I chose to walk down a narrow path along the back of the pond in a wooded area. Little Ricky twisted his sleek back and neck side to side as he snuffled up the numerous doggy and wildlife odors. A huge, dark pine tree with a cushion of soft fragrant needles underneath it was a comfortable place to sit. I hadn't had anything to eat since early morning and forgot all about food during the stress and tension of the shelter. Now, after a just short walk, I was feeling a little faint.

Little Ricky sat down and pressed his side up against mine in a companionable way. I put my arm around him and we rested on the damp, cool pine needles, watching the ducks swim around the pond in the distance waiting for bits of bread to be tossed to them. I already felt a very strong bond forming with this dog.

Then, out of the corner of my eye, I caught a glimpse of a dark gray movement nearby. Little Ricky had seen it just a second before I did. His hackles sprang up from the short hair of his back like a row of orange spikes. A large man in a shiny parka was standing in a row of scrubby bushes nearby and was staring at us from under lowered eyelids. I've lived in the city for many years, and walk in parks frequently, so the sight of a strange man lurking in the woods was not unusual. Still, something about this man made me more nervous than usual. He was shuffling back and then forth as if trying to make up his mind about something and emerged from the bushes suddenly and started moving towards us.

Little Ricky sprang up to meet him, his teeth bared and throat emitting a low murderous growl. That sound meant business. This was the kind of growl I'd dreaded hearing moments ago in the shelter. Fortunately, the anger wasn't directed towards me. The man stopped motionless in his tracks and Ricky pressed his body hard against the front of my legs while he let loose with a torrent of snarling barks towards the man. He formed an impenetrable barrier of teeth and muscle.

The man took a few tentative steps backward and then ran back into the woods. Little Ricky relaxed and returned to lay in the pine needles at my feet. I sat down and hugged him tightly. I lost all fear of Ricky. He was clearly on my side and was very intuitive. He knew who was good and who was evil. I was sure of that and I was overwhelmed with admiration and respect for this new dog in my life. He'd known me for only an hour yet was willing to lay his life down to defend me if need be.

We walked slowly back to the van. We passed several groups of women and their toddlers laughing and feeding the ducks. I tightened my grip on his Ricky's leash but he wagged his friendly tail at the groups of happy people and at the ducks. He was a good dog.

12. The Tightest Bond

It was clear within two short weeks that Little Ricky and Hawkins were never going to be best buddies, or to even to be able to live together at all. The first walk we tried to take with them both ended in a nearly disastrous dog fight on a downtown street corner and bitten hands for both me and Mark. Briefly, I thought that maybe after a week or two of getting used to each other's scent in separate rooms we could try again, but it was clear that Hawkins and Ricky wanted to kill one another on sight. Hawkins' aggression seemed to escalate. He was actively searching for doors left ajar and for any way to get at Little Ricky and kill him.

Sadly, I had to accept that if the two were live in the house together it would be not in separate rooms but on separate floors. So, for the time being, Little Ricky moved up to our bedroom and Hawkins became the resident living room dog. Maggie was the go-between dog - preferring to lay around with Hawkins on the sofa during the day then tagging along upstairs with us at night to curl up on our bed with Little Ricky.

The Internet-based pet adoption websites were ramping up in popularity fast, so I decided to post Ricky on the Hidden Falls adoption page. Hector and Bliss agreed reluctantly. Hector had worked with Hawkins before I brought him home and warned me that he thought he could be aggressive with other male dogs. He wasn't at all happy that Ricky was living at my house and he didn't want to place an unknown entity on the shelter adoption site.

Soon, I started bringing Ricky to Hector's Saturday morning classes that he said were for punk dogs. To my surprise, Ricky was perfectly happy to run and play with the just about any other dog at the class - male or female. He was extremely attentive and intelligent and gazed up at me with guileless, discerning eyes that seemed nearly human. He learned obedience commands quickly and Hector looked on with admiration, saying that Ricky was a really good dog, he could see that he was motivated by our bond, and not just the treats I was slipping him.

I felt more optimistic about finding an adoptive home for Ricky, at least more responsible anyway, but sadder because with each class I felt our friendship and trust growing stronger. How was I ever going to betray his trust and take him to some stranger's house, turn my back and walk away to my van with Little Ricky staring after me, his golden eyes burning a hole in my back?

Reluctantly, after his neck wounds became less visible, I placed his photos online and started getting calls and emails from all over New England and throughout the rest of the country. Ricky's red fur, golden eyes and tiny cat-like ears attracted many people to him. Also, to my dismay, was the fact that he was being called a damn big Pit. As soon as someone used those words, or anything like them, they became ineligible as adopters.

Everyone at Hidden Falls thought that Ricky probably come from a dog-fighting situation. I was learning, with increasing sadness, too much about the cruel ways humans tormented dogs to create a fighter. Bliss thought that the imbedded collar was not accidental but probably a tactic to cause constant pain and frustration that would result in a hostile dog that was ready to lash out and fight.

But it hadn't worked. In spite of his encounters with the foulest human beings, Ricky remained a loving, patient dog. There was no way I was going to let him go to a home where he was not treated well, or was ignored, or used as a guard dog or a macho status symbol. In spite of the difficulties of having dogs on separate floors, we'd hold on to Ricky until the perfect home was found for him.

After all, I thought to myself, there were many other workers at Hidden Falls that had dogs and cats in separate living situations in their homes. Various systems were set up to avoid the dreaded battles between packs - combinations of baby gates, half doors, audible alarms, and locks - human daily routines ever changing with the growing or shrinking packs and conflicts.

I'd hear stories about these houses and lives and think, never, never will I do that. It's crazy. Dogs are supposed to add pleasure to our lives, to blend seamlessly in with us, to be companions, not permanent shelter dogs that have to be jostled and manipulated so they don't kill each other. Humans shouldn't live out their days filled with stress and fear of the next fight while constantly dodging baby gates.

Then, I was idealistic and intent on finding Little Ricky a good home where he would live with friendly dogs and good people that would lavish him with the love and attention he deserved. I didn't pay attention to Hector when he told me that in spite of Ricky's beauty and success at training class he'd be a tough adoption, but it was turning out to be true. No golden happy family with a house and yard with a high white picket fence seemed interested in adopting a pit bull. The only people responding to his post seemed to want a guard dog.

Still, I optimistically kept his photos and biography posted online. I looked through dozens of adoption applications but there was always something wrong. It was shelter policy to only adopt pit bulls to people who owned their own home since most landlords didn't want the breed on their properties. Most people who called about Ricky were renters. We always did a brief background check on potential adopters by calling their veterinarians about the care given their other pets. We called the tax assessor's offices to find out if they really did own their own property and then Bliss called the animal control officers in nearby towns to find out if there were any former violations filed for animal neglect or abuse against the prospective adopters. In Ricky's case, our investigations negated almost all of the applicants. People wanting to adopt pit bulls seemed to be professional liars.

For the first time in my life I felt trapped by my pets. I was longing to take another winter road trip, and so was Mark, but the thought of loading Ricky into a crate along with Maggie and having Hawkins lunging as we drove along seemed impossible and crazy. And, I couldn't bear to put Hawkins in a crate after his two years living in one at Hidden Falls. And, I couldn't bear to put Ricky in a boarding kennel after his recent stint at the shelter, so the fall trip to view sparkly snow and revel in the crisp cooler air of northern New England were put aside.

Then one morning I got an email in response to Ricky's photo on Petfinder. It was from a teenage girl who had fallen in love with his photograph and his rich autumnal orange fur. She wanted to meet him right away but she was four hours away in Conway, New Hampshire. I normally don't respond to emails from teenagers wanting to adopt a dog unless their parents call first, but the girl's father called soon after and we discussed whether Ricky might be a good dog for the family.

The situation sounded better than I could hope for Little Ricky - former street fighting pit bull – with a country home in the mountains of New Hampshire and a family of older children used to large-breed dogs. The father claimed to be a zealous amateur dog-trainer and all his work and vet references checked out. According to the tax assessor's office for Conway, the parents owned the home they were living in, and several acres of wooded land behind their home.

The only thing that made me worry was the lack of any opinion or voice from the mother of the children, something I wouldn't ignore these days, but at that time I was just happy that Ricky had possibly found a new home in the country. I longed for days we'd be able to travel around the country in the beloved motorhome my mother had given us, travelling north to the woods and lakes of New York State and the Green Mountains of Vermont of my childhood memories.

I had some horrible pains of guilt and regret as I looked at Ricky curled up on our bed snuggled into our comforter like a baby deer curling into leaves in the forest. I felt misgivings about the New Hampshire family and an awareness of the fact that no matter what happened, from here on, I would always wonder what had happened to Ricky for the rest of my life.

I felt as if I were giving away a child and Ricky had only been a part of my life for two months. Ricky lay on the bed and watched me pack some small bags for our trip to New Hampshire. I felt he knew he was leaving us at this point and was sad, yet resigned, as he had learned to be in his short life in the hands of human beings.

So, our long-anticipated snow trip took place under the guise of delivering Ricky to his new home.

Bliss and Hector both looked over the application and references and thought they were good. Hector said, "It's probably the best shot this guy's got." We drove Ricky northwards sadly, but feeling good about our role in helping him find a new home and better life.

Just as I expected, Little Ricky lay calmly in a blanketed crate in the back of the RV with Maggie and Hawkins stretched out luxuriously on the fold down side bed. Once in a while, when he thought we weren't looking, Hawkins would rush back to Ricky's crate to hassle him. I'd grab Hawkins and drag him by the collar back up to his bed perch as he looked up at me innocently. Hawkins could get away with just about anything if he gave me that sweet look and he knew it.

Little Ricky's new home appeared as we drove over a low farmland hill several miles outside of North Conway. A peaceful orange and purple misty valley sunset greeted us as we pulled up in front of the classic New England white, one-story house. It had a huge sugar maple tree with a few straggling leaves left on it out front with a wooden dog house underneath. I pointed out the dog house to Mark nervously as we walked up to ring the front door bell, pulling Ricky along reluctantly behind us. The dog house had a large, heavy chain trailing out of it and was crammed full of hay. It looked as if it had been set up for a dog to stay outdoors in year round.

A large, heavily-bearded bald man opened the door and a teenaged boy peered out from behind him. A tall red-haired girl rushed out past them and introduced herself as Sharon, the girl I had first spoken to on the phone. She ran over to Ricky squealing and, before I could say anything, dropped down on the ground to hug him. "He has my hair color," she said. "He's a real ginger head. That's why I wanted him. He matches me perfectly."

I hoped she felt connected to Ricky in more ways than their shared hair color, but Ricky seemed happy and was basking in her attention with a big smile on his face. A short, stocky middle-aged woman came out of the house to join us and introduced herself as Sharon's mother.

"I really didn't want another large dog. As you can see," she said as she nodded towards the dog house, "we had one – a big Lab. Just passed. Old age, hip dysplasia, the works. But, he was a good dog. But me, now, I wanted a small dog, a Maltese or something like that - easy to walk. But, nobody ever listens to me in this house."

She looked at Sharon and Ricky sitting together on the grass and said, "Well, it looks like he'll work out okay. He's a beauty all right, and my husband likes to have a big dog to walk around the neighborhood with."

Her husband came out of the house and joined her with a think heavy chain in his hand that looked large enough to be used for towing cars.

"I make these for all my dogs," he said proudly. "I think the heavy leash gives them a good workout plus gives them a sense of security."

He walked towards Ricky, who hopped up nervously, and clipped the heavy chain onto his collar without any problems. I was more nervous. I didn't like the look of the leash or the dog house under the tree. And, I didn't like that the mother pined for a little safe lap dog. Ricky would be happy to sit on her lap, but he certainly wasn't small. I whispered my misgivings to Mark.

"Let's just see how it goes. Give him a shot," he said. "Remember what Hector said to you. This may be his only chance for a family life. You've got to let him go."

I knew Mark was anxious to get back to our more comfortable and anxiety-free life with only two dogs.

Bob said he'd like us all to take Ricky for a walk to help him transition to his new family. We walked down the hill into the low valley that looked like an old hand-colored postcard with shades of dusty pink and blue pastels. The air was cold and misty and smelled thick with decaying leaves. The scene was so beautiful that it was coloring my judgment. I wanted to live there. Therefore, I thought that Little Ricky would enjoy living there, too. It was heavenly in northern New England and I momentarily longed for myself the country life I wanted for Little Ricky.

As we passed the dog house I said to the father, "I thought you told me on the phone that you didn't tie your dog outdoors. I don't want Ricky to live outdoors in a doghouse. And, it's in our adoption contract. We don't adopt to people who keep their dogs outdoors."

"Oh, don't worry about that dog house. We were just going to tear it down. That was for our other dog. He didn't like living indoors. A real outdoors dog was old Rocky. Even in deep winter. If we tried to bring him in he'd just sit at the front door and howl until we let him back out. Right, honey?"

Bob's wife nodded silently, but she wasn't smiling. Ricky's head hung low under the weight of the heavy chain. My instinct was to unclip it from his collar and hustle him back into the RV. I ached with the urge to do it. But just then Sharon ran up and she and her brother unclipped Ricky and ran with him through the front door of the white house. They were laughing and romping around on the bed by the time rest of us caught up with them.

"You see," said Mark. "It's okay. Ricky didn't even look back at us. Look how happy he is with those kids. Let's get going now. Please? It's getting dark and we need to find a campsite for tonight."

"But, I said and starting to cry, "I think I should at least give Ricky a last hug goodbye before we leave."

"No, no, no. Don't do that," said Mark, a little panic sounding in his voice. "You won't leave him here if you do that. And, you know you've got to learn to give him up! This is for the good of Hawkins and Maggie."

We said our goodbyes to the parents and walked sadly to the RV. We would drive away and Ricky wouldn't look back at us, as Mark said, because he wouldn't have a clue what was happening to him. He didn't know we were going to drive away. Maybe he'd break away from his playtime with Sharon and her brother, look up, walk and sniff around and wonder where we were and be confused and upset. I couldn't keep the tears from flowing. I could hear all their voices chiming away in my head now - Mark, Bliss, and Hector - all saying. "You've got to let him go. Let him go, let him go…"

I was pretty sure I was going to be a lousy foster pet parent by this point. I just couldn't let go of an animal I'd grown to love, especially not Ricky, not after that first day of our meeting; seeing him cringing terrified and torn-up in that awful shelter. He'd come such a long way and was just learning to fully trust people. But, the voices of the rescue experts were right. If I couldn't let go of this one dog, how was I going to foster any others?

And, wasn't that what I had signed on for, so idealistically and innocently, as a shelter volunteer? I wanted to provide as many dogs as possible with a temporary foster home, a sanctuary, and a new shot at life. It was the hardest thing in the world for me to do, it would haunt me forever, but I kept telling myself that I had to let go of Little Ricky.

I went to the RV and grabbed the adoption contract. Hawkins and Maggie were waiting and looking very smug at the fact that Ricky was no longer in their RV. Bob and his wife read the contract perfunctorily and signed it. I reminded them that the contract stated that Ricky was not to be kept outdoors, and that they understood that he was not good with cats. I'd seen a couple of cats running under the side porch as I was returning to the house with the contract.

"Oh, we don't have any cats," said the husband, Bob. "At least not really, they are outdoor cats that our neighbors left behind when they moved. They adopted us, right honey? We never let them indoors - we just leave some food for them outside sometimes."

"Ricky will chase them down if he has a chance," I said.

"Oh don't worry about them," Bob assured me. "Really, they are not our cats. They know the score. If they've lived this long without being eaten by coyotes, they aren't going to be scared about a dog. Besides, they always did just fine with old Rocky."

"Ricky is not a mellow Lab."

"Oh, we know. We know. We have lots of friends with pit bulls. Lots of people have them around here. I've worked with them plenty before. Believe me, Ricky is going to be just fine here. Although, we'll be changing his name to Red, for Sharon's sake you know."

"Come on!" Mark said, pulling on my elbow. With tears in my eyes and nerves burning a hole in my stomach, I grabbed my copy of the signed adoption contract and walked out the door into to the fragrant purple air. I could hear the kids still squealing and shouting as they jumped around with Ricky on the bed. I sighed with resignation. If Ricky seemed frightened, or wasn't enjoying himself so much, he'd be with us and driving away. But, he was in there playing in a bedroom, a part of a family, having fun, and, most of all, he was safe from Hawkins. I had to let him go.

We found a campsite by a cold, dark peaceful lake. The campers next to us left their campfire to come over to pat and compliment Maggie but looked at Hawkins with trepidation. This often happened when we brought Hawkins into rural areas where pit bulls are fewer and far between. We took a leisurely walk around the little lake and watched the campfires flicker nostalgically on the surface of the water. I was starting to relax. It felt good to not be stressed out with an extra dog whining in a crate back in the RV. I suddenly felt as if we were getting back to our normal, sane and controllable lives.

Traveling in my parents' old RV was a big step up from our usual tent camping adventures and was much better for winter camping. Yet, if felt strange to be sitting in it without my parents there with us. I thought about my mother in her assisted-living home separated from my father living in his nursing home and felt a crushing feeling of loss.

The RV still smelled strongly of cats, an odor we didn't seem able to purge with any amount of cleaning. My parents were able to travel in their later years by staying free of dogs and keeping only cats as pets. Cats were easier to travel with, and to disguise in campsites that didn't allow pets. My parents joyously drove this tipsy vehicle through every contiguous state in the nation and then through Canada and Alaska with their four cats riding high up in the cabin top bed.

I was usually repelled by the cat odor, but that night it was oddly comforting, as if my parents were right there in the RV with us, as if I was traveling with them again as I did as kid, up to Maine, up to magical Acadia State Park, my mother struggling to keep her cats and our Springer Spaniel, Pepper, hidden and quiet on the bottom of the floor as we passed the ranger stations.

That night, Mark tossed and turned for a while after opening the windows wide and complaining that he couldn't sleep with the odor. But, soon he and the dogs were all snoring away comfortably while I lay awake staring at the dark tree tops and wondering how Little Ricky was doing. Did he miss us? Was he freaking out? Was he lying in bed with Sharon or her brother and snoring away? I hoped so.

Gentle wind and night sounds lulled me to sleep finally. I was exhausted from driving and struggling with my emotions. Early in the morning, when the night was still dark and cold blue, I woke up with a start. I knew I'd been dreaming and could see remnants of the images lurking just behind my eyelids - shadowy and indistinguishable from the sound that had woken me up. It was the heart-rending sound of a howling dog. It was Little Ricky! I knew it was Ricky's voice coming clearly and loudly over the rolling hills and low mountains that lay between his new home and our campsite.

I shook Mark awake. "I can hear Ricky howling. He's crying for us. I can hear him crying," I said.

I was so upset that I felt cold and shaky all over. "It's just coyotes crying," said Mark. "Listen to them. Listen. It's more than one dog. It's not Ricky. Ricky is twenty miles away. You can't hear a dog howling that far away. That's crazy. You were just having a dream about him. That's all."

As I listened I could hear that it was indeed a big pack of dogs, of coyotes, shrieking in excitement over their breakfast. Still, I couldn't shake the feeling that the cry I'd heard was Ricky trying to communicate with me. I knew then that he wasn't happy. Something was wrong. I knew I'd been dreaming about him. The flickering images left on the back of my eyelids from the dream had been Ricky's face.

"You've got your phone," said Mark logically. "If something is wrong, the people will call you. Or, you can call and make sure everything is okay later before we drive home."

That is exactly what I did, as soon as it was late

enough in the morning to not be rude. The night anxiety and my urge to drive right back to Conway to get Ricky was dispelled by Sharon's cheery young voice telling me that everything was indeed okay. Ricky spent a peaceful night in his new home she said and was settling in nicely. I felt immense relief and again happy and elated with our recovered sense of freedom as we walked the dogs around the lake a last time, packed up and headed back to Massachusetts.

Over the next couple of weeks, I had several phone calls from Sharon telling me how well Ricky was doing, how much her father was enjoying walking him, showing him off to his friends, and working on his training. Then one day I got an email from her. It seemed odd that she would send an email instead of calling me and I was immediately filled with dread. Maybe she was just sending me photos of Ricky in his new home. But, there were no attachments in the email.

I opened it and the first lines seemed unbelievable, even though they were really what I'd expected. "Please, please come and get Red. Right away. He hates, hates, hates our cats. He wants to kill our cats. My mom says he has to go right away or he's going to a shelter. Can you please come get him right away? Please?"

I felt sick to my stomach. Those people told me several times that the cats in the yard were not theirs. My negative suspicions about that home, that family, were right all along. I learned in the few minutes it took my mind to process this email that I had to learn to trust my own instincts, no matter what people told me to think or feel.

But, mainly, I was overwhelmed with panic. Not a shelter. Not another shelter for Ricky. That bitch of a mother said they'd take Ricky to a shelter. It was written in the adoption contract that the adopters were forbidden to take an animal to a shelter without contacting the original rescue and returning the animal.

I grabbed my phone and called Sharon. "What is going on up there?" I shouted when I heard her meek little voice on the other end of the line.

"My Daddy says Red, I mean Ricky, has to go. He tried to kill our cats."

"I thought they were outdoor cats and not yours," I said. "We discussed this. Do you remember?"

"No, I mean, yes. I mean it doesn't matter. My Mommy will take Ricky to a shelter up here if you can't come and get him right now."

My thoughts rushed around in my head. Mark was at work teaching. It was four hours back up to

Conway on a weekday. I'd wind up passing Boston in rush hour traffic, alone. I'd have to leave Hawkins and Maggie at home and drive up and back myself - eight hours on the road at a minimum. But, I was already grabbing my purse, setting out bowls of water and extra food for the dogs. I'd get gas and coffee on the way.

Then I heard a deeper voice coming through my phone, angry and accusatory in tone, "Hello, hello...Bob here, I think my daughter has explained to you. We can't keep this dog. I can't work with him. My wife wants him out. She wants to get a Poodle and she can't do that with this dog. He's a mean dog. He tried to kill our cats."

Trying hard to keep my voice calm and patient, I explained to Bob that we'd discussed the cat situation and Bob had said that the cats were not his. But, I knew it was pointless to argue any further. I heard the finality and resolve in Bob's tone of voice, and didn't care about anything besides keeping Little Ricky safe from a strange shelter.

I'd found that many people really don't want to work with dogs, not even people like Bob who claimed some minor expertise in dog training. No matter what people said on adoption day, they really just wanted a dog that would fit seamlessly into their home with no work and no trouble. If the dog didn't assimilate and conform fast, it was often given back to the shelter, quick as a blink. People didn't want to invest in a problem dog as they might be forced by law to invest in a problem child. A dog can easily be dropped off at a shelter and forgotten. Someone like Bob could turn his back and walk away feeling he did the right thing. He would justify it by thinking that the shelter would find a new home for the animal. A problem dog could easily be dropped off at a shelter, or set loose in the woods. Out of sight, out of mind.

I was furious, but I didn't want to argue with Bob and make it more likely that he'd drive Ricky right to a shelter. I spoke with him very calmly as if to a spoiled and stubborn child. I sympathized with the trouble Bob was having with his difficult wife who now wanted a Poodle. Of course, women were so difficult and, yes, it's hard when you want a man's dog, like Red, but can't ever have what you want because your wife and kids want Poodles and cats.

I listened patiently to Bob complaining about his difficult life for about a half hour before he finally said, "Know what? I can keep Red until Saturday. Then I'll have time to meet you half way. I just don't want to drive through Boston on a weekday. On Saturday we can meet at a rest area on the state border and I'll bring Red to you there, how's that?"

That, I knew, was the best I was going to get from Bob, and I was very relieved. "You have to promise me you will not bring him to a shelter, or let your wife do it before Saturday," I said.

"Nah, once she knows you are going to take Red back, she won't do anything like that. I'll see you on Saturday."

I hung up and sat down and cried. I was relieved and happy to be getting Ricky back. I'd been tossing and turning most nights thinking about the howling dream every night since with left him behind. I was disappointed with the adopters and overwhelmed with that increasingly familiar feeling of being trapped by my dogs. And, I knew one thing without a doubt; all people were liars; whether they knew it or not.

We waited anxiously until Saturday, worried the entire time that Bob and his wife wouldn't be able to stand Ricky in their home for one more day and take him to a shelter, or worse. Finally, Saturday came and on another bright blue and white morning we drove to the designated rest area on the state border. My stomach churned as I worried that Bob and Little Ricky might not show up. But as soon as we pulled off the interstate we immediately saw Bob's red pickup waiting in the parking lot.

My heart leapt to see Little Ricky sitting in the front seat between Bob and Sharon with the huge heavy chain wrapped around his neck. Ricky saw us drive up and I'll never forget the expression of surprise and joy on his face as he tried to jump out of the window of the pickup and scramble into our van. We all got out of our vehicles and walked towards each other, but Ricky pulled away from Bob and still trailing his chain ran up to sit by the van, wagging his tail with gusto.

"See that," said Bob. "That dog is really dominant, very pushy, very tough to train. It's sad really. I don't know what you are going to do with him."

"Yeah," Sharon chimed in, "He's strong too. He actually pulled the chain right off the dog house trying to get at our cats."

I thought you said you were taking down that dog house," I said. "Ricky was not to be a tied-out dog. You signed a contract agreeing to that. Remember?"

"Oh, right, right." said Bob. "But, once we could see what Red was like we couldn't keep him in the house - not with my wife's new dog there."

I was about to ask him what dog he was talking about. We had never discussed another dog in the home. But, I stopped. I just want to get Ricky away from those awful lying people and bring him home. Mark was already sitting in the driver's seat of the van with Little Ricky sitting up high and ready to ride shotgun on the passenger's side.

Mark reached over and detached the heavy chain from Ricky's neck and pushed it out of the window towards me with a look of disgust. I gave it back to Bob and walked to the van. Bob seemed to want to talk more, to defend his actions with Ricky, but there was no need for further discussion and no more time in our lives to be wasted on these lying people. Ricky sat in the front seat between my legs in way that was to become a habit - his feet hanging off the edge of the seat like a human kid with his front paws on the dashboard. His was panting hard, with his tongue hanging down huge and drooling, but he had a great happy smile on his face.

We stopped at the Winchester Fells, just outside of Boston, on the way home for a walk. It was a perfect New England winter afternoon, with sharp, cool air and deep blue sky in glorious contrast to many shades of snow. Little Ricky's dark red fur provided a perfect camouflage as he trudged happily through paths of snow and rotting leaves. Watching the sun glittering on his fur I knew with certainty that Ricky was our dog now. My dog. He was not going through another trial adoption. I knew that all people were liars and I was not about to expose Ricky to any more awful humans. We'd stop at the hardware and pick up more baby gates before we got home.

13. Sable for Christmas

I knew, looking at all the eyes staring at me when I first walked into the dog runs during shifts at Hidden Falls that I wanted to do something to salvage these sad lives beyond giving them a little comfort, beyond giving out fresh, clean blankets, refilling empty bowls, refreshing water pools and wiping away smeared poop so days can be spent sprawled out on concrete that is, at least, clean. Sometimes I met a pair of eyes that were a little more intense than the rest. Eyes that expressed knowledge of what was happening to them and what might happen in the future. There was fear in those eyes along with that weary resignation. But one look or bit of attention from a shelter volunteer could spark a look of hope and intense longing. Those eyes are what made doing shelter work worthwhile for me.

A pair of those intense eyes confronted me when I walked in to the Helping Paws and Claws Low Cost Veterinary Clinic one day in November to get some medication for a persistent skin itch suffered by Little Ricky. On a crate on the floor behind the receptionist's desk was a dog that looked like a much smaller version of Ricky. The dog was also dark golden orange with white socks, chest and tail tip. She had a stubby pit bull pinkish nose and delicate white feet that looked more like human hands than paws.

The little dog was barking her head off and every time she opened her mouth she'd jump and bang her head on the top of the crate, just like Hawkins used to do at Hidden Falls. The pink mouth was pressed up against the metal of the crate door and spittle was flying in every direction with every high-pitched bark.

Alison, the receptionist, asked me if I'd like to meet the dog outside of the crate. I wasn't sure I did, but Alison assured me that Sable was a very sweet dog, once she was free, and that if she decided she didn't like me she'd only bark at me, not bite me. So, I told Alison to let Sable have some freedom. Alison just started to open the crate door when Sable took some initiative and bashed out of the small opening and sprang across to the floor to where I was sitting on one of the sticky orange vinyl waiting room couches.

I jumped up to meet Sable. Not knowing her, I didn't want her to jump up in my lap, near my face. She ran right up to me and put both feet on my knees and looked me straight in the eyes with a look that was so determined, so intelligent and knowing that it startled me and it took my breath away. It was like looking in the eyes of a defiant and determined child. Sable's eyes showed that she took an immense amount of enjoyment from life, no matter what the circumstances. She clearly possessed a strong will to live. Sable looked directly at me with a challenge gleaming in her eyes.

"I want to live," she seemed to say, "I want to live and what are you going to do about it?"

I thought "Oh no," Ricky had looked at me with those eyes and so did Maggie and Hawkins. I sighed and asked Alison what Sable's story was. She explained that she rescued Sable last winter from a tenant farm in a nearby town where pit bulls, horses, goats, chickens, ducks and even peacocks were being bred, sold and horribly neglected by the amateur farmers. Sable and some of the other animals at the farm had been confiscated by animal control and being held as evidence in the abuse case being tried against the farm owner by The State Department of Agriculture. Alison was fostering Sable until the case was wrapped up because Sable had such extreme kennel stress she couldn't be kept at Hidden Falls.

"Oh, you should have seen the place," Alison said while I cringed. I knew she wanted to vent about the horrible things she'd seen at the tenant farm but I hated hearing animal abuse horror stories. In just my short career as an animal rescue volunteer, and just as I had feared at the beginning, I was feeling overwhelmed with new knowledge of how humans were capable of such shocking atrocities.

Alison explained that Sable was kept as a breeding mother in a small plastic dog igloo for the past couple of bitter sub-zero winters. Hay was tossed in occasionally to keep her body warm enough to stay alive but the hay rotted and she'd contracted a body-wide skin infection that was resistant to treatment. Indeed, Sable's skin was flaking off all over the place and her beautiful coat was powdered with it as if she'd been out in the snow.

Sable ran circles around the waiting room. Each time she made a round she'd jump up on my legs, then looking at me straight in the eyes, she'd do a little punkish push backwards as if to say she didn't really want or need my attention. Then she'd spin around a couple of times and sit down to dig at her itchy skin with her hind feet.

Months ago, at the beginning of the abuse investigation, animals couldn't be removed from the farm as paperwork made its way through the court system. Alison was panicked by the horrible condition of the dogs during the winter so she and a group of rescue workers went to the farm twice a day through the bitterest coldest months and fed and brought blankets to the animals trapped there.

Sable suffered most from the cold, with her skin condition and because her hair was so thin, so Alison rigged up battery-operated heat lamp system to the top of her plastic igloo and prayed she'd survive when the temperatures hit sub-zero.

Finally, in the spring rescue workers were allowed to remove the animals and Helping Paws and Claws, and other local animal rescue and welfare organizations, moved in to gather up and distribute the dogs to foster homes and low-kill shelters.

With Alison's help, Sable was tough enough to survive the winter. She soon began to put on weight and gain strength but her skin condition was getting worse. Several vets tried treatments but nothing helped stop the itching and peeling. Now, Alison was worried because her husband wanted Sable out of the house as she didn't get along with his two huge Dalmatians and the vet at Helping Paws and Claws suggested that perhaps the most humane thing for Sable, considering her painful skin condition, was to put her to sleep.

"No way! Not after all that work," cried Alison, "All those days and nights of sneaking into to that stinking farm in the dead of winter. I could have been shot by one of those crazy farmers for feeding those dogs and now they want to put Sable down? It's not going to happen!"

I dreaded asking because I already knew the answer, but I did anyway, "Is there anything I can do to help her?"

"Oh, could you?" Alison said, "Do you think you could foster her for just a little while?"

I hadn't actually offered to foster Sable, but I agreed to take Sable home for a couple of weeks until Alison could find a long-term situation for her. I knew that Mark would be upset at first, as he had been with Ricky, but then he'd start to enjoy her company and she'd become part of the daily routine. Besides, for just the two of us humans, we did have a big rambling house with five bedrooms. We had the space to do this. And, after Little Ricky came back home, I'd given up any dreams of future travel for now. Alison needed us now, living as she did in a tiny mobile home with two huge aggressive dogs and a husband much less tolerant of her rescue habit than Mark was of mine.

Sable came home with me that day. And then we had four dogs living in relative comfort in our city house, confined within a network of baby gates. Technically, we should have applied for a city shelter license, but since Sable was just a foster dog I told myself there was really no need for that, and why call attention to the situation anyway? The dogs didn't bother the neighbors and they were well cared for to the point of being spoiled rotten, so I thought it best to fly under the radar of the local authorities for the time being.

Hawkins soon proved again that he did not get along with any dog other than Maggie. Maybe it was because he thought Maggie was his mate for life or he knew she was here first so would always hold a place of honor and superiority in his mind. Or, in training him to be a fighting dog, his former owners poisoned his mind against any pit bull or dog that resembled one. Probably his hostility towards Ricky and Sable was a combination of both, but from then on we entered into a serious system of pack separation. I added solid-half doors to our arsenal of baby gates.

Sable and Ricky looked very much alike and I allowed them to meet face to face after just a day. They took to each other immediately. They began with a joyous romping and seeming recognition of their similarities as pit bulls. Perhaps, they were actually related. I was learning that many, way too many, of the homeless in dogs in New Bedford and Fall River began their lives at that nearby tenant farm.

Sable and Ricky ran back and forth across the narrow upstairs hallway. I'd toss a tennis ball so it would hit the wall on the far end and ricochet off the walls in a crazy pattern, with the dogs chasing wildly after it. It was amazing how much exercise and action could be generated in a limited space. Finally, they'd splay their legs out and lay on their bellies frog style side by side in companionable exhaustion on our king-sized bed.

The autumn nights were cold when Sable came home, and the second night with us she used her nose to push up the covers after I'd climbed in bed and crawled right in next to me, skin-to-skin, under the heavy comforters just like Hawkins did when he first came home. I had some regrets about Hawkins being relegated to the downstairs sofa with Maggie, but it couldn't be helped. Soon Ricky crawled in and snuggled up next to the other side of my body, and I became part of a very warm pit bull sandwich. and we slept that way many nights thereafter. Hawkins didn't seem to mind as long as he had a cozy place on the couch, and his woman Maggie to keep him company.

There were a few problems though. Mark had long since come to terms with dogs sleeping in the bed, but Sable's itchy, flaky skin condition got on his nerves.

"How can you bring that disgusting, itchy dog into our bed?" he moaned. "What if she has something contagious?"

I worried about the same thing, but I didn't want to admit it. The vet couldn't find any remaining bacteria, fungus or virus in her skin scrapings. She thought that the continuing itch was just a result of stress and change. But it was unnerving. Still, I just couldn't bear to boot Sable out of her little cave of warmth and cozy comfort after all the freezing nights she'd spend in a dog-igloo on the sad marshy wasteland of the tenant farm. So, we put up with digging and scratching and washed the sheets daily.

Soon her skin condition began to clear, and within two weeks the itching stopped. The skin healed completely and her hair grew back in all the bald patches. The vet was right. Once free of the stress of discomfort and struggling for daily survival, Sable developed a coat that was worthy of her namesake. Her dark orange and brindle striped fur had a golden glow that seemed to emanate from within her little body.

I brought Sable over to Helping Paws and Claws

so Alison could visit with her. Alison and all the staff were amazed at her speedy recovery. The vet said that she secretly thought the skin issue was incurable and was worried it was a symptom of something eventually fatal like lymphoma. She hadn't wanted to disappoint Alison with this news, so didn't share it with either of us. She hoped we wouldn't be too sad when Sable's health eventually declined.

But, her health certainly did not decline. Her appearance was handsome and her personality grew spunkier and brattier by the day. She now greeted everyone with her characteristic gesture - bounce up, put paws firmly on thighs, then push off hard with an expression of defiance. This movement endeared her to me at our first meeting. Dependent as she was on us, this act was her little declaration of independence from humans. She was a survivor and she knew it.

Like many pit bulls, Sable could be a tough disciplinarian with other dogs and Ricky soon learned to be subservient to her wants and needs. She was the pack leader and no dog was ever allowed to question her authority. Sable and Ricky were great car companions and they began to accompany me to my volunteer shifts on alternate days with Hawkins and Maggie. Sable and Hawkins always claimed their right to ride shotgun. Maggie and Ricky always rode in the backseat.

On tolerably cold days, either pair would curl up together in the back of my van while I tended to the animals at Hidden Falls. Then, I'd take them for a short walk along the dirty estuary flowing around the granite factories and 1920's former factory workers' homes of Fall River. My dogs enjoyed hearing the raucous barking of the Hidden Falls' dogs and seemed to taunt the residents who were still stuck inside a shelter but could smell the presence of strange dogs walking outside the shelter. Most of all, they loved to roll in the dead and rotting tidal wash that constituted the only beach in this part of the city.

After the Baltimore trip, the winter holiday season was already over and we were faced with the longest dreariest months of the southern New England winter season - February and March. This year seemed particularly oppressive because of the sudden absence of phone calls and activity surrounding the care of my parents.

Before my brother and his wife swept my parents away from their Ashville home, winter included phone calls every day from my mother asking me advice about caring for my father, complaining about things in general and gossiping about the rest of the family members who were scattered all over the world. She was my only real connection to them.

This holiday season had not seemed to contain Christmas at all, since mostly we were just going through the holiday motions in Asheville while planning for the inevitable. All the pre-holiday daily journeys to the university, my studio, and the Hidden Falls Shelter seemed laden with sadness and mourning, the gray skies heavy but promising little snow to add a bright cover to the gritty grime of early-winter New Bedford and Fall River. I put up a little Christmas tree in our front window and Mark found one of his mother's favorite menorahs to put in the other and that was the extent of our home holiday decorating and festivities that year.

Oddly, it turned out that many of the shelter volunteers and staff at Hidden Falls had a rotten or depressing Christmas that year. Bliss's mother was in the hospital with a terminal illness. Many people seemed to have lost family members in the late fall or had children who couldn't return home for the holidays. Everyone had a grim story to report about Christmas morning disappointment. So, we decided to have a new Christmas celebration at the shelter in January and call it Fake Christmas.

The Fake Christmas morning at the shelter turned out to be a nice peaceful soft rose-purple day and in gentle contrast the ground was covered with a crust of sparkly light blue snow when I got into my van. The ten-mile drive to the shelter was beautiful and invigorating. The scrappy woods along Route 195 between New Bedford and Fall River were transformed by the snow and icy sunrise into lovely drooping crystalline forms and a soft mist rose from the low spots and wetlands.

Ricky and Sable were up and ready to hit the road when I grabbed my keys, while Hawkins and Maggie were snuggled tightly together under the blanket on the sofa with the electric fire turning softly on low. They didn't even raise their heads to look as we opened the front door. I leashed the other two and let them jump into the back of the van.

Pulling into the shelter parking lot, a really frigid breeze hit me from the river and I wished I'd left the dogs home safe and warm in bed with Mark. I couldn't turn around and go home because nobody else seemed to have shown up for the morning shift and I could hear dozens of frantic barking dogs waiting for food and fresh water and further agitated by the sudden onset of frigid weather. With disappointment, I thought everyone else had forgotten about our Fake Christmas idea.

I grabbed the extra-large coffee I'd picked up at

Dunkin Donuts on the way over anyway, and prepared myself mentally for a morning of icy grimy hard work. The sheer amount of physical activity facing me pushed any thoughts and feelings of loss and emptiness out of my mind. I went into my robot mode as I did when faced with large amounts of unpleasant work. I'd stop thinking, start doing, grab whatever task was in front of me and do it with as much vigor as possible without analyzing anything and working without a break until a welcome exhaustion invaded my body.

I started with the cat crates - the least emotionally taxing for me since I didn't connect with cats emotionally as tightly as with dogs - quickly transferring cats to another clean crate while I placed crusted food bowls and clotted litter boxes on the floor for later scrubbing. I glanced around me and felt a bit desperate. There were over twenty cat cages to clean, plus the ten indoor dog crates and then the back runs, plus scrubbing dishes and feeding. If I were lucky I'd be out of there by three o'clock. And, I was worried about the chilly dogs I'd left out in the car. I'd have to find a free run and bring them in, exposing them to the potential parasites from contact with a bunch of strange dogs.

I tried to push away thoughts of Ashville and the drive down there - past Harrisville and into Virginia passing all those Blue Ridge towns with soft fairy-tale sounding names like Stroudsburg and Wytheville, and how we pulled into Ashville very late on Christmas Eve, my father with his very last wood fire roaring away on a Christmas Eve and the welcoming smell of wood smoke. I was overwhelmed with a sudden rush of loss, like a punch to the stomach, and a feeling of exhaustion followed - I didn't know how I'd get through the shift.

    Then I heard the creaking of the heavy metal front door and a huge box of Dunkin Donuts doughnuts appeared followed by Hector, our resident dog trainer. Behind Hector was Berta, and Diane from animal control followed her inside. Several other volunteers arrived and then finally Bliss walked in carrying a jumbo Dunkin Box o' Joe and packet of foam cups.

    When Bliss saw me already scraping the litter boxes in the cat crates she exclaimed, "What are you doing here so early? We decided not to come in at 7:00 on Fake Christmas morning. We thought we'd give you all a little break and start at 8:00, didn't you get the message? Oh well, it's good you're here and cleaning already. We'll all get out of here a little earlier because of it. Okay, everyone, gather around, we're finally going to have the fattening Christmas morning treats not all of us got at home this year, but that all of us need and deserve!"

"Yes, first things first," said Hector, as he opened the big flat box of doughnuts in all their sticky glory - cream filled, chocolate covered, jelly filled, sugar powder covered delights.

We all stuffed sticky frosting and jimmy-covered doughnuts into our mouths and drank coffee until we'd reached a giddy, peaceful energized high from the mass amount of caffeine and sugar. Then we turned to the cleaning tasks. The dogs were barking and hyper from smelling the doughnuts and we saved all the plain ones for them. I took dogs out of the rows of crates and walked them one by one out into the icy parking lot and down to the river to sniff around and roll on the cold crackling sand.

Inside, Hector, Bliss and the others scrubbed filthy crates and fed the cats. When I was finished walking the dogs I let the other ones in the back runs out in the yard in pairs to romp around in the cold. I wanted to take each one of them home and wrap them up warmly in comforters on the sofa, as I knew Hawkins and Maggie were at the moment. The greatest satisfaction I've had from almost anything in life is bringing a dog home that has never experienced any comfort in life and just load on the coziness - comforters, fake fur blankets, lots of good food, people-food snacks - and watch for the glow of appreciation of life to appear in its eyes.

 Many rescued dogs were once relegated to a life of servitude - chained in a side yard, penned in a small run behind a house or business without much interaction other than a daily pat on the head when water and food bowls are exchanged. Others, like Sable, Ricky, and Hawkins, have experienced extremes of neglect and cruelty - deprivation and pain to enhance training for dog fighting and guard duty, or plain brutality for the unjustifiable enjoyment of inflicting of pain on something helpless. Dogs, more than any other animal, seem to appreciate creature comforts. Providing comfort for neglected dogs led to a bond of trust and love that I've only rarely felt with other people.

 Hector shouted for everyone to clean up and gather around the front desk. He had a Fake Christmas gift to give to Bliss. All the volunteers came up to front of the shelter to watch Bliss unwrap her package and to pick at the remains of the doughnuts. The dogs and cats were busy eating breakfast and were quiet except for the peaceful sound of kibble crunching. Hector found some classical music that could pass for Christmas music on the old boom box radio that sat on top of the refrigerator.

More than on a holiday with blood family, on that Fake Christmas morning at Hidden Falls, everyone seemed to be content to be where they were at the moment - clustered around an old metal Army desk covered in paperwork and doughnut crumbs - waiting for Bliss to tear the wrappings off of the only present anyone had thought to bring. Everyone was tired, filthy, and chilled by the damp winter wind coming through the cracks in the building from the river, but everyone was in good humor and feeling friendly.

Bliss undid the last piece of Scotch tape on her present and pulled out a little statuette.

"Oh my god! It's The Thinker," laughed Doris. The Thinker was a little resin statue of a dog sitting on the toilet with his paws on his chin in a position that was similar to that of Rodin's famous statue, The Thinker. Bliss had one of these Toilet Thinker statues but it seemed to have come to a bad end. The Thinker was once the shelter mascot and sat proudly on top of the toilet tank. Members of the board hated The Thinker.

"It's so tacky," exclaimed one of them, "It's just symbolic of everything that's wrong with this place."

"White trash," muttered another.

Eventually, the Thinker mysteriously disappeared from the back of the tank, never to be found, not even in any trash can or dumpster. Most volunteers had a suspicion of what happened to The Thinker and glanced towards the dirty river whenever they spoke of it.

"It was just a joke," said Bliss, after The Thinker disappeared. "What is with those people anyway? Who do they think they are? Are they better than me because we all just want to have a laugh around here once in a while, after everything we deal with every day?"

The missing Thinker wasn't mentioned but its disappearance became a symbol of the growing tension and divisions between the board and Bliss and the volunteers at Hidden Falls. It came to represent presumed and resented class differences. On the Fake Christmas it was funny, and a big relief, to see the work-hardened veneer of Bliss' face dissolve into tears over a silly resin figurine of a dog sitting on a toilet. But she held it in her hands as if Hector had given her a bundle of red roses.

Bliss smiled at everyone warmly, which was a very rare occurrence, and said, "You guys give a shit about me and I appreciate it. I really do. You made up for the crap I had to deal with on the real holiday this year, for sure."

Then Bliss went and placed The Thinker on its

rightful place on the back of the toilet tank while we finished the Box o' Joe and got dressed in our heavy coats for the chilly walk back to our cars. We made the rounds of the runs first, distributing to all the dogs and cats a holiday handful of treats and the new catnip toys that Berta had sewn. I hated leaving the shelter for home, and leaving the feeling of companionship we had that day.

Thinking again of Ricky and Sable curled up together in a pile of sleeping bags in the back seat of the cold van, I put on my coat and walked out the front door with the others. We didn't hug each other. None of us were really demonstrative huggers. But, somehow, as I walked towards my car I felt as if we had all given each other a prolonged bear hug that day.

The dogs were snuggled up together on the front seat of the van. Together they looked like one big pumpkin-glazed doughnut. They jumped up when they saw me and I thought about walking them along the dirty riverfront but the city in the distance looked so gritty and depressing that I decided against it. Still, the dogs needed a good walk and I didn't feel like returning home. Mark would probably still be in bed and the silence and the empty anticlimactic feeling in the house was more than I could face.

I decided to take the longer rural route home. Southeastern Massachusetts is home to our two small old industrial cities - New Bedford and Fall River - only ten miles apart. Between the two cities is some of the most beautiful oceanfront farmland in the county. I decided to drive down to the u-shaped spit of land between the two cities and walk the dogs at a reservation that overlooked a long silver estuary snaking miles inland from the gray Atlantic.

Old 1920's converted farmhouses dotted the landscape. This part of the countryside still remained impervious to suburban tract developments and three-hundred-year old gray green stone fences wound over and around fields and forests. That morning they were covered with a fine shiny frost.

The dogs piled out of the car as I wrangled with their leashes. I never let my dogs run free. My old Springer Spaniel romped along beside us as we hiked as kids, chasing anything that moved, but always returned to our sides in a minute. Once the pit bulls start the chase they are so intent and singular minded on achieving their goal that they will run after a deer for miles without once turning around to consider from where they started. So, I took one leash and each hand and let Sable and Ricky pull me around the isolated reservation.

It seemed that everyone else was indoors lighting their wood fires. I could smell the sentimental tang of wood smoke. But, once out and moving through the tangled forest and open fields of the frozen reservation I stopped feeling sad and pining for the past. I was solely in the moment, enjoying the air and the day, just like my dogs were enjoying it - openly and to the fullest.

A massive gray Heron heaved itself up from the estuary beach and rose closely over our heads. I had a sudden feeling of the presence of my mother and father, walking with us, laughing and breathing in the bitter cold air. My parents always loved weather - bad weather, storms, wind, waves dashing dramatically along piers - it always brought them outdoors when everyone else was huddled inside for safety. I am the same way.

We walked for miles that cold day, until my feet felt frozen solid in my boots and until I could tell the dogs were lifting their feet away from the frost in discomfort. Then we headed back to the van exhausted and drove home to our own electric fireplace and to Mark who was watching TV with Hawkins and Maggie and waiting impatiently for me to come home.

The Fake Christmas was the first Christmas holiday in my life without the presence of my parents.

It turned out to be the best possible gift I could have received from my friends because it helped me realize I could survive the real holiday, the following year, without my mother and father.

 **14. Bliss**

By the time the dirty snow had completely melted out of the Hidden Falls parking lot that spring, the division between Bliss and the board of directors had become irreparable. Unknown to most of the staff and volunteers was the location of a new shelter site that the board had been breaking ground on since the early thaw. They'd contracted with a local vocational high school, and the staff and students began building a large, modern shelter building through grant funding and some large, silent donations.

Most of the Hidden Falls volunteers, like myself, were both excited and angry. We couldn't understand why we weren't made a part of the new shelter planning, and wondered why Bliss, the owner of the current shelter building, had been left completely in the dark about everything.

"She's a complete obstructionist," replied Alice, when I asked her about Bliss's snubbing. "She and her brother have put up road blocks from the get-go."

Bliss and her brother owned the old Quonset hut, parking lot and dirt-filled land that comprised the current Hidden Falls Animal Shelter. The Hidden Falls board of directors owned the name of the non-profit charity.

"They're going to take our name, my name," shouted Bliss, when she finally learned of the new space. "Because, I'm not moving. Once the shelter leaves my property they will never do things my way. So, I'm staying here, and they are taking the name I created for this shelter years before there ever was a board of directors. And, to think I ever called any of those people my friends!"

I felt sad for Bliss. She was tough and angry. She was difficult to deal with and very abrasive, but I felt she had inherent integrity and, most importantly, put the welfare of the animals in her care above any other person or political consideration.

I also was excited about the new shelter, mainly because the board told us that once it was complete, they would be better able to serve the city of New Bedford animal control department - meaning all those poor, sad animals going to that awful shelter with the dark Elvira and her security guard minion lurking at the front desk would soon have the much better option of coming to Hidden Falls.

    Bliss informed the volunteers that she'd be staying at the Quonset hut. She would give up the Hidden Falls name and would later come up with a new name for the small shelter she'd continue to run there. I was sad for her, but felt it couldn't be anything but positive to have two animal shelters running between two cities where there was so much need. I, and the others, offered to continue to help Bliss while we worked at the new shelter, but she wasn't on board with that idea at all.

    "No way. It's all or nothing with me," she said firmly and stubbornly. "Either you are with me or against me."

    I found it heartbreaking that Bliss would take my offer to volunteer at the new shelter as a betrayal, but then I really didn't know all the details about the years of growing animosity between her and the board.

    So, on one of those spring days, with dark clouds accentuating the brilliance of the azaleas and cherry blossoms, we loaded up truck after truck with crates and supplies - any object the board could legally remove from the Quonset hut. Bliss stood by watching stoically as the stacked crates that had been home to Hawkins and hundreds of other dogs were shifted into the vans. Finally, the mounds of unruly paperwork were dumped from the top of her metal military-style desk and the desk itself was forced out the front door, past Bliss, and onto the last truck.

"Stupid, is what it is," said Bliss. "They aren't even going to be near the underground river anymore and they want to keep calling the new place my shelter name; Hidden Falls."

Bliss was referring to the river and falls that were paved over when the city was built right over on the top of it during the textile boom era. The falls are still hidden under paved roadways, and flowed right under the Quonset hut and parking lot we were standing in. Then she reached over to hug me quickly, something she'd never done before, then turned away and walked back into the now empty, old shelter.

In spite of Bliss's with me or not with me statement, I still stopped by to visit her from time to time, played with some of the dogs in her newly named shelter and helped find some of them homes. But, the former zeal for animal rescue seemed to be gone from her. We slowly drifted apart then, a few years later, I saw her at an animal rescue fundraiser. She was no longer rescuing dogs and cats, but was rescuing humans. Bliss told me she would appear in family court and take custody of any sick, unclaimed or unwanted child and bring her of him home to her fifty-acre inherited farm a few miles north of the city. Her sister and husband helped her raise dozens of babies, toddlers and teenagers and so they could launch them into more stable and productive lives.

"You wouldn't believe it," she said, her old intensity restored. "People, mothers even, will just leave their babies at the court. If they don't show for the hearing, the poor kids become wards of the court - nobody to care for them. That's where I step in. I take them, no questions asked, and we get them healthy again."

I smiled at Bliss because I loved her. I loved her compassion and willingness to work and support any creature she found in need. I wondered for a second about how her abrasive personality might affect a small child, but I quickly set the concern aside. I felt that the love emanating from a true rescuer like Bliss could shine through any rough surface. Bliss survived and evolved after the betrayal over Hidden Falls, and she was happy, her true heart still strong and intact, and best of all, she was putting all her rescue energy into helping human beings. If Bliss, a few years ago the most misanthropic person I'd ever met, could find a place in her heart to embrace her fellow human beings, I could too.

 15. Kindred Spirits

By late spring, the new Hidden Falls shelter held dozens of dogs, hundreds of cats, and even a few rabbits and parrots. The dream of saving more animals was becoming a reality as all the animals taken in by

City of New Bedford animal control officers could come to Hidden Falls for care and adoption - a vast improvement over the dark, sad shelter on the wharves.

The new Hidden Falls was bright, clean, spacious and surrounded by fields, forests and walking trails for the dogs. The cats had a light and airy built-out addition with a screened-in patio so they could watch the birds and squirrels playing in the many trees surrounding the shelter. It was very different from the sad, dank, dark rows of cat cages I'd glimpsed when we were liberating Little Ricky. I couldn't wait to see the truckloads of animals arriving at Hidden Falls from that nasty old shelter.

Instead of walking dogs along the brown river with its tangled muddy piles of sticks and refuse, volunteers walked them up a hill through the woods and then through a tiny cemetery, overgrown but beautiful with flowing, fragrant wild roses and gnarled lilacs. We were careful to carry a good supply of poop bags. We didn't want to show any disrespect for the cemetery that was such a welcome retreat from the rows of barking dogs in the shelter. Nice as it was, it was still a shelter and stressful for animals. There was plenty of love there, but it was still not a cozy, comfortable home.

Hector approached me one day as I was returning

from a cemetery walk with two dogs in tow. He wanted to talk with me about Trixie, a dog that had been transferred to the new Hidden Falls from the old Quonset hut. Trixie was a mixed breed of a type common to area shelters: feisty, small dogs which were a mixture of pit bull and Chihuahua that we called Chippits. Backyard breeders are hobbyist genetic experimenters looking to create new dog breed mixes lucrative for quick corner sales or drug deals. These experiments generally include some kind of pit bull, for perceived toughness, and something small for savings on food costs and ease in hiding pets in rental properties.

Chippits, like Chihuahuas, had very spunky and shrewd personalities and Trixie was exemplary. She'd recently bitten the shelter vet. Trixie, like so many of the shelter dogs, had a fear of men. Since moving to the new shelter, a new male veterinarian had replaced the female one at the old shelter. Trixie promptly bit the new vet on the leg.

Hector said, "She has to go. The Board voted on Trixie and she can't stay on at the shelter with a bite record. There is no way we can adopt her out now."

I'd heard other volunteers, especially Melissa, talking about Trixie. All were worried about her fate. In spite of her cantankerousness, or maybe because of it, she was a volunteer favorite. All of us were worried that Trixie would be put down. It seemed unfair, as her irritability was a manifestation of early abuse by humans. But, I understood that the shelter couldn't adopt her out and risk a potential lawsuit, especially not now, with so much more to lose.

Hector continued, "Melissa submitted a letter to the Board offering the services of a local boarding kennel, one near you, actually, to house Trixie for the rest of her life. The kennel owner is a pretty well-known rescue person around here and she's on board with it, although I don't really know why. It's just no life for a dog living cooped up in a kennel, you know?"

"In my opinion, Trixie would be better off dead than living out her life in a kennel, but The-Powers-That-Be say that Trixie shall live. The reason I'm telling you all this is that I wondered if you could take Trixie along with you when you leave today and run her out to the kennel, seeing as it's on your way home."

I agreed with Hector about doubting the wisdom of keeping Trixie in a kennel for the rest of her life, but I was relieved, too, that Melissa had taken the initiative to plead her case with the Board. So, at the end of my shift, I loaded Trixie into my van and let her ride shotgun on her way to her permanent and final home.

I was also very curious to meet the rescue woman

who lived so close to me and had a kennel where difficult dogs could be boarded. I was getting very antsy for a nice summer vacation trip, and was starting to accept the fact that with four dogs, we'd have to board at least one of them to make any travel feasible.

Trixie had a huge smile on her face as she sat in the front seat and took in the sights. We drove out of the stony, bumpy, rural road and onto the highway towards Massasoit, a rural town just a few miles outside of my New Bedford city neighborhood. We stopped on the way at the drive-up doughnut shop, a shelter ritual with long-term dogs, and got an iced coffee for me and a plain doughnut for Trixie that she consumed in one gulp.

The kennel was set behind a huge, old-fashioned gingerbread Victorian house. The only indicator that there was a kennel business on site was the sign out front with the name Fantastic Fur-Babies Boarding and Grooming. The woman who had agreed to house Trixie for life was named Sherri. Barking coming from the long low kennel area was deafening and soon Trixie poked her head out of the van window to join the chorus.

The office door in the kennel was locked and the area dark. I walked tentatively onto the front porch that hung low around two sides side of the house and rapped on the door. It too was locked tight and the connecting kitchen was dark. I knew that I was on time for the appointment Hector had made for us earlier in the day. I glanced back at Trixie. It was a hot, late spring afternoon and she was drooling and panting, drips sliding down the outside of the open van windows.

    I took her out and walked her behind the kennel. I figured that Sherri had been held up somewhere and we'd wait for at least a half hour; besides, I had no place else to bring Trixie. She didn't like other dogs or men or I'd bring her to my house. She couldn't go back to the shelter because Hector had said, "Once she's out she's out, got it?"

    I glimpsed woods and gardens, glowing golden in the late day light. The scene was so bucolic and tempting I wanted to immerse myself in it. We wandered in and I realized that we were in a graveyard. I stooped to read some of the stones. They were old, corroded and close to the ground, and they were not in memorial to humans. Judging by the names they all were for animals (Buster, Ditsy, Bella and Blue) and some were dated from as far back as the 1920's. The landscaping of the pet graveyard was carefully maintained and incredibly beautiful, though antiquated and odd with distorted old yews, and twisted vines spouting orange trumpet flowers in pure contrast to the faded plastic animals and flowers left on some of the gravestones.

I was so immersed in the otherworldliness of the place that Trixie and I spent nearly an hour wandering about reading the quaint, sentimental inscriptions before we wandered back to the kennel and saw that it was as tightly locked up as before. I tried calling Hector but he didn't answer, not that he would have been any help. I didn't have a number for Sherri. I couldn't think of anything to do but to bring Trixie home and try to manage for the night.

I'd bring a crate up to the kitchen and keep an eye on her there, then call someone from the shelter and get a number for Sherri so I could bring her over there in the morning. Mark would freak out, I was sure of it, when he walked into the kitchen and saw Trixie there. But, oddly enough, he didn't.

In fact, Trixie was so calm in the little crate that we decided to let her out to wander around the kitchen while we did the dishes after dinner. We thought that maybe she was really a well-behaved dog now that she was out of the stressful environment of the shelter. Maybe…we could foster her instead of consigning her to a life in a cage. I opened the cage door.

Suddenly, Trixie transformed. She was like the

symbolic Chinese Red Celestial Dog changing from Yang (unswerving devotion and fidelity) to Yin (destruction and catastrophe) in a mere second. She tore out of the crate and went straight for Mark, who was loading a pile of plates into the dishwasher. The plates hit the tile floor and shattered was shards flying everywhere as Trixie grabbed the ankle of his pants and started to tear at them ferociously. Her teeth showed narrow, white and long under her curling, snarling lips. Luckily, Mark had his hiking boots and jeans on, because Trixie was doing whatever she could to make contact with flesh.

    I saw drops of blood beginning to accumulate on the floor and started to panic. I pulled at Trixie's hind legs, lifting her off the floor, as we were told to do, to break up a dogfight at the shelter, but she didn't relax her grip on Mark's ankle, not one bit. I realized, with partial relief, that the blood was just coming from Trixie's paws as her front feet were scrambling around in the broken glass from the plates.

    All this time, really just a few seconds, Mark didn't say a thing. He just looked shocked and a little distanced from what was actually happening. Fortunately, Trixie was holding onto the leather ankle of Mark's boot and seemed satisfied to keep her teeth in one place as she probably thought she'd latched onto a really nice, thick piece of flesh. Then, I noticed the pitcher of iced water on the kitchen table, grabbed it and threw it with a slap against Trixie's side. She dropped Mark's leg immediately and he ran for the door to the deck. Trixie sat looking at me and panting, her tongue hanging out of her mouth like a thick piece of ham. The look in her dark brown eyes was both joyful and confused, as if she were saying, "What did you do that for? I was getting him for you! And, I got him pretty good, didn't I?"

 I grabbed her by the collar and pulled her into the crate. She went in happily and I shakily tossed her some dog treats. There was absolutely no use in punishing or correcting Trixie for attacking Mark's leg. It was very clear that she thought it was her duty to protect me from an awful, frightening man. Trixie seemed to think that men were some alien and dangerous species - her reactions to Mark were so different than the friendly gregarious persona she shared with women. Tentatively, I braced myself to go out on the deck and check on Mark. He had his boot off and was holding it up sadly.

 "Just look at what she did to my Salomon's," he sighed. Mark had a penchant for collecting high-end hiking boots and these favorites now sported several large tooth holes that penetrated nearly all the way through the thick leather. "You are lucky you insist on wearing those hiking boots in warm weather," I laughed.

I was relieved that Mark wasn't injured, and also that he wasn't angry and yelling at me for bringing Trixie home. I was almost giddy with laughter as he sat holding his boot in the air, his jeans shredded and torn up the side of both ankles. I was also relieved to find how effective a pitcher of cold water could be in breaking up a dog bite situation. I was relieved that we were still at home and not heading down the road to the emergency room. I was also happy that I was living with someone who understood.

In spite of his taciturn demeanor and seeming lack of emotion, Mark really did share my love of animals, especially dogs. In spite of his declarations of agnosticism, his love for nature and animals was truly spiritual. At that moment, I could see with clarity that it was that quality that I sensed in him from our first meeting and was the main reason I had stayed with for so long.

Mark's mother kept a pristinely clean home. An animal hair never dared land on any surface in her perfectly designed and comfortable house. Mark certainly was never allowed to have a pet, particularly a messy one like a dog. But, he always longed for one, and played with dogs owned by the parents of his neighborhood friends so experienced dog connections vicariously. But, not having grown up with dogs in the house from early childhood, Trixie was a bit too much dog for Mark.

"That beast is going somewhere else tomorrow, right?" Mark asked.

"Yes, oh yes, definitely," I replied.

But, I really didn't know where Trixie was going. What had happened to the owner of the Our Fantastic Fur Babies kennel? Why hadn't she been there when I went to drop Trixie off? Had she changed her mind? I started to feel less giddy and started to feel the weight of responsibility and fear that was an inherent part of rescuing these strange dogs.

What would I do if Trixie had no place to go? I couldn't bring her back to the shelter. Hector had made that quite clear. I couldn't adopt her out to anyone else. That was clearly not an option after what just occurred. If Hidden Falls couldn't risk a lawsuit by adopting Trixie out, we certainly couldn't. If Trixie attacked an adopter in the way she attacked Mark, especially if the victim wasn't wearing heavy boots, we would stand to lose everything we had and worked for, including a home where we could keep our rescued dogs. We'd either have to commit to keeping Trixie, or take her to a vet to have her euthanized. Making that awful decision myself was something I'd hoped to avoid.

My mood went from buoyant to depressed, but I didn't tell Mark about the problem with the kennel. I assured him that Trixie would be on her way first thing in the morning. All my tentative ideas of fostering Trixie were set aside as temporary madness. There was no way I could risk having her attack Mark again, or one of my other dogs. The thought of Hawkins and Trixie meeting up made my blood run cold.

But, I just didn't think I could bring myself to have a young and healthy dog like Trixie put down. Of course, dogs in shelters were put down for much less egregious offences than the ones that Trixie had committed. Trixie was dangerous. Her pretty eyes were the problem. I adored the look of loyalty and love in her eyes gazing up at me even after what she'd done to Mark. She thought that was her duty to me - protecting me from a nasty man like Ricky had protected me that first day in Buttonwood Park - just with a little more energy. I knew I couldn't bring her into a veterinarian's office and have her killed.

As I sat on the deck staring miserably into the leaves of our old maple tree, my phone rang. To my great relief, an unfamiliar shrill female voice came over the phone through sounds of raucous barking in the background. The woman sounded as if she was continents away, not just a few miles down the road as she squawked, "Lori, Lori is that you? This is Sherri, from the kennel. I am so, so sorry. I got your note but I thought you were coming by with Trixie tomorrow afternoon. I know Hector said it was tomorrow you'd be coming."

I assured Sherri that everything was just fine. It was just a simple mistake on Hector's part, after all, no harm done - not really. I'd be over with Trixie first thing in the morning instead of the afternoon if that would be okay. Sherri said it was, and we agreed it would be nice to finally meet. I hung up with the most exquisite feeling of relief. I felt a little guilty not informing Sherri about the incident with Mark's ankle. I didn't want to pass on a problem to some unknowing person. But, I was also afraid that Sherri might refuse to take her at the kennel.

Besides, I rationalized, Sherri knew what she was getting into with Trixie. She was one of the people advocating for her life after she bit the veterinarian. And, according to Hector, Sherri always took Hector's last-chance dogs - the ones deemed unadoptable because of little incidents or the ones too traumatized in their former lives to ever live in an uncontrolled space again. Besides, I thought, there was no need to add to Trixie's existing list of transgressions.

I fed Trixie her dinner in the crate, then fed and reassured the other dogs, who were frantic after overhearing the struggle in the kitchen and from smelling a new dog in their territory. I took Trixie out for a short walk after dinner, being very careful to stay clear of anyone walking down the sidewalk nearby. I was surprised to find myself feeling that I'd actually miss the little hell-raiser. I had that familiar leaden feeling of loss in my stomach that I had whenever I had to give up a dog, even one I'd only spent a few hours with.

I hoped Sherri's kennel would be a good option for Trixie and that she'd find the peace and security she'd never experienced in her short troubled life. Besides, it was the only option open to her - other than death.

The next day was one of those clear, warm and dry spring New England days I value so much, before the soggy coastal humidity settles in for the summer. I put Trixie in the back of the van without a crate and let her race back and forth from window to window, banging her nose hard on the glass each time she saw a moving creature, all the way out to Massasoit.

We pulled back into the long gravel drive and this

time a tall, pale, fragile-looking woman with red hair and wearing shorts was pulling tangled weeds out of the ragged rose gardens surrounding the gingerbread Victorian. I guessed this was Sherri, but she looked nothing like I'd pictured her with her tough, masculine, cigarette-husky telephone voice. Trixie let loose with a cacophony of excited squeals and barks when she spotted her.

This was something I'd see over and over again with Sherri. Trixie's barks weren't the usual half-stressed, half vicious barks she used when she saw new people, like Mark. These were excited, friendly barks. Without even having met Sherri in person, Trixie seemed to recognize a kindred spirit. In time, I'd witness even the most hostile dogs reacting positively to Sherri.

Trixie practically pulled me to my knees while tangling herself in her leash as she scrambled frantically to get out of the van. She was small but incredibly powerful, and she made a beeline towards Sherri before I could get a good grip on the leash. She pulled free and charged full-force into Sherri's knees, sending her back a few steps without upending her. My heartbeat accelerated to near tachycardia as I watched Trixie confront Sherri. Trixie seemed to like Sherri, but I still didn't trust Trixie at all after last night's experience. I could only picture the fragile-looking Sherri being knocked to the ground and mauled by Trixie before I could get over to them to help.

But, nothing like that happened. Trixie put both front feet on Sherri's knees and gazed up into her face, tongue lolling, drool dripping, with a look of devotion I'd never seen in her eyes before. Sherri was laughing and reached down to give Trixie a hug, not minding the strings of drool that were oozing their way down her jeans.

"Is this another one of those evil, vicious killer-hounds that Hector is sending my way?" laughed Sherri. "Just another terrible beast coming to our little prison. Hector loves saving society from the ravages of canine career criminals, and sending them to me."

I liked Sherri immediately. I could see right away that she understood the politics at the various shelters. She seemed very young, but premature wrinkles on her forehead and around her eyes, and some long dull pink scars on her cheek, hands and legs, hinted at a lifetime of accumulated stressful, violent, incidents with dogs and possibly people.

I was finally able to yank Trixie's leash out from under her scrambling legs and wriggling butt. We decided to give her a good walk around the pet cemetery to help her blow off some steam before introducing her to the kennel run in which she would live out the rest of her life.

Again, I appreciated how the cemetery was a tangled splendor - kind of like how I had pictured the secret garden when I was enchanted with that book as a kid. Through the low granite gravestones grew huge twisted English yew trees, their dark branches reaching up to the sky like twisted grasping fingers. Cemetery maintenance was sporadic at best, and many invasive vines were winding themselves up and around and choking the yews and walnut trees that lined the entrance. Cherokee roses, a beautiful spring invader, were already in full bloom and spilling down white waterfalls of fragrant flowers that we had to push aside or crawl under.

Trixie never stopped pulling on her leash for a minute as she charged down each pathway, sniffing wildly, and nearly separating my elbow from my arm.

"Do you want me to take her for a bit?" asked Sherri.
I declined the offer, looking dubiously at Sherri's thin reed-like arms and fingers.

"I'm not as weak as I look," she laughed. "I've been working with animals most of my life. And, I used to work on a farm with the horses and stock animals. I didn't like that though. I did like the horses. I wanted to have some here, but my husband, George, said absolutely no way would he let me have horses here. So, I have really big dogs instead."

We walked to the furthest end of the cemetery, a good half-mile back. There, all the sounds of the roadways disappeared and we were surrounded by huge old white pines. The ground was padded with many years accumulation of pine needles and they gave off a soft golden scent in the warm air.

Trixie's was panting and her tongue was lolling out triple its normal size. She'd had enough walking and pulling. She lay on her stomach and stretched her hind legs way back out behind her like a frog, a position Hawkins and other pit bulls I'd met seemed to prefer when they were very tired and very relaxed. I'd never seen Trixie even close to being relaxed at the shelter. She sighed into the pine needles. Sherri and I sat down on either side of her.

"Now I feel really good about leaving Trixie here," I said. "I'm just so relieved. I can't thank you enough. I didn't want to see her put down, but I can't keep her at my house."

Then, I told Sherri about what had happened with Mark's leg. I felt much better getting it out in the open and Sherri understood. I knew she would. She told me about other dogs and cats with issues she'd been caring for at the kennel over the years, most coming in from Hector and other local shelters and rescues, or from neighbors or dog grooming clients, or animal control officers, or just dumped in the night on her front porch.

I asked her where this great accumulation of animal graves had come from and who owned the pet cemetery. I'd never seen so many gravestones in a cemetery, let alone one for pets. The contrast between the sentimental odes to their pets that people carved on these stones existed in stark contrast to the yelps and whines I could hear in the distance from the many unwanted rescue dogs in Sherri's kennel.

The cemetery was not owned by Sherri and her husband, George. I was shocked to learn that it was owned by a non-profit foundation that supported that nightmarish city kennel from which we rescued Little Ricky. That small, dismal shelter, clearly not adequate housing for the multitudes of unwanted animals coming through there on a daily basis – the shelter that would soon be sending all their animals over to Hidden Falls.

But, this cemetery, though not well maintained, spoke of money - lots of money - and people who could afford the luxury of an inscribed headstone for their dead pets, and fees for the plot and upkeep. I told

Sherri about my experience at the shelter with Ricky and asked about the seeming disparity between that place and this expensive secret garden cemetery.

"You're not kidding! "she said in her husky voice as she lit a cigarette and took a long drag, "I really shouldn't be telling you this, so don't say anything, okay? We bought this house and kennel from the lawyer that runs that foundation and that shelter. The house used to be offices for the shelter. In my opinion, he just runs that shelter as a service to the city so he can keep his non-profit foundation going. That's the moneymaker for him. He, his wife, and the board of directors are all about money, for themselves, their big homes on Rocky Neck, their summer homes, boats, whatever. And, they can puff themselves up for their rich friends by saying they are saving animals but they don't give a shit about animals! They kill most of them that wind up in there."

"Then why do the dead ones here have all these fancy expensive gravestones? They must at least care about their own animals."

"Nope," Sherri said in a weary voice. "These graves are sold to a bunch of naïve, sentimental people who give big money to the shelter foundation. They don't ever go to the shelter to see what really goes on there! They don't want to know! All these people are just big wigs living out in their 10-million dollar houses on Rocky Neck. They aren't going to leave that safe little gated-community to come into New Bedford to see a filthy rundown shelter and get their shoes dirty. Which is good for the owners, because it's all a freaking scam!"

I thought about Ricky and the other dogs and cats I'd seen at that shelter that day I got him out of there. I thought of the poor terrified dog that tried to suck on my finger in a desperate wish to return to puppyhood and leave the hell and smell of death in that shelter. I felt suddenly dizzy and sick.

"Well, someone should do something about this bullshit," I said. "Why don't the papers write about this? Why don't people who do know, do something about it?"

Sherri looked at me sadly and indulgently. "You haven't lived here all that long," she said. If you'd grown up here, you might know. These people - these idiots who run the shelter and foundation - they own everything in the city. The city is their little non-profit playground. They are on every board - profit and nonprofit. They have friends. And they watch out for each other, especially the rat lawyer who sold us this house, Louis Harrington.

We wanted this place for the grooming and

boarding business really bad and there was just nothing else like it on the market and available. So, old Harrington, in order to sell it to us, made us sign an agreement that we'd never have rescued animals here - do you believe it? He thinks we might become competition for his disgusting shelter. But, of course, without that shelter, how would he get people to cough up money for his foundation? The situation sucks all the way around."

"But," I said, "you do have rescued animals here. Almost the entire kennel is full of rescued animals isn't it? How do you keep him from finding out, and really, why would he care? There are so many unwanted animals. I'm sure there's enough to go around for you both."

"Well, I think the deal is that our kennel used to be the old city shelter kennel and Harrington just doesn't want anyone associating his shelter with this one. I don't know why. He's just a control freak. So, I tell him all the dogs here are boarding clients, and some are, so I'm not lying entirely."

"I still don't get it," I said. "That shelter is pure evil. And, it's not even run by the city, so the city council or mayor can't even do anything about it! It's awful, and anyone who's been there must know it. They do know it! So, if this kennel is sold to you now and the deal is done, how can he have any influence over you at all. Why don't you speak up?"

"Well…unfortunately, we took a bridge loan out from Harrington personally to buy this place when our old house in the city didn't sell right away. We still owe years on that. He made us sign papers that said if we keep rescued dogs here and adopt them out, he'd call in the loan. And, we just can't pay that in full right now. No way! So, that's why I asked you to say nothing of what you see here.

Not that people don't know, almost everyone knows, we have animal control officers bringing their lost causes here, for God's sake. But, as long as everything is cool and everyone pretends that we are not a shelter, Harrington seems to be cool with that. He wants to be the only show in town so the old-money people keep pouring money into his foundation."

"Still, what's in it for him, really?" I pressed. "He's a lawyer. The piddling little amount an animal shelter must pull in for donations can't possibly make or break his lifestyle, can it?"

"It's this place," said Sherri, sweeping her hand across the stonewalled rose vine-covered vista of the pet cemetery. "When those old bats living out on Rocky Neck lose their little Princess or Skippy to old age, they want to bury their baby here and they want to donate a vast amount in their baby's memory to Harrington's lovely shelter downtown. Like I said, they don't want to get their hands dirty. They take it on his word - or choose to be blind - that it's a wonderful place. They don't know that they kill almost everything that walks in the door on four legs, and they don't really care. They just want to feel that they are doing something good, something in their social comfort zone, if you know what I mean?"

"I do, sort of, but I still don't understand how there can be much money in it," I said.

"Well, you'd be surprised! When one of those old folks die, they sometimes leave millions of dollars to Harrington's foundation. He has parties; he invites them out there to Rocky Neck, if they don't live there already. He sets them up and grooms them, feeds them so much bullshit, that when they are getting ready to die they couldn't imagine leaving the world without giving Harrington the animal lover at least a few hundred thousand. If there are no heirs there will be plenty more than that coming in, too. They've had a couple of million-dollar-plus donations come in from a couple of old Swamp Yankee widows just this year alone!"

We sat in silence for a few minutes listening to the

rose-fragrant spring breeze blowing through the tops of the huge pines. Trixie was fast asleep and snoring into the pine needles, peaceful at last. My mind couldn't process someone committing such a despicable type of fraud - killing animals and fooling kind, sentimental old animal lovers for profit. What could be more evil? My heart and head felt heavy and full of hopelessness. How would things ever get better for animals, or humans, if people like Harrington existed in the world? The more I learned about the animal rescue world the worse people seemed in general, except for the true rescuers like Bliss. I hugged my knees and put my forehead down on them. I was so tired.

Sherri broke the silence. "Don't worry about Trixie," She said. "Either, me or George will bring her for a walk out here every day. That's the best thing about this place - the fact that the foundation doesn't mind if we walk our dogs back here. I don't want to lose this place, ever. It makes things tough for me morally, though. I want to tell people about Harrington, but if he lost the foundation this land could be sold and gone forever. A housing tract could be built here and that would suck in so many ways for everyone living around here."

"I can certainly understand that," I said. "But, wouldn't it be good if someone were to expose this

Harrington asshole in a way that couldn't hurt you? He's committing fraud with his false advertising. It's sad those old people think he and his shelter are so great and it's just a dirty death house. Maybe I could say something. He couldn't do anything to me."

"I'd watch myself if I were you," said Sherri laughing and lighting a fresh cigarette. "A part of me wants to say 'Yeah. Go for it. Write all about it. But, I wouldn't if I were you. Harrington's an old wharf-rat lawyer. He's a lawyer to the fishing boat owners and he's as corrupt as they make them. If you come up against him, you just might find yourself tangled up in a fishing net and sunk below the docks downtown one night."

"Are you just kidding me and being dramatic?" I asked, smiling.

"A little of both," Sherri laughed. "But, seriously, I'd watch out. I'm not just saying that for my sake, so you won't repeat anything I've told you. The guy's a real creep and I don't want to see you get hurt."

We got up at last and walked Trixie back to the kennel. I was already thinking of ways I could challenge Mr. Harrington, but I put those thoughts aside for the rest of the walk. I'd wait until I could do some research before deciding what to do. Trixie didn't pull on the way back to the kennel, and was happy to walk slowly on her leash between us, looking back and forth into my face and into Sherri's. When we got to the dog runs Sherri took the leash and led us back past dozens of barking dogs to a long run that led out into a sunny patch of concrete surrounded by a cluster of tall pine trees.

Sherri had laid out a soft pad on top of a raised platform bed and covered it with a blanket. There were two bowls of fresh water and a bowl of kibble. The place looked roomy, comfortable and clean. Not bad, really, for a doggy prison. Still, I felt that dragging heavy sad feeling again at the prospect of leaving Trixie there.

Sherri seemed to sense it and said," She'll be just fine. Dogs like Trixie actually prefer the kennel sometimes. They've had so much trauma and they know life is unpredictable and they enjoy the daily routine of kennel life and the security of their run. You'll see. She'll be okay. And, you are welcome out here any day to walk her. I'm almost always here. Just ring me a couple of hours before you come."

And, we left it at that. Trixie jumped right up on her new bed and heaved a big sigh. She seemed to know she was safe and at home and seemed more relaxed than I'd ever seen her at Hidden Falls. I arranged to come back the next day to take her for a walk. That walk led to many, many walks with Trixie and Sherri, and with many of the other dogs at the kennel, through the tangled secret garden landscape of the pet cemetery through the seasons. We watched the leaves turn yellow and orange and mound up on the graves and vines, kicked snow off the graves in the winter, and witnessed the glorious fragrant house-high mounded roses mingled with the comfortable scent of the damp pines each spring for as long as time would allow.

 16. Ten Black Dogs

On our final day at the old Hidden Falls Quonset hut, Bliss watched with resentment as her former volunteers and staff emptied the building and loaded all the kennel stuff into an array of waiting vans and trucks for the trip over to the newly constructed shelter on the other side of the city. The metal walls of Quonset hut - that once vibrated with sound of barking dogs - only echoed the hushed voices of the volunteers.

Nobody spoke to Bliss directly and evaded her

gaze as they walked by her with their final loads of paperwork or other last-minute salvaged items. Bliss hadn't wanted to part with any of the stuff at the shelter and a good fight ensued between her and the board, including a final discussion with the board's lawyer, before Bliss was convinced she had to let many years of accumulated shelter supplies go to the new place.

When we drove up to the new shelter we saw a large, clean, bright yellow building surrounded by a pretty ribbon of pine trees that filtered the afternoon light into rows of straight golden lines - a vastly different scene from the old Hidden Falls. The board did battle with Bliss to keep Hidden Falls as the name of the new shelter and they won. It was peaceful and quiet. Spring birds were chipping and chattering in the woods and squirrels were running around gathering up kibble dropped outside of the runs of the few dogs that were residing there.

"I never thought I'd say this about any shelter, but it's too quiet! We need to get more dogs in here as soon as possible," said Melissa, the new shelter manager.

I still felt guilty leaving Bliss behind at the empty Quonset hut all alone. After twenty-plus years of dealing with stressed, dangerous and hyper dogs, frightened semi-feral cats, and any other animal in need, wild or domestic, that came her way, it was the actions of people that took the worst toll on her energy and her crabby enthusiasm. The circumstances made me sad and angry.

"We need to get adoptions going and get the word out to people that we are here. And, we need more dogs. I don't know what we're going to do for animals," Melissa continued. "And, this is just between you and me, but I think the board is going to submit a proposal to get the animal control contracts for several towns and cities this year. Now, that would really bring in some dogs."

My mood lightened a bit at hearing that news. That would enable Hidden Falls to take control of all those pathetic animals at the death house shelter in New Bedford, the nightmarish place that Ricky came from, and from that dreadful wharf rat lawyer that Sherri spoke about when I dropped Trixie off at her place. Sherri may have been exaggerating the scam story out of dislike for Mr. Harrington, but I believed some of what she said about the connection between the dodgy foundation, cemetery and shelter.

I stopped feeling as sad about Bliss at that point. I began to think that if the move to the new shelter would improve the fates of more of the stray animals of the two cities, the transition change would be all worth it. Fall River would still have a good, small nonprofit shelter run by Bliss and New Bedford would have our big, new, modern shelter that could house all the unwanted pets with relative comfort and kindness.

Until the contracts came in, the brand new shiny runs, puppy rooms and kitten play cages would be empty and available for any random dog or cat in need. For the time being Hidden Falls would have to operate mainly with owner turn-ins - the sad animals that are dumped at the shelter by people who no longer want or can no longer care for them. They are often older pets, or sick, or have ingrained behavior problems that Hector would try to work out of them before they could be adopted. But, Hidden Falls needed some quick adoption income and most of the owner turn-ins found homes only after a long, slow process of rehabilitation.

At the same time, Petfinder.com and other Internet pet adoption websites were becoming extremely popular and were increasing adoptions in shelters across the country exponentially. Online shelter pet-watching became an addictive pastime for all of the Hidden Falls volunteers. We'd take time off from grunt work to peek at the office computer screen and squeal over the photos of the cute animals up for adoption in shelters in Florida and Texas and, like children, dream about how one day we'd buy farms to house all our rescue dogs and set up sanctuaries for the old and unwanted ones that we'd care for forever.

The increasing online communication between shelter workers in different states was facilitating a burgeoning rescue transport network whereby shelters that were overloaded with one type of pet would shift the animals across state lines to shelters that were seeking that type of pet to fill their cages and increase adoptions.

Southern states were not as active in promoting low cost spay and neuter programs to the public and therefore were swamped with litters of puppies and kittens. Shelters in the northeast, where spay neuter activism has resulted in decreasing numbers unwanted litters, were often short on younger animals that got adopted quickly.

Transporting dogs seemed to be a good opportunity for Hidden Falls, and some of us internet-addicted volunteers decided to approach the board with the idea of establishing relationships with a couple of shelters in West Virginia and North Carolina, that had extremely high euthanasia rates to arrange rescue transports to bring some of these animals to fill the beautiful new empty cages at Hidden Falls.

The board tentatively voted to give the idea a try.

We'd bring a couple of batches of southern animals up for a trial run and then later vote on policy to continue to populate a fixed percentage of the shelter with southern pets and animals from other overpopulated states.

From then on, groups of volunteers sat for hours around the computer searching for dogs to save from the southern shelters. We had a notebook in which we'd jot down our favorites for the board to review for final decisions. Looking at these photos was fun, but we knew we were making life or death decisions about these dogs and cats. Which filters should we use to make our choices? Should we look for young animals, fluffy puppies and cuddly kittens that would be quick and easy adoptions and much needed income for the shelter? And, how could we purge our memories of the eyes of the older animals peering longingly out at us from the computer screen? Culling the few animals we could afford to rescue and transport from these lists of hundreds and hundreds of beautiful lives was an addictive but heart wrenching activity. Fun at first, it soon left me exhausted and depressed.

The very first transport was finally arranged with a rural shelter in North Carolina. Hidden Falls would have a group of dogs coming up, some puppies, a few middle aged ones of desirable breeds - meaning no pit bulls. I was angry about that decision from the board but they said, "Why bring in more of what we have trouble adopting already?" The southern dogs were travelling north via a group of extraordinarily well-organized volunteers who called themselves the Canine Rescue Railroad. They arranged runs which were shifts of drivers each driving an hour or two up the highways in trucks and vans loaded with animals for delivery to northern shelters or to volunteers from the shelters who would meet them at hotels or highway rest stations along the way.

Nobody at Hidden Falls was enthusiastic about travelling to meet the transports so I volunteered to drive down I-95 to the border of Connecticut and New York to get the dogs. I knew I could talk Mark into going along. We always enjoyed road trips for the sake of driving. We'd turn off our phones, turn on the radio and listen to music or innocuous chat shows. It was relaxing to know we couldn't be contacted by anyone or see anyone we knew for those few precious hours on the road where we felt we were in limbo and the rest of the irritating world couldn't annoy us.

We left the next Saturday, which was an unusually hot early spring day, when all the plants were still mostly naked but sprouting green and pink buds. I loved looking at the muted colors of the trees against the bluish, ash gray clouds as we drove. We were very relaxed when we got to the right exit and located the nearby Holiday Inn parking lot where we were to meet the last leg of the transport coming up from their connection in Maryland.

When we pulled in I saw a middle aged man and woman both with long silver and gray ponytails wearing florescent orange hoodies and holding a group of ten black shepherd-types dogs by leashes - five dogs per person - and the dogs were jerking the couple all around the parking lot. My relaxation was replaced by panic as I thought that any second the dogs would free themselves from the humans struggling to hold them and run out onto the highway. I had a quick vision of the four of us chasing ten frightened dogs down the road and watching them get plowed under the wheels of the roaring tractor trailers.

Mark and I walked tentatively up to the tangled group of bodies and ropes, not wanting to excite the dogs any further. We were about five minutes late for our appointed meeting time. That was early for us. Considering we'd just traveled down I-95 from Massachusetts to the Connecticut/New York border overlapping the rush hour, I considered our timing was pretty good.

But, the ponytailed woman strode towards me and

demanded to know why we hadn't called to tell her we were running late. The dogs were jumping up on my legs or stooping to sniff my shoes and Mark stood a little behind me not knowing what he should do to assist the struggling couple. That was of no consequence because the orange-hoodie-wearing man had already opened the door of our van and hustled his five dogs into the back seat. They immediately started hopping from the back seat to the back storage area where I'd loaded in a couple of boxes of dog biscuits at the last minute.

I was about to tell the woman to wait - I needed to get all the paperwork straight before I could take possession of the dogs. Melissa had warned me several times not to take the dogs until I was sure each one matched a set of paperwork showing an interstate medical clearance and vaccination history. Before I could ask for the paperwork, the woman pushed her set of dogs into the back seat of our van with the others. Then all the dogs were scrambling over one another and squirming from the far back to the front of the car and sitting in our seats. I could hear a few growls as a dog tore open a treat bag and they struggled to scarf down as many biscuits as possible before the other dogs took notice.

"Sorry," said the woman, "One of the drivers

didn't show up for her leg of the trip so we had to continue past New York City. We really weren't planning to be on the road all day. We both have to be at work early tomorrow and now we've got to head back by the city in rush hour."

The woman's face was flushed red and sweat was running down her forehead. She was panting her words out and I was worried for a second that she might be having a heart attack. Her husband meanwhile was reaching into the back of their van and emerged with a big damp folder of crushed up paperwork.

"Here are all the records," he said, shoving them into my hands. I had to scramble to keep the folder together so the documents wouldn't escape from the folder and fly around the parking lot.

"Wait a minute," I gasped, "I have to check each vet record to each individual dog. Didn't these records come with any photos?"

I was starting to feel panicked as I leafed through the sheaf of soggy paperwork. There were no photos of dogs on any of the documents. The wrinkled cover of each vet record had a description stating 'medium-sized, black, mixed-breed Shepherd.' The entire group of dogs fit that description! Also, how could I tell if the records were actually for this group of dogs? What if they weren't healthy? And, worse, what if Melissa and the shelter board wouldn't accept the dogs with these dubious health records?

The weight of what we were doing suddenly struck me. This wasn't just an adventurous weekend outing, or a pleasant drive down the interstate to pick up a group of needy dogs and feel good about ourselves for doing it after they were all safely tucked up in the shelter. We could actually end up being responsible for these dogs! We could wind up with 14 dogs in our house tonight. At the least, we could end up paying for vaccinations and health checks for ten dogs ourselves. Or worse, we could be responsible for adopting the dogs out, and where would they stay in the meantime? With relief, I thought of Sherri's kennel. That would have to do in a pinch. I knew that Sherri would help me out with the dogs if I needed her.

After Mark and I had sorted the dogs into backseat and rear storage area, I turned back around to ask the transport people to help me sort out the paperwork. They were already in their truck and waving goodbye as they quickly exited their parking space. I turned back to the truck and saw Mark hunched over in the driver's seat. One of the larger dogs had placed its paws over the back of Mark's neck and was enthusiastically licking his hair. Two other dogs were now ensconced in the passenger's seat with their tongues lolling and looking joyful at the prospect of riding shotgun.

I left them there and squeezed into the back seat with the remaining seven dogs that were jumping back and forth from the cargo area to my seat. They were still trailing leashes and getting tangled as they leaped. The two large bags of dog biscuits were long gone but the dogs were still voracious and kept returning to the empty bags to snuffle around and make sure they hadn't missed a crumb.

"Well," I said meekly, "At least they seem to be pretty friendly."

Mark didn't say a word. He'd pushed a dog off his neck but I couldn't tell if his expression was grim or smiling.

"Let's just hit the road and get this trip over with," he said evenly.

During the all this ruckus, one smaller black dog sat crunched up against the door on my right side and didn't seem all interested in participating in mischief with the other dogs. I looked more closely at him as we pulled onto the interstate and I could see his yellow eyes were large and frozen with terror. Under his fur I could feel that his body was trembling all over, his tongue was sticking and he was rapidly panting. I put my hand on his back for reassurance and he flinched a bit but didn't attempt to shake it off. After an hour or so he seemed to relax and fell into a twitchy sleep.

The other dogs did not tire themselves out. They continued to leap back and forth checking the treat bags. They seemed so frantic for food that we decided to stop at McDonalds and buy them each a burger. We pulled up to the drive-up window and ordered twenty plain burgers as the clerk peered into our van in amazement. The hamburgers disappeared in two seconds in a flurry of flying slobber.

The only dog not interested in the burgers was the little fuzzy one squeezed tightly to the side of my leg. I tried breaking off a bit of meat and feeding it to him and he took it tentatively then spit it out on the seat. He was just too traumatized to eat. I understood how he was feeling from my experiences in the hospital as kid - not knowing who means you harm and who is helping, not trusting the little-explained actions or intentions of the large people looming over you, yet knowing that any active resistance on your part will probably result in punishment. That kind of stress ties your stomach in knots and food sits like dry cardboard in your mouth. I pulled the dog closer to my side and held him tightly for the rest of the trip.

We finally arrived back at the shelter in the early

evening. Mark was muttering about never being able to get the van smelling clean again. Melissa was waiting for us at the front door and we unloaded the dogs out of the van and into comfortable shelter runs, each with a raised bed and blanket, a pile of dog toys and large bowls of food and water. They seemed happy and grateful, and not at all resistant to being placed in the locked runs.

The new accommodations must have been far superior to the hot, crowded, filthy southern shelter that had been described to me by the transport coordinator. We left them happily slurping water and crunching on their kibble.

We all went to the front office and sat down to try to sort out the tangle of paperwork. That's when we realized that we'd only brought nine dogs into the shelter. I ran out to the van in a panic. The most nightmarish event on a rescue transport would be to lose one of the animals. I peeked into the darkened backseat and with great relief saw the littlest dog still crunched up against the door of the car. He had his paw over his face and seemed to be trying to make himself invisible by covering his eyes. I pulled the trembling, resistant lump of fur out of the van and with a painful heart carried him into the shelter.

"Oh, thank goodness," cried Melissa when she saw

the dog," What's wrong with the poor little thing? He must be totally traumatized. Well, that's understandable. He'll get over it in a day or two."

We tucked him up carefully in his bed and blanket, but the blank look of fear didn't leave his eyes and he didn't stop trembling. He didn't even glance at his food or toys. He just stared straight ahead, eyes frozen and wide. I felt sick at the thought of leaving the poor puppy alone at the shelter overnight.

I asked Melissa if I could bring him home and she said no, the dogs had to be quarantined for ten days. The paperwork was such a hopeless mess that there was no way to sort it and assign it to a particular dog. Therefore, there was no proof of vaccinations and she couldn't allow me to bring an unvaccinated dog home. As sad as it was, the little dog might threaten the health of our own dogs. I understood, but it hurt dreadfully to walk away from the little shaky dog, turn out the light at the end of the hallway and exit the shelter without him.

Over the next two weeks nearly all of the southern dogs were adopted from the shelter quickly. People were excited to find what they claimed were pure-bred Belgian Shepherds available for adoption at a shelter. I'd had no idea what the van load of black dogs had been in terms of breed, and couldn't have cared less really, but if being a pure-breed helped them find them homes it was all for the best.

The shelter board was excited that the southern transport had worked out so well, and started bringing up more and more dogs from shelters all over the south and the mid-west. Mark and I schlepped down to the Connecticut/New York border many more times, driving up the interstate with a load of excited, ravenous dogs and developing a ritual of stopping at the same McDonalds to order a bag brimming with plain hamburgers that disappeared in a feeding frenzy.

Sadly, during all those weeks of arrivals and adoptions of dozens of southern dogs, the sad little depressed dog that sat next to me in the back seat on the first transport was still at the shelter, passed by and not adopted. "He just doesn't show well," said Melissa. "He cringes in the shadows of the back of the run and nobody knows he's there. If someone tries to drag him out of there, he nips. You might as well prepare yourself, this one might not make it."

I knew what Melissa meant. He'd be put to sleep if shelter space was lacking, or if the board decided he was never going to be adoptable and be a continued burden to resources, as Hawkins had once been. Hector tried working with him but had determined that he was probably feral, meaning he'd had no socialization from his puppy months on through adulthood. Hector told me he'd talked with the shelter he came from in North Carolina and they told him he was found with a pack of stray farm dogs, trapped in a ditch. He'd never had a real home.

Hidden Falls was taking in stray animals from New Bedford and during the following months the shelter became crowded with older, local dogs. The southern transports slowed down a bit. I was impressed that these new dogs were adopted out pretty quickly with the help of Petfinder.com, but the little southern guy was still there. Melissa reluctantly sent him in to be neutered when I begged her to, but she admonished me that it was a waste of money if he wound up having to be euthanized.

The following week was very stressful as suddenly and mysteriously a large number of the shelter dogs began to fall ill. Some were coughing constantly. Others lost their appetites and became lethargic. I felt a prickling of panic as I thought back to the messy pile of indecipherable medical records on the first transport. What if there was some type of strange disease that came in with some of these transports? I started to feel guilty about ever suggesting the idea of the transports. But I told myself this couldn't be an epidemic. The dogs had been carefully quarantined and vaccinated when they got here to avoid spreading new diseases.

The increasing numbers of animals with the mystery illness was taking a toll on the shelter volunteers and staff. We'd never had this many animals at the old Hidden Falls. There were now hundreds of cats, dozens of dogs, and even some birds, rabbits and hamsters all needing care and attention. And, more dogs were becoming ill daily, while the ones that were already sick were getting worse.

One morning, I walked into the shelter and into Hector's office. He had his head down on the metal desk, his untouched Dunkin Donuts coffee beside him and still full - a very unusual occurrence for Hector. I sat down by the desk to talk with him and waited for him to look up. When he did, Hector's eyes startled me. They were starry and glassy, as if he'd had too much to drink or had a high fever himself or was on some kind of heavy duty medication. He was out of it. He was clearly overwhelmed and depressed.

I asked him if I could walk the little southern dog. Most of the dogs were quarantined again in an attempt to contain the ravaging illness. Hector just nodded slowly and said to go ahead. He didn't seem to care about much at all - behavior very unusual for this gregarious and passionate man. Hector just leaned backwards in his rocking chair and rocked slowly forward and backwards, staring at his desk cover with boxes brimming with paperwork.

I walked back through the runs trying to avoid the eyes of the other dogs. I kneeled down by the little dog's run and saw that he was lying on his side in what looked like a pool of water. He was moving but his eyes were glassy and fixed. I flung the gate open in panic and scooped him up off the floor. I realized what I thought was water was particularly foul smelling urine and it ran down my arms as I held him. His head flopped limply over to one side, but he was still alive.

I ran into Hector's office and told him I was taking the dog to the vet, to the shelter's vet, and I was going to put whatever treatment was needed on the shelter's bill. I was furious that this little gentle, fearful creature had been left to rot on the concrete floor of his run - ignored and alone. I didn't care how depressed and overwhelmed Hector and Melissa were feeling. They needed to suck it up and do the jobs they'd taken on with this new shelter. I thought, "Bliss would never, never have let this happen."

I drove as fast as I could to the vet in the nearby town of Bristol, Rhode Island, the little dog lying limp in the front seat next to me. I grabbed him and ran into the vet's office in tears and begged the receptionist to ask the vet if he could see the dog quickly. The doctor wasn't busy and came out to see what the ruckus was all about. He grabbed the dog from me and we all walked back to a treatment room where he laid the poor thing out on a metal table.

"It doesn't look good," he said. "My first guess just looking at him is a massive infection. Just look at the hind legs. They are swollen twice what their size should be."

"Wasn't this one of the dogs we just had in here from the shelter for neutering?" asked the vet tech.

"Yes, I think he is one from that batch," said the vet.

He looked at the neuter scar and saw that it was red and inflamed. I explained that things were hectic at the shelter and the runs hadn't been cleaned as often as they should be. The little dog was lying in a pool of urine for days with an open scar just soaking up the bacteria.

I felt horribly angry but very guilty, too. Bringing the southern dogs up here was just too much for the shelter. It was all my fault. Why had I ever suggested it? The staff and board were new at this. I should have come in every day after work to help. The new staff and volunteers weren't as experienced or as tough as Bliss was. The little dog looked up at me with pure misery in his eyes and I started crying. I put my arms around him and begged the vet, "Please, please save him. Please save him."

He put his hand on my shoulder and said gently, "I think he'll pull through this."

I went back to the waiting room for a couple of hours as the dog received several bags of intravenous antibiotics and saline solution for dehydration. In the meantime, I thought of names I could call the little guy. I had no doubt in my mind. He was coming home with me. He'd been through too much trauma in his short life - some of it my fault. He wasn't going to be euthanized, and he wasn't going to suffer any more pain. I decided to call him Poirot in honor of my beloved Agatha Christie stories.

Finally, the vet came out with Poirot in his arms. He still looked limp but his eyes were definitely brighter and he looked hopeful. The vet gave me two large bottles of antibiotic pills and instructions for Poirot's care.

"The next couple of days will tell the tale," he said sternly. "You have to watch him closely and make sure he gets all of his pills on time, and subcutaneous water constantly."

"No problem at all," I replied.

I didn't even call Mark to tell him another dog was

coming into the house. I knew he'd remember Poirot from the first transport run and understand. I placed Poirot gently on the front seat of the van and wrapped him tightly in a blanket with only his yellow eyes visible. Those eyes had already softened and lost some of their hunted look. He stared at me with what looked like hope and love during the entire drive home, as they still continue to do the same nearly thirteen years later. Hawkins accepted Poirot as one of his pack right away, since he wasn't another pit bull. For many years, on cold days Poirot, Hawkins, and Maggie all piled up on each other in the corner of their favorite couch.

# 17. Worldwide Woof

One morning not long after Poirot joined our dog packs, I got a call from Sherri at 6:00 in the morning.

That was a very early call for Sherri. She'd just be opening up the runs in her kennel and beginning to transfer the dogs to yard so she could scoop the poop. She didn't usually communicate or even have a cup of coffee until she'd swabbed the runs and they were spotless. Then she'd call me and we'd talk dogs over coffee for half an hour.

When I picked up the phone I could barely hear Sherri. Her words were slurred or garbled and she seemed to be crying. I had a premonition about what might be wrong. Lately, Sherri had also been transporting southern dogs to her kennel and adopting them out from there. She made a little extra money with the adoption fees and felt good about helping save their lives. But, in recent visits I'd noticed a little gleam of obsession in Sherri's eyes as she perused her computer for new southern rescue dogs. I think to her, rescuing these dogs was a bit like online gambling - finding a good prospect to bet on, feeling the excitement of surprise when the dog arrived and then making the final deal when the dog was adopted. She loved the whole process.

Instead of our usual conversation about canine quirks and antics, I struggled to make out what Sherri was saying as she stuttered away, her words struggled to come through the phone. I finally got a grasp on what was going on. Sherri had placed a transport order for a van load of dogs coming up from a shelter in Kentucky and, for some reason, the entire van - drivers and dogs - had been arrested and detained by the police at the border of Rhode Island just after entering Massachusetts.

It took me another half hour on the phone to understand as she explained in tears that the Department of Agriculture had been thinking up ways to ban the importation of pets from out-of-state shelters and across state lines for years. Surprise raids were the action they chose to take on transport vans as soon as they were a mile over the border. Such an action would cause the news to travel quickly through word-of-mouth and the Internet. It would serve as a warning more effective than any written or televised campaign against interstate pet transports.

I tried to get Sherri to calm down enough to tell me what had happened to the van full of dogs. Where had the authorities taken them? Were they going to be euthanized? Where were the drivers? What was going to happen to them and their vehicles? I knew many of the drivers that made the runs from Connecticut through Massachusetts now, and even became friendly with the pony-tailed couple that had dumped the ten large undocumented dogs into our van. I hoped it wasn't this couple who'd been arrested on this run. They'd have a complete emotional meltdown.

Sherri cried, "They called them junk and trash. They literally said to the drivers, 'Don't you be bringing your Southern garbage up here and polluting our state!'"

"Who said that? What garbage?" I asked naively. I couldn't figure out what Sherri meant by the term garbage.

"The dogs! The damn dogs. Those fucking Department of Agriculture cop assholes or whoever it was who pulled the van over called the dogs trash - as if those dogs asked to be born in some scumbag southern state with a shelter system that does mass electrocutions. Dogs are not garbage. I bet all those cops have dogs of their own. Do they call their own pets trash? They are living, breathing creatures. They're probably terrified and they've done nothing, absolutely nothing, to deserve the way they are being treated right now."

Sherri continued, "Worse, they've now got paperwork tying those dogs to this kennel as their destination. And, the idiot drivers actually lost the medical paperwork at their last stop when they were transferring the dogs to their van. They left it in the other van. Now the cops are saying that I'm transporting dogs across state lines without proof of vaccinations. Do you know what that means? They can shut me down. They can come and confiscate all the dogs I have here, too. In fact, they are sending someone over to inspect my kennel this week. They would never have done that if they hadn't stopped the transport."

"Okay, okay," I said trying to sound calm. "What if they do come over to your kennel? You take good care of your animals. Your place is clean. What are you worried about?"

"I don't have any medical records for the dogs that are still here from the last transport. The shelter forgot to send them."

"Can't they just fax them to you?"

"No, no, they don't have them anymore, or I mean that I didn't actually pay them for the vaccinations prior to the transport. My vet can do it so much cheaper here. I just haven't had time to get the shots yet. Can you help bring all the dogs over to the vet today?

I started to feel a little sick. Sherri transported dogs knowingly without up-to-date vaccinations. Sherri's heart was in the right place, and I knew she cared deeply about the animals, but she never believed in playing by the rules. And, now, she was going to be in for big trouble and so was the shelter that had sent the dogs without the vaccinations. And, most tragically, the dogs would suffer a long quarantine or even death for this idiotic screw-up. All to save a few bucks. I was seeing a side of Sherri that was part skinflint and part gambler. I was very angry.

"I'll help you get them to the vet," I said shortly. Belated vaccines would probably make no impression at all on the authorities, or avert the fate the dogs were likely to suffer, but it was worth a try. I hung up the phone and grabbed my keys.

Mark was at work with the van, so I took the new truck I was hoping to keep fresh and untouched by dog hair and odor for a little while. That was a futile idea. The wind blew rain onto my windshield the entire way out to Massasoit. Sherri was waiting by the kennel with her big Tundra pulled right up to the door and was pulling reluctant dogs out through the rain into the car crates. I put several of the more malleable dogs, ones that we hoped could ride together without fighting, into the back of the truck and a couple more into the back seat. Of course they both jumped into the front seat, tracking mud throughout the truck. Oh well, it needed breaking in sooner or later.

We managed to get all dogs safely to the vet clinic and back to the kennel with their vaccines up to date. I hoped that would be the end of the drama surrounding the confiscated rescue transport, but for Sherri that particular gamble would wind up being disastrous.

The very next day a team of officials from the Department of Agriculture, the MSPCA, and local animal control officers were knocking on the door of her house demanding to do a surprise inspection of her kennel operation. It turned out to be very fortunate for the poor dogs that we'd taken them all in for their vaccines the day prior. Otherwise, the officials would have gathered them all into a waiting van and driven them straight to the municipal shelter, futures uncertain without a current record of vaccines.

Nobody fell for the claim Sherri made that yesterday had just happened to be her regular date to take all her dogs to the vet for shots, but they accepted the lie and let the dogs stay with her, temporarily. Two days later she was informed by certified letter that her kennel would be forced to close in a month if she didn't relinquish to the MSPCA all of the dogs she had taken in from any of the southern transports. They had already taken charge of the dogs confiscated at the state border, claiming they would shelter them after a six-month quarantine period, then adopt them out to good homes.

"Fucking liars," cried Sherri. "They'll do nothing

of the sort. They'll just kill them all. They're probably dead already."

I thought that Sherri was being overly paranoid. I went over to the kennel a couple of days later to be with her during the inspection of the kennel with the officials. All of the officers, the local animal control agent, and the Rescue League officer who came down from Boston, in particular, seemed kind and sincere and very concerned about the plight of all the southern dogs that were barking loudly throughout the kennel. I knew that Sherri was overwhelmed.

Sherri meant well, like so many shelter volunteers I'd met at Hidden Falls, by taking in so many animals. The fact that there were no homes for these animals was too hard to bear sometimes. No volunteer or animal rescue person sleeps well with the knowledge that many animals are born to die - never to have a full life, to experience fun or love or peaceful restful days, or even a few minutes of kindness. No rescuer sleeps well with the knowledge that human beings are selfish creatures that breed other animals for profit, and toss away the discards as if they were stuffed toys. I knew that rescuer frustration was driving Sherri to take in too many animals. I was afraid I was starting to do the same thing myself.

I watched as the officers looked with dismay at the

clutter in the kennel, the crusty food and filth that had built up over that last few weeks on the bars and wires of the dog runs, the bits of dog food and poop that covered the floors and mixed with the poop from the mice that came in during the night to nibble on it. For the first time, the place smelled bad. It stunk. I was never more aware of the putrid odor that on the day of that inspection and I for a minute I felt ashamed and embarrassed to be associated with Sherri and her smelly kennel but it was partly my fault.

I felt very guilty. I knew she was overwhelmed and that she didn't get much help from her husband. She couldn't begin to afford to provide vet care and good food for all the animals she had gathered since she'd been transporting southern dogs up to her kennel.

Sherri was so small, and although of an athletic build, the amount of physical effort it would take to properly clean and sanitize the place was beyond her ability. She needed several full-time employees to keep up with all these dogs. But, being perpetually broke and in debt she just couldn't afford to hire help. And, being a bit of a reclusive misanthrope, she didn't have the mindset to start a non-profit animal rescue organization and to recruit volunteers. I knew all this, but I hadn't helped her much. I was too involved with my own growing pack of dogs at home, with the drama of the shelter break-up at Hidden Falls - with my own life in general. I didn't see Sherri slipping down the hole.

The next day we loaded all the southern dogs in Sherri's kennel into her massive SUV and drove them through back roads northward to the town of Pembroke. An Animal Rescue League shelter there would house the dogs, vet them, and work with the behavior issues that developed as a result of poor breeding, poor treatment, and being shuttled around from place to place without consistent attention from one human companion. Sherri drove and cried though most of the trip. She was sure the kindly ARL officer, Dave, was just putting on an act and intended to kill all the dogs as soon as we drove away from the shelter.

Dave was waiting at the front door of the beautiful modern shelter that looked similar to the new Hidden Falls shelter. It was such a contrast from the low dark city shelter that Ricky was saved from, and from the narrow stinky hallways of Sherri's kennel. This shelter was surrounded by well-kept gardens with huge orange lilies drooping over the sidewalks. At the rear of the shelter was a wooded area and yard that was filled with dogs and volunteers playing with tennis balls and Frisbees.

"This looks like a good place," I whispered to

Sherri as we started unloading the dogs one by one from the back of vehicle.

She just glanced at me coldly. I'd learned that Sherri never changed her opinion about people or events. Her distrust ran to hatred and it could run cold and deep. Dave came outside to help with the dogs. He was a large man, middle aged, with warm honest eyes. They looked at us directly as I asked questions about what the destiny of these dogs would be. Dave smiled, though he seemed to always have a droopy-lipped, sad expression, and a slow, deliberate gait like a large fat pit bull.

"We're going to temperament test all these dogs right now," he replied, "All three of us."

"Really? I thought we'd just be dropping the dogs off and leaving," said Sherri. It was clear she was surprised and maybe a tiny bit less distrustful.

"I'm not out to screw you around," said Dave slowly. "I really want to help. This is a bad situation and I don't want any of these animals to pay for it. If any of these guys don't pass the temperament test you can take them right back with you. We'll just say you are adopting them yourself. And I will expect you to do so, and not turn around and adopt a difficult dog out to anyone else." We followed Dave into a large pleasant, window-walled, wood-floored room filled with afternoon light. We'd placed all the dogs into separate glass runs surrounding the training room and brought each one over to Dave so he could perform the temperament testing routines.

    The dogs seemed to think Dave was a dog as well. He certainly moved like one, and the dogs seemed to like him, trotting briskly after him as he jogged around the room, then sitting and looking attentively up at him as he slowly offered them treats. Even Cowboy, a dog that was rumored to be a wolf-mix, took the treat slowly and gently from the palm of Dave's outstretched hand. We were in the habit of tossing treats gingerly into Cowboy's run because he was usually aggressive in snatching them out of our fingers.

    Dave brought out a big red hand on the end of a broom handle and started pushing it towards the dogs. He pushed it hard and aggressively into their faces and not one dog reacted with aggression. Some sniffed at it and Brandy, a fat little beagle, ran for safety between Sherri's legs. I knew that no matter how dirty Sherri's kennel might be at that point, the dogs loved and trusted her like nobody else in the world.

    The testing session went very well and Dave was willing to accept every single dog into the adoption program, even Cowboy. We left the shelter and got back into the SUV that seemed huge and barren without the horde of dogs jostling each other and trying to climb into our laps. The sun was shining through the mist. There were flowers blooming in all the gardens surrounding the place and the air was golden and peaceful at the shelter. We could hear the distant yapping of dogs playing with volunteers on the hillside behind us.

"Well," commented Sherri, "I guess if there is a heaven for each of us this would be it for me."

I agreed with her. I could take the time to really look around at the scenery as Sherri drove though the winding back roads and short cuts she always managed to find. She had a phobia of highways and complete lack of trust in any driver other than herself. I was surprised at how antiquated this part of New England seemed, with tiny weathered cedar cottages mingling with larger colonial clapboard homes. Even the messiest yards were filled with some kind of blooming tree or flower bed. It was peaceful and beautiful as if we were the only vehicle around - time travelers passing through ephemeral farm country.

Even in the midst of all this beauty, Sherri remained tense and hunched over the wheel, her thin fingers gripping hard as we rounded the tight turns of the rural streets. She was silent but I knew she was thinking about how much she distrusted Dave and was still worried about the futures of all those dogs.

I said softly, "I really think Dave is a good guy. I don't think he's lying to us. I can't imagine that he'd go through the motions of testing all those dogs today if he was just going to have them killed."

"I don't know," said Sherri, "I can't help it. I just don't trust anyone who works for the state. I don't trust cops, shelter workers, or animal control officers. They are either out for themselves, or they are jaded and don't give a damn anymore. They'd like to see small rescues like mine shut down."

I told Sherri that I doubted that was true but I remembered how Dave and the others had looked at the filthy walls of her kennel with concern and disgust. I thought that they did probably want to shut down kennels and shelters like Sherri's, but not for the reasons she was thinking. I felt that many of the officials had a lot of compassion for animals and that was probably why they were in this difficult and heartbreaking business. They certainly could have made different career choices.

"Well," she said turning to look directly at me, "I am going to make sure that every single one of those dogs gets into a good home. I am going to be calling Dave every day, starting this afternoon, in fact, to make sure those assholes don't even think about killing one of those dogs without contacting me first and letting me take it back. I'll adopt them all if I have to. They are not going to be put down because of idiot people that only care about red tape and the bottom line. State assholes, I don't care they are, they all on a power trip. They don't give a shit about the animals, only about controlling other people."

    Sherri turned back to stare at the road and I looked at her sadly. Like many of the animal rescue people and shelter volunteers I'd met, Sherri was harboring too much hurt, hate, distrust and bitterness inside. I didn't have a clue how it had originated with Sherri. She never talked much about her past or her family, other than her husband. She and I talked about dogs and other animals and that was about it. Had Sherri been abused in some way? Had she experienced a tragedy, or did her bitterness just grow naturally over the years from having had so many sad experiences with animals?

    She looked very small and lonely hunched over the wheel of her massive truck. I wanted to reach my hand out and put it on her bony shoulder but I knew instinctively that she'd jerk away from my touch. I was the same way. Both of had this trait in common, and both of us seemed to be able to intuit it in the other without an outright rejection. So, we rode along in silence for a while.

When we were nearing Sherri's kennel, I looked at her and said, "I really, really think those dog are going to be okay."

The kennel was much quieter than when we left it and the pet cemetery looked lonely, sad and golden in the early evening light. Sherri was fighting back tears as she parked the car and faced all the empty runs.

But, in the end the dogs were just fine. Dave beat Sherri to the phone and spoke with her everyday about the training and health progress of each dog and about the various adoption prospects for each. Sherri shared her own opinions about what she thought would be an optimum home for each. Dave really listened to her and that cheered her up while calming her down.

Sherri even managed to extract from Dave the name of Cowboy's adopter. She was most worried about his fate due to his wolf genetics. His new mom turned out to be a woman who lived near us behind the Freetown State Forest - a location that Cowboy would love greatly. Sherri and I, along with Poirot and some of our milder mannered dogs who could tolerate the hyperactive Cowboy, met his new mom in person to share some beautiful hikes though the forest.

We watched the dogs tugging on the ends of their leads to keep up with the inimitable Cowboy.

Surprisingly, he was the only dog allowed to romp leash-free through the underbrush because he didn't chase after deer or ever seem to want to go far from his new mom's side. The fall leaves drifted down in golden swirls around us, and I thought that this is why we put up with all the stress and heartbreak and annoyance and filth. The beauty of a day like that could overcome the heartbreak.

18. Freewheeling Disease

Sherri's kennel was quiet for several months, and since she didn't need my help as often, I headed back to the brand new Hidden Falls shelter to help out there. The board had managed to successfully bid for several municipal animal control contracts. In contrast to the quiet vacant hallways of the new shelter just a few months ago the place was raucous and filled to capacity. The new-building smell was long gone but in spite of the chaos the building still looked clean and well run.

There was an entire wall of windows built out into

a glassed atrium filled with cats lounging in the sunshine. Local residents had donated dozens of cat beds, carpeted cat trees and cat houses. High and low, cats covered every surface. The dogs filled several long hallways of runs branching out towards the opposite side of the building so their barking wouldn't disturb the cats. They had a large grassy yard behind the shelter that rivaled the pretty landscaping of the Pembroke shelter and pine woods surrounded the entire place.

After the illness scare that never amounted to anything major, Hector was himself again and giving a dog training class in the back yard. Melissa was staring at the computer at the front desk, still perusing shelter websites for southern dogs. She was happy to have me back as a volunteer and waved me over to the computer to see the photos of the dogs she'd lined up for this weeks' transport up from Kentucky. I commented that I was a little surprised that the shelter was still taking in southern dogs since the place was now filled with stray dogs from various towns. I'd hoped that the mystery illness that brought Poirot to our house would make her think more carefully about bringing up more southern dogs in the future.

"Well, most of these stray dogs don't get adopted real fast. A lot of them are pits, as you know, and as sweet as they can be, but not everybody is willing to adopt a pit. So, I'm looking for breeds of dogs that people want so we can keep bringing in more money."

    I watched over her shoulder for a while as Melissa looked at photos of dogs from the shelter she was ordering from in Kentucky. She clicked on a box next to her choices - an Australian cattle dog puppy, a couple of young hound dogs, and a litter of small puppies that looked like crosses between dachshund and poodle. I was happy for those dogs that would soon be making the long, stressful journey up the interstate because I knew they would soon find homes here. But, I was sad listening to the city strays we could hear barking through the wall just behind us.

    I lingered, looking at the computer for longer than I should in order to avoid going into the runs to face them. The southern dogs of more desirable breeds and ages would get adopted fast while the city pits would linger on and on, living out their lives in these runs.

    The runs were small, but comfortable with raised beds, a little pile of toys, and bowls of kibble and clean water. That didn't stop the dogs from jumping up at the gates and scratching desperately at the wires to get my attention. They were all longing for a little affection.

Berta came up behind me as I was sticking my arm into one of the runs allowing the big gray pit bull inside to cover it enthusiastically with slobber.

"I'll help you walk all these guys," she offered.

"I'd love that," I replied.

Berta was almost eighty years old and had a couple of large dogs of her own. She lived in a duplex a couple of miles away in downtown Fall River. She and her husband had a big RV crammed into their narrow driveway, as her husband liked to take frequent road trips, but Berta preferred to spend her time at the shelter walking the dogs. She claimed it kept her alive and she usually had more energy and stamina than I did.

Berta loved pit bulls and was reaching enthusiastically for the leashes that were hanging on hooks next to each run. She handed one to me and I opened the run with the gray pit I'd been petting and hooked him up as he danced around on his hind legs with joy. Berta clipped a leash on a smaller orange and white female pit. We'd carefully read the signs hanging on each run that indicated which dog could safely be walked with another. For some reason, just like people, dogs develop an instant dislike against a particular other dog. I did not want to be breaking up a dog fight with an eighty-year-old woman in the middle of it, no matter how spry Berta was.

I kept the large male pit carefully a few feet away from the younger female as she pranced and pulled happily towards him. Berta dragged her along and we walked towards the row of beautiful pine trees.

Someone cut a nice path through the underbrush so we could take the dogs for a long walk through the woods. It was a perfect fall New England day with cool air and brilliant dry blue sky. The day reminded me of when I'd first started volunteering at Hidden Falls; the companionship of Bliss and the other volunteers, and Hawkins and his warm brown eyes smiling at us as we picked off his ticks.

This big pit bull looked much like Hawkins though his fur was light and silvery. His name was Chowder. I didn't know who named him but he did look a bit like a big bowl of New England clam chowder. He was easy to walk and didn't pull, just trotted happily along sniffing at the greenery around him - probably a new experience for him.

Berta's dog, on the other hand, was pulling her to the left then the right, dragging her over stumps and rocks to get to the next fascinating smell. She reminded me of Trixie. I offered to exchange dogs with her but I knew she'd refuse. Berta always liked to take on the difficult dogs. We walked along the path until we could see a bright yellow field in the distance. It was swampy and low but lush and filled with old gravestones - some dating back to the early 1800's.

We walked through graves, being careful to not let the dogs pee or poop near the stones. This was a human graveyard but it reminded me of the pet cemetery behind Sherri's kennel and I wondered why animal shelters were so often sited near graveyards or town dumps. To me these animals were the most precious things in the world, but to so many they were considered refuse.

Looking at the joyful innocent faces of Snappy and Chowder, that thought made me feel very angry. These animals never did anything but want to love and bond with people and it was heartbreaking that people could betray that trust so abominably. But, the company of Berta and the dogs on that day was so peaceful and beautiful that I couldn't dwell on the negative. I knew that we'd work relentlessly to find real homes for both of these city strays and all the other ones in the shelter, and we'd succeed. Other volunteers could work with the southern dogs but we'd focus on the city pit bulls.

The autumn and winter months passed fast as I drove north every other day to teach, returning in the late afternoons to walk the shelter dogs through the woods and graveyard. The southern dogs came and went, quickly finding homes and not allowing much time for volunteers to get attached to favorites as they did with the city dogs. Sherri's kennel stayed quiet and she was content, for a while, to run her grooming and boarding business and leave the southern dog adoptions to the larger shelters.

My mother passed away in February. My brother called to let me know she'd had a stroke and had not regained consciousness. Michigan was snowed in with huge blizzards blowing over the Great Lakes and I had to wait a week to get a flight out.

I stopped at the Slocum's River Reserve with Little Ricky one day on the way back from my volunteer shift. I always brought one or two dogs to the shelter on days with cool weather so we could stop and walk in some woodsy area or on the wintery beach.

That day, the park was empty except for the two of us crunching over the icy top of the two-day old snow. The air was frigid but felt sharply clean. The river in the distance was a brilliant cornflower blue. Ice patches reflected the sky back at us. Suddenly, two huge white swans rose up out of the frozen marsh grasses and flew with whistling wings right up over our heads and away over the river, leaving us startled and breathless.

I felt a heavy chest-wringing sadness overtake me and I knew, I just knew in my heart, that my mother had died. I returned home and found out that my brother had been calling all afternoon on our landline to tell me that my mother had passed away before I could even schedule a flight to Michigan. That was the hardest day of my life.

Soon, spring revealed that the grounds of Hidden Falls were filled with wide swaths of old plantings of daffodils and crocus. Berta and I put some decorative fencing around them to keep volunteers from allowing the dogs to brown the flowers. My mother cherished the first spring crocuses better than any of her well-loved plants and I couldn't bear seeing these little clusters get trampled this year.

Berta met me outside the main kennel one day after I'd taken a week's break from volunteering at Hidden Falls to attend a conference for work. It was a gentle warm day and I thought she was just enjoying a cigarette in the sunshine but she wanted to talk to me away from earshot of the other volunteers. We walked over to the wilting daffodil patches and Berta told me that she thought something was wrong with the all dogs in the shelter again.

We went in to the kennel and walked up and down the runs. True enough, the dogs that were normally leaping at the gates and barking in anticipation of a walk were just sitting quietly or lying on their sides. They didn't have any dramatic symptoms of illness like coughing or vomiting, but they were just too peaceful for kennel dogs on a prime walking day with a cool spring breeze blowing tempting scents in through the runs.

We approached Melissa with our concerns and she responded, "Why is there a problem with the dogs being peaceful for once? It's nice and quiet in here for once. Maybe they are just enjoying the warmer weather. Maybe they are less stressed out now that the new shelter is starting to get a routine to it. As far as I can see, they are just napping."

We wanted to believe Melissa. And, we knew that the expense of bringing a vet in to check all the dogs would be great and we'd be in trouble if we did it without getting the approval of the board. We dragged a couple of the dogs out for short walks and they dutifully sniffed the ground and trees and, while not pulling as hard on the leashes as usual, they seemed fairly normal.

I returned to the shelter the next day to find Berta and several other volunteers standing outside the front door of the shelter.

"I think we have a real problem here," said Berta

shakily.

"The dogs are really bad today," said Diane. "They are panting a lot and not eating and some of them puked up their water and most aren't drinking much anyway. I'm starting to freak out."

"What is Melissa doing?" I asked with annoyance.

A pattern was clearly developing. None of the volunteers wanted to say anything that upset Melissa but were wary of taking any necessary responsible actions themselves out of fear of being reprimanded by the board.

"Where is Hector?" I asked.

Hector wasn't able to make any major shelter decisions, but he was usually the voice of reason and able to approach Melissa and deal with her bad temper effectively. Hector was in his office sitting at his desk and looking very worried.

"I don't know what we are dealing with here," he said, shaking his head sadly. "Clearly the dogs are ill. All of them are ill. Or, at least the dogs in the southern-dog runs. It can't be good, not something simple, not with all of them sick. The cats are all okay, fortunately. There must be a bacteria or virus passing around among the dogs. Melissa is in denial."

My temper bristled at the mention of the southern runs. Melissa placed all the southern dogs on one side of the shelter and the local strays on the other. When potential adopters came to visit, she brought them over to the southern side first, where she felt the more desirable dogs lived. The local dogs were left to be seen last.

While the southern dog adoptions were booming, the local dog adoption rates were slow. And, the more time a dog spent in the shelter the greater the possibility of shelter stress - a set of anxiety-based behaviors exacerbated by isolation and lack of socialization and difficult to overcome. The more time a dog spent in the shelter, the greater the possibility that he or she would be euthanized.

I left Hector in his office and led Berta, Diane and the other volunteers down the hallways to look at the dogs in the southern runs. The first thing that hit us at the door was the putrid smell of diarrhea. The floors of every run were coated with slippery liquid poop and the dogs, having not much room to move, were lying in it. There was poop in their untouched food bowls and in their water. They were all panting and clearly feverish as the day was much cooler than yesterday.

We all stood still in shock. The volunteers hadn't looked in at the kennels for their daily cleaning shift yet. It was late afternoon and the dogs hadn't been tended to since early morning. We all were worried sick about the dogs but also dreading the massive task of mopping up and sanitizing the filthy runs.

I ran to the front of the shelter and saw Melissa hunched over her computer still perusing southern dogs.

She looked up at me and said, "Please get the runs completely clean back there, deodorize the entire place and then don't feed those dogs anything, just give them water, no food. We clearly have a bad batch of dog food here and I just ordered some new kibble."

"I don't think they are suffering from bad dog food." I said, trying to keep my voice calm so Melissa wouldn't shut me down. "They are really, really sick and you need to call a vet right now. It's probably very contagious."

"No way," responded Melissa. "These dogs are all up to date on vaccines. They have only been sick for a day or two. We just switched dog food brands. That can have a bad effect until they get used to it."

"We need to get a vet out here to make sure," I said.

"I just put in a call to the board," replied Melissa. "When they call back I'll ask them if we can call the vet. But, I'm not risking getting a vet out here for a site visit without board approval. It's too expensive."

"It's going to be more expensive, for the dogs

especially, if this is a virus or something and you wait all night to get someone out here. It's 4:30 now and if you don't call a vet soon they'll be leaving for the day."

"Nope, no way. Not until I hear from the board."

I left Melissa sitting at her computer and went back in to see Hector.

"We need to call the vet now," I said. "We can't wait for the board members to get home from their day jobs to make the call."

"I agree," he said. "It will be on my head. But, all of us are here as witnesses as to how bad these dogs are. We've got to call."

Hector reached for the phone and as I left his office I could hear him telling the shelter vet what was going on and how urgent he felt the situation was. I started pulling an old towels and blankets from the clean pile in the laundry room and went into the runs. Berta was waiting with several other volunteers. We figured the best way to get on top of the incredible cleaning task facing us was to start soaking up the mess with lots of washable fabric.

One of the volunteers was stationed in the laundry room to keep the washers and driers full and running non-stop. We shifted sick dogs from run to run as we scrubbed floors with bleach and shelter disinfectant. We worked well past midnight and I didn't know how

I'd ever get up to teach my class in the morning.

    I finally drove home exhausted and ran upstairs after tossing my clothes into the washer with some bleach. I didn't want to touch my own dogs until I'd scrubbed my skin raw in the shower. I had no idea what was infecting the shelter. I didn't have a good feeling about the fates of the poor dogs we'd just left in the temporarily clean runs.

 19. Deadly Insects

    Poirot recovered nicely from his massive infection and was romping and playing with his new dog pack in a matter of days. He simply loved all dogs. He was equally wary about people. He did decide that Mark was lovable and to be trusted, at least after his first angry outburst at seeing me walk in the door with another dog. Still, after a day, he was sitting on Mark's lap in the evening while he was watching TV and working on his computer. Poirot's reaction to any other person, for the rest of his long life, would be to run and hide and snarl, peering warily with his black beady eyes out of his corner or from under the couch.

But, happily, Poirot bonded especially tightly with Ricky, and even Hawkins, and we loved watching the two dogs run around and around the border of our small yard – through the shrubbery and under the shady umbrella of the weeping holly tree. Ricky was a perpetual bed spud and at night Poirot would snuggle up tightly into his layers of warm fatty flesh and they'd both snore. Even Hawkins enjoyed Poirot, just giving him the look that all dogs understand when Poirot attempted to jump up in Hawkins' favorite couch spot. The pit bulls, Ricky, Hawkins and Sable, cattle dog, Maggie, and now the little feral Belgian shepherd, Poirot. This was our family and these misfit mutts were truly our children. I didn't have any regrets in spite of my mother-in-law's dismay that her only grandchildren were going to be dogs.

After the big clean-up, I took a few days off from volunteering at the shelter, but Berta soon called to talk about shelter events. She told me that Melissa was fired the very evening of the illness crisis. Members of the board came by and talked with the veterinarian who treating all the sick southern dogs. The vet told them they were dealing with a highly infectious disease, of origin yet unknown, but potentially very lethal. The board and the vet interrogated Melissa. She admitted to hiding evidence of the dogs being ill for several days. That's when she was fired. Then Hector took over unwillingly as shelter manager until they could hire someone new.

Berta told me that all the southern dogs had been removed from the kennel and were being housed and treated at another shelter that had a sanitary, isolated quarantine space. They'd stay there until the veterinarians could figure out what was wrong with them.

The kennel runs were filthy again and Berta needed some help to clean them. I didn't ask where all the other volunteers were because many of them were students and in school most days or others had young children at home and wouldn't want to get themselves dirty scrubbing down runs covered with dog diarrhea from some mysterious disease.

So, I went to the shelter to help Berta and Hector scrub down the concrete floors of the runs, wash the raised beds, use big brushes to scrub the encrusted wire gates, and finally disinfect all the units with an intense-smelling liquid cleaner designed to kill most bacteria and viruses including the parvovirus. I couldn't understand why the board wanted us to disinfect so intensely since all of the dogs were inoculated against the deadly parvovirus before entering the shelter building.

In addition, all of the cats were inoculated against panleukopenia, a disease similar to parvovirus in cats. Nobody yet knew what could be causing the sickness of the southern dogs. But, I knew that Poirot was fortunate that he'd become ill from infected stitches and removed from the shelter before the worst illness struck. And, all of the local dogs seemed to be doing just fine. Ironically, Melissa's segregation of them may have saved their lives.

The three of us cleaned the southern dog runs until they looked new again. They also looked very empty and sad. We still didn't have any word on what the disease might be. We put the beds out to dry and disinfect in the warm sun. The dishes were either tossed away or left to soak in buckets of disinfectant.

Finally, towards the end of our shift, Doris and Althea from the board stopped by the shelter to give us all an update: Two of the southern dogs had died but the rest were holding on with the help of massive infusions of intravenous liquids. Horribly, the dogs were all found to be infected by a new strain of parvovirus, and one that could be transferred between dogs and cats. We all just looked at one another with horror as Doris went on to inform us that the southern dogs had probably been the carriers of this deadly new strain to the shelter. Prior to this outbreak, it had only been diagnosed in the southern states.

We all stood still in shock. I felt sick and very guilty. I'd been dismayed that Melissa had started to favor the southern dogs over the local dogs and lost interest in the pit bulls, but I had been the originator of the southern transport idea that fueled both Melissa's and Sherri's addictions. How could what I thought was such a good idea, such a humane idea, go so wrong? Bliss's voice echoed in my head, "Shit happens with dogs."

I thought anxiously of Poirot. At that moment he was probably curled up tight with Ricky and Sable. Could he be a carrier of this new strain of parvovirus? Was he infecting our dogs at this very moment? I wanted to race home and grab him up and bring him back to the shelter. But, it wouldn't matter. He'd been in my house for too long. It was too late. The best I could do was go home and call our own veterinarian.

It turned out that Poirot missed the parvovirus bullet. I took him out of the shelter before that one sick dog came in. He was a lucky dog. My dogs were all lucky. Mark and I were lucky. Sherri was lucky that she'd stopped transporting southern dogs a month earlier. Sometimes staying alive for a long time on this planet seems like just a matter of luck.

Doris and Althea announced that all the animals remaining in the shelter would be quarantined for a month. In that time, the disease would make itself known in the dogs that didn't yet show any symptoms.

All volunteers would still come in and care for the dogs and cats but we'd have to adhere to a strict disinfection protocol upon entering and leaving the shelter. I called my vet the next day and Mark and I drove all the dogs over to get booster vaccinations to guard against the new strain of parvovirus. Poirot was checked and was bursting with good health after overcoming his bacterial infection.

Hidden Falls lost a lot of money during this entire parvovirus fiasco. Doris and Althea were anxiously planning a big emergency fundraising event. They'd have preferred to keep the news of the infection secret, but funds were dwindling fast. And shelter supporters came out in huge numbers when they heard of the disease and plight of the sickened dogs. They were always generous, and even more so this time.

I felt bad for Melissa. She seemed to have suffered some kind of emotional paralysis when she realized the dogs were all sick. She couldn't do anything but stare at her computer and pretend it wasn't happening. She needed to be fired, obviously, but I felt that anyone might react in a similar way in such circumstances.

Hector took me aside at the fundraiser and said, "This isn't your fault, you know. Every big shelter is bringing up tons of southern dogs now, and it's a good thing to do, for us and for the dogs. We just have to learn more about what to do and what not to do, that's all. Who knew there was a new virus or new variation of an old virus? None of us knew."

It was true, but it took me a long time until I could look at little Poirot and not feel guilty about the devastation I could have let him bring to my trusting little family of dogs. But, I couldn't dwell on the guilt too long. There were over twenty local dogs under a month-long quarantine at the shelter and plenty of dog walking to do for all of the volunteers.

The daffodils and crocuses wilted and were replaced with mounds of intensely fragrant wild roses and honeysuckle along the edges of the piney woods. During the quarantine, the shelter was quiet and relaxed without the usual coming and goings of visitors and adopters. The public was banned from entering the shelter during the quarantine period. I'd pick up a tray of coffees at Dunkin Donuts on my way to the shelter for the other volunteers and we'd drink it slowly and walk dogs through the sweet smelling woods from late afternoon to evening.

On my way home one evening I kept reaching up

and scratching one place on the back of my head. I felt a small lump there and when I got home I had Mark take a look.

"Oh gross!" he said as he plucked at my scalp and pulled out a large brown tick. "Well, at least it's a just a big dog tick. You'd better go pour some peroxide up there."

We always worried most about the tiny black and red ticks that infest the forests and fields of this region because they are carriers of Lyme disease and babesiosis. Many people refuse to hike or bike outdoors from April through November because of these nasty little deer ticks. We didn't worry as much about the large dog ticks as a bite was less likely to contain infectious agents and didn't usually cause problems other than a lot of itching and swelling. I put a blob of hydrocortisone on the bite and forgot all about it in a couple of days.

School was ending for the year as my university held finals week early in May. I'd decided not to teach any summer classes that year. We wanted to go up to our cabin for an extended period of time, and looked forward to seeing the dogs romping in acres of forest instead of around and around in circles in our tiny city backyard.

Then, I started to get some intense headaches that

I attributed to my spring allergies and sinusitis. One morning I woke with a doozy of a headache that didn't go away with one dose of ibuprofen, or even with several doses and cups of coffee - usually a sure cure for a headache. By evening I was alternating between rushes of heat with lots of sweat and shaking chills. And the frightening headache was getting worse and worse - pinching my forehead over my eyes and expanding like an elastic band around the back of my head. Then it started to move into the back of my head and neck. My neck was so stiff I could barely turn my head.

 Mark went into the bathroom cupboard and dug out the old mercury thermometer we hardly ever used. I smiled and stuck the thermometer in my mouth thinking his concern was sweet. I was sure my fever was probably around a hundred degrees. I figured I was probably just getting my usual end-of-semester cold since most of my students had some sort of cough.

 I pulled the glass thermometer out of my mouth and squinted at it. Then I shook it down and put it back in my mouth. I thought the stupid thing must be so old that it wasn't working right. It was showing that I had a fever of a hundred and three. I didn't remember ever having a fever that high, even during all my childhood illnesses. I pulled the thermometer out again and brought it over to look at under some brighter light. It was the same reading. I was really sweaty and my head was aching so badly that my vision seemed to get momentarily brighter and dimmer with every beat of blood through my heart.

    I decided to go and take a lukewarm shower to cool off and, in the part of my mind that was in denial that anything was really wrong, wash away any taint of germs that might be causing me to be coming down with such a terrible cold or maybe this was influenza. But, my nose wasn't running. My ears didn't itch. I didn't have any of my usual cold symptoms. And, most alarming, when I looked down at my feet in the shower I could see a red rash. I hadn't noticed it in the morning when I was getting dressed. There were masses of clear, round, bright, hard red bumps on both of my feet and, shockingly, they seemed to be crawling up my legs as I watched. They were visibly multiplying, one new one after the other, in just the few minutes I stood soaking in the shower.

    I jumped out of the shower and grabbed a towel to dry my hair a bit and then threw on some sweat pants and a t-shirt. I ran down the stairs to the kitchen where Mark was cooking dinner.

    "We need to go to the emergency room," I said as calmly and as firmly as possible. "Now!"

    "What?" cried Mark. His voice was getting the

high raspy sound it had just before we had an argument or when he was headed for a complete meltdown of exasperation. "I'm just making dinner. Why do you want to go to the hospital for a cold? They'll keep us there all night waiting for nothing."

That last comment was true. Mark was the last to land in this emergency room for a broken collarbone he obtained in a biking accident. We'd sat in the dreary gray halls for hours. But, I thought, I went to the hospital with him then and he was going to sit with me now. I was starting to panic thinking about what might be wrong because in the back of my mind was a recent news report of a meningitis outbreak at a local college very close to the university where I taught.

"It's not a cold. We need to go. Look!" I pulled up the leg of my pants and pointed down at my shin where the red bumps were growing rapidly. They were now almost up to my knee - in just five minutes.

Mark watched the crawling bumps for a few seconds then said, "Okay. Let's get the dogs all settled. We're going to be there all night."

There were a couple of rows of people sitting in the chairs lined up along the windows of the emergency department at the hospital. Some had small children scrambling on the floor and in their laps. Others were leaning over to the side taking naps. Mark found a couple of empty seats and sat down with a sigh. With all of these people waiting, yes, we would be waiting all night. I went up to the receptionist and gave her an overview of my symptoms and headed for the restroom.

I splashed cold water on my face and looked at my legs. The rash was still creeping upwards and starting to cover my thighs. What would happen when it got to my face? Oddly, I wasn't sweating any more. My forehead, my entire body, felt hot and very dry. I looked in the mirror and tried to suppress my rising panic.

The rash hadn't made it close to my face yet, but I could see bumps appearing on my hands and they were heading towards my wrists. I was glad I'd thought to take a Xanax before we left home. I couldn't imagine sitting in that waiting room with all those people while I was in a state of panic. With the pill, at least I could push the physical panic to the background. My thoughts were panicky but my body just felt dry and light.

Someone knocked on the bathroom door. It was Mark telling me that the nurse was looking for me already. I couldn't believe it. I was going to be let in to the emergency room before all those other people. I was happy we didn't have to wait all night, but it was not a good sign. The triage nurse must have been thinking this was something very bad and very contagious.

Mark sat in the waiting room while the nurse led me into a little square white room with a thermometer on a stand. She sat me down in a chair against the wall and reached over with the thermometer covered in plastic. She seemed to be trying to keep as far away from me as possible. She was stretching hard to keep her body away from me and her reaching hand was also covered with a thick blue latex glove.

"Your temperature is a hundred and three point five," she said matter-of-factly. "Wait here a minute."

She came back with a wheelchair. I didn't feel faint or nauseous but I was happy to sit in the chair as she wheeled me into the labyrinth of little cubicles. Where was Mark? Would I have to spend the night here? I dreaded the thought of spending the night in the hospital. I'd spent so many days and nights in the hospital as kid with kidney problems. Procedures were never explained to me. Everyone told me the things that were stuck into me were going to be good for me, but they always hurt or made me feel dizzy and sick.

The nurse put me into another square cubicle way at the back of the emergency department - away from the other patients that were lying in similar cubicles alone or with anxious loved ones standing next to them. The nurse put me in an isolated part of the ward with thick curtains around the cubicle and where it was very dark. I started to feel some serious panic pushing at the wall of the Xanax so I asked the nurse for a cup of water. I had a few more pills in my purse. The mannerisms of the nurses and the attendants were telling me that they thought something was very wrong. None of them wanted to touch me.

Finally, Mark came in and asked me what was going on. I told him I hadn't seen a doctor yet, so we sat in the dark and waited. Finally, a kindly male doctor in his thirties came and put a hand on my shoulder. I was so grateful for his attempt to be reassuring that I relaxed a bit until he told me what he thought was wrong, it was exactly what I had been dreading.

"We think you may have contracted meningitis," he said trying to sound calm. "We hear you are a teacher, right?"

I nodded. None of my students or any other student in the university had been reported to have meningitis. I couldn't believe I could have contracted meningitis. But, a couple of weeks ago I'd been assigned to oversee student teachers at many area schools, and worked with students of all ages. It was possible, maybe, that I'd picked up something in one of those schools. But, how could we trace where the disease came from now? What were we going to do? People died of meningitis. I was glad I'd taken two more Xanax pills before the doctor came in.

The doctor wanted me to sign a consent form for a spinal tap. It was the only definitive test to tell if I had meningitis he said. I dreaded having a spinal tap. I'd heard horror stories about them, but by now my body and mind were so limp from all the tranquilizers that I was starting to not care what was happening. I signed the form and waited.

The spinal tap turned out to be, like so many other things that happen in hospitals as an adult, not nearly as bad as the scary stories everyone told me. After the procedure I rolled onto my back and oddly felt very relaxed. The panic had passed. I was physically strong. We'd deal with this. Mark was nodding away in the chair next to my bed and we waited for several hours the doctor to return.

"Some good news!" said the doctor as he pushed the curtains to my isolation cubicle back. "You don't have bacterial meningitis - which can be deadly. Your spinal fluid is clear. We think that you may have viral meningitis, though. We can't treat it other than support you with fluids, so you can stay here tonight for IV fluids or you can go home. But, if you do choose to go home, be sure to drink fluids constantly."

I was so relieved that my excitement broke through the Xanax cloud. I sat up in the bed and I was ready to hit the road. Mark looked at me warily and asked wouldn't I rather spend the night at the hospital just to be sure everything was going to be okay? "No," I said. I wanted to get out of there. I wanted to get home and curl up with Ricky and go to sleep forever. I was exhausted but I wanted to be as far away from the hospital as I could get. Hospitals made me feel trapped and claustrophobic, especially when waking up in the morning in one, after the tranquilizers wore off.

So, we headed home. The attendant wheeled me out to the car and tucked me into the front seat. Once in bed, Mark brought several liters of seltzer water and orange juice upstairs and sat them on the table by the bed with a bucket of ice so I could continue to hydrate constantly, as the doctor had advised. Other than that, I just took a couple more ibuprofen for my awful headache and fever.

The next day was Sunday and I stayed in bed. The phone rang and I picked up the landline by the bed. It was my father-in-law's usual Sunday call. He asked how we were and I told him about my strange symptoms and our experience at the emergency room.

Half an hour after I'd hung up the phone it rang again. It was my father-in-law again telling me I needed to get back to the hospital right away.

"I'm telling you," he said. "You do not have viral meningitis. You have all the classic symptoms of Rocky Mountain Spotted Fever. Have you been bitten by a tick recently?"

I remembered back to the other day when I found the tick on my head while driving home from Hidden Falls. I didn't think much about it afterwards. With five dogs that we walked outdoors and walked dozens of dogs weekly in the woods at Hidden Falls. I was always getting tick bites. I had my doctor test me for Lyme Disease each year, but Rocky Mountain Spotted Fever? We were in New England for goodness sake. I was in complete denial that I had a tick-borne illness. I did not want to go back to the hospital. Besides, the doctor had given me the okay to go home.

Mark's father had formed his own expert opinion. He was a biological chemist and he lived in North Carolina where there had been recorded cases of Rocky Mountain Fever. I was worried. I knew in my heart that Mark's father's diagnosis was probably the right one, but I stubbornly refused to face up to it and go back to the hospital.

My in-laws called all day trying to convince us to

return to the hospital. They were starting to wear me down, except that at that point I felt too sick and weak to go anywhere in a car. Mark would have to call an ambulance to get me. But, I was starting to get so lethargic that I just didn't care about anything anymore. I was so hot I felt my body and head were on fire but I wasn't sweating at all. I kept drinking the orange juice and water mixture - liters of it at one time. Oddly, I didn't need to urinate. Which, at the time, I thought was fortunate because I was so weak in the legs that I would have to ask Mark to help me to the bathroom.

Call the ambulance, begged Mark's father as evening rolled around. But, I didn't want the ambulance attendants in the house riling up all the dogs. I told Mark I was feeling better, but really I felt terrible and I was no longer rational. All I could imagine was the attendants coming into our house and letting the dogs get out onto the street, or getting bitten. And, I didn't want to go to the hospital. I was afraid I'd die there. I didn't want to die in the claustrophobic, impersonal hospital. I'd rather die in my own bed. I wasn't rational or sane at that point but, as usual, Mark listened to me and took my advice. We didn't call the ambulance.

The next day I lay in bed watching television with

Ricky, Sable and Poirot all lying around at different places near my body. Ricky lay near my feet and was watching the movie "1001 Dalmatians" on the TV with interest – turning his head this way and that as one of the black and white spotted puppies popped up on the screen. Ricky always responded to television dogs.

I was enjoying watching him. Sable was pressed tightly against me left side as I lay on my back and Poirot was pressed tightly against the right. This was the closest Poirot had ever come to me. Since I brought him home from the shelter he'd been friendly, but kept his distance. But, that day, he was pressed against me as closely as he could get.

Earlier, I had Mark help me to the bathroom. For the first time in twenty-four hours, in spite of all the water I drank, I needed to go. I looked in the mirror and was startled to see that the whites of my eyes had a strange brownish-yellow tinge to them. The rash had spread over my entire body now and there was even a row of bumps along my hairline. The bumps were bright red and hard and were starting to itch.

My fever was still a hundred and three and a half. Mark asked me again if I wanted to go to the hospital. Again, I refused to go. I was as stubborn as my father about hospitals. I just wanted to flop down in the bed with my dogs and watch Cruella DaVille.

My chest became so heavy I could hardly take a breath and was aware of every one that I did manage to pull into my lungs. I lay flat on my back with my dogs as Mark puttered around downstairs. I felt as if a stack of encyclopedias had been placed on my chest. My mouth was sore and my skin felt very, very tight. In fact, the skin on the ends of my fingers and toes was starting to get hard and crack and peel off in chunks. In spite of all the physical discomfort, I felt a strange relaxation and euphoria, even though I hadn't taken any more Xanax.

I kept nodding off and waking up, though I could hardly breathe, my lungs felt so heavy. Still, I felt very pleasantly relaxed. Then, suddenly, I felt my body divide into duplicates of itself. One of us floated out of the one lying on the bed and drifted up and through a hole in the left side of the ceiling of my bedroom. My entire consciousness was in that floating body as it made its way upward, higher and higher. I finally hit a tangle of roots hanging down from what looked like a flat table of sky. Then, I floated up through the roots and into a beautiful pasture full of weeds and flowers. I stood in the field and looked around and saw a nice pine forest, like the one at Hidden Falls, except wilder, in the distance. I walked towards the trees.

To my amazement I saw my mother walk out of a path emanating from the trees. She waited for me without saying a word and I followed into the woods and back down the path. It was beautiful in the forest. The path was covered with a thick layer of pine needles, and twisted and turned into the distance through multitudes of tall healthy pines with the sun filtering down through them in moving patterns. I felt so relaxed and so happy to see that my mother was happy and at peace in her new home. I knew this was her personal heaven. It was perfect for her.

And, she was real. I could tell this wasn't just a dream because my mother was still criticizing me! She had a basket of purple iris bulbs and she was planting them alongside the path as we walked down it. The instant she put a bulb into the ground it popped up in brilliant bloom. She kept admonishing me to not step on her flowers, just as she did when I was a kid. Blue irises were my mother's favorite flower. In life she was a master at growing them, as she was now in death.

We walked and walked and then finally my mother turned around to head back the same way we came. I followed her. I had no choice. When we came near the beginning of the path and the edge of the forest I could see the field I first walked through in the distance.

My mother starting planting the bulbs right in the path behind us. When we got out to the field I looked back at the woodland path. It was filled entirely with brilliant blue irises in full bloom. I thought I'd never seen anything more beautiful and relaxing. I felt euphoric and tingly, light and free of anxiety, and better than I'd ever felt in my entire life.

"I want to stay here with you," I said to my Mom as I turned to walk back down the path into the woods.

"Wait," she cried. "Don't step on my new iris flowers!"

Just like in life, I turned to argue with her but she tapped my arm. "It's not time yet," she said. "You need to head right back to your husband and dogs, now. They need you."

She turned to walk back down the path and when she trod on them the irises remained standing and unbroken. I tried to follow her. I was desperate to stay with my mother, but the irises seemed to emanate a power that kept me firmly in my place. I turned away to look back across the field and as soon I took a few steps in the opposite direction from which my mother walked I felt my new body rejoining my old one in the bed.

Little Poirot was in my face sniffing my breath and licking my cheeks. This was an act I'd see him do again and again, to other dogs that were nearing death. I opened my eyes and looked at him and he heaved a sigh then returned to his place pressed tightly up against my side.

   Strangely, as soon as I woke from that vivid dream I knew that my fever had broken. I reached to the table next to the bed for the thermometer and stuck it in my mouth. Sure enough, my fever was down to only a hundred degrees. And, while I was dreaming, my rash had changed. The bumps had flattened out into an intricate red and purple lattice all over my body. I knew the worst was over. I never felt so peaceful before or after that strange afternoon. And, whether I'd had a vivid dream or near-death-experience, I was never as afraid of death as I'd been before.

   On Monday, I felt well enough to go to my own doctor so she could check my rash and I told her the whole story.

   Her main comment was, "I can't believe that idiot doctor in the emergency room let you go home!"

   My doctor was sure I'd had Rocky Mountain Spotted Fever - a disease many don't survive without intensive antibiotic treatment early in the course of symptoms. My doctor explained that a big dose of IV antibiotics would have helped in the beginning, when I first got the headache, but by the time the rash appeared it would have been much less effective. By the time the fever broke, antibiotics would be useless. So, my father-in-law had been right all along. I'd managed to survive Rocky Mountain Spotted Fever without any drugs.

I felt like a very fortunate idiot. Yet I wouldn't trade that vivid dream, where I saw my mother happy again, for any change in events. That dream made the entire ordeal worthwhile. It gave me a peace of mind that will last a lifetime and I know in my heart that it wasn't just a dream. That pine forest filled with irises is my mother's final resting place and it is beautiful and it is perfect. My Mom saved my life then, but I will see her there again someday, although maybe I'll be bringing the ghosts of some of my old dogs along with me then. They'd love that pathway through the pines, though we will all have to be very careful of my mother's flowers.

20. Elvira

    Thankfully, the whites of my eyes turned from tea colored to white after about a month. That weird eye color was the most frightening aspect of the entire illness ordeal. I had to find a substitute to take my classes for the semester finals week. The Rocky Mountain Spotted fever turned my legs wobbly, while the rash continued to morph from small red lattice-like patches to large purple bruises. Months later the bruises began to fade and I could, finally, think about those few days spent burning up in bed without going to the hospital without guilt. I couldn't believe that I was so out of my senses that I'd endangered my dogs, and myself.

    I didn't think Mark would be able to deal with the whole pack of dogs if I died. He would try. He would become frustrated. He'd persist and then maybe later he'd give up. I couldn't blame him. He didn't have dogs or other pets besides a short-lived turtle when he was a kid. As Mark's mother was a supreme housekeeper, it was interesting that Mark grew up to be a sloppy person who seemed to get joy and a sense of freedom from disorganization and clutter. He enjoyed the chaos of a five-dog-house most times, but it certainly wasn't his idea to have multiple dogs living here. I felt so guilty. He shouldn't be burdened with them if I died. I decided to make some plans for that eventuality.

    By June, my legs became stable and I finally felt

enough energy to head to the shelter to walk the dogs with Berta. Hector was sitting at the front desk as I walked in the door. He told me he'd been made shelter manager after Melissa was fired and that the board also decided to hire an assistant manager for checks and balances. They wanted to make sure a disaster like the parvovirus crisis never happened again. A single manager might panic alone, but two would likely maintain their cool in a crisis. We all hoped so.

I thought hiring the assistant manager was a great idea and was glad the board was being so generous with the funding for the position. The shelter manager job was nearly overwhelming and included maintaining the health and wellbeing of hundreds of animals, interacting with local animal control officers and police officers and prodding dozens of staff and volunteers to stay organized and get their work done.

It was too much work and stress for one person, as the fates of Melissa and Bliss had proven. Hector was too gentle and caring a person to suffer a nervous collapse and be fired. I looked forward to meeting the new assistant manager.

I felt extremely fortunate to be alive and walking dozens of dogs, one after the other, out to the graveyard through the fragrant June woods. Since my fight with Rocky Mountain Spotted Fever every scent seemed stronger, every color brighter, and every sound clearer. I'd been suffering from depression before I ever started volunteering, but after the deadly disease the feeling lifted and I was grateful to be alive and able to enjoy the objects and beings I encountered.

One day, Berta and I were walking two hard-pulling pit bulls back towards their runs when I saw a woman with long straight black hair walking towards the shelter from the parking lot. She looked familiar but it was hard to place her at a distance. We settled the dogs with treats and new toys and walked to the front of the shelter to talk with Hector. It seemed odd to be at Hidden Falls without Melissa hunched over her computer, and without helping her choose a dog or two from her online lists of southern shelter animals. The Hidden Falls board had decided to forego any more southern transports.

The dark-haired women we'd seen outdoors was bending over the front desk speaking with Hector. When she turned towards us I realized with a shock that it was Elvira, the surly woman from the city shelter where I'd rescued Little Ricky. What was she doing here, I wondered? To me, she was the epitome of evil.

Sherri was familiar with Elvira and we'd discussed at length Sherri's many confrontations with her over the years. According to Sherri, while working at the old city shelter, Elvira enjoyed picking and choosing which animals to send to the euthanasia room. Dogs who didn't take treats from her hand, cats who were frightened and reached out to swat her hands away from their cages - these animals ended up on the top of the weekly death lists.

Of course, I didn't take this information entirely seriously as it was coming from Sherri. She was like the rook in a chess game. She could only move forward or backward in dealing with people. Everyone was either all good or entirely evil. She saw the world in sharp contrasting colors. She couldn't perceive of anyone at an angle or acknowledge that someone might cross the boundaries of the good and evil squares diagonally and touch the corners of each now and then.

Berta and I approached the desk and Hector took my breath away by introducing Elvira as the new assistant manager. What if Sherri's story had contained even a grain of truth? Did we want a euthanasia advocate working at Hidden Falls? I greeted her reluctantly and shook her long-nailed hand. Of course, her real name wasn't Elvira. She had just reminded me of the cheesy 1980's television character "Elvira: Mistress of the Dark" because she looked so much like her with her lank black hair and dark lipstick. Her real name was Paula, a name I somehow associated with gentleness. I decided to try to keep an open mind about Paula.

I could tell she recognized me from our encounter at the other shelter. Her black eyes glittered for a second when we touched. The next day Paula cornered me in the hallway after my shift walking the dogs. Berta was home with her grandchildren that day, so Paula led me alone into the little room we used to introduce dogs to their new adopters and shut the door behind us. We sat face to face on the hard metal chairs. I didn't like being alone with this woman and I wondered why she wanted to talk to me.

Paula came right out with it, "You don't like me much, do you?" she said slowly.

"I don't really know you," I replied looking at the little window in the door to see if anyone was passing down the hallway.

"Well, I think you should know - I didn't have anything to do with the policies at the other shelter. It was all Louis Harrington. He's the money behind that place. It looks like a dumpy little shelter but the fundraising they do all goes straight in to his pocket. Have you ever seen his place on Rocky Neck? That's all shelter foundation money."

"I have no idea who Mr. Harrington is," I replied, though Sherri had talked about him in connection with her property and the pet cemetery behind it. "That's terrible if he's misleading people but I don't know why you are telling me this."

"Well...I'm telling you because I could see how much you care about the animals when you came in to pick up that Pit at the other shelter. And, you seem like a fairly reasonable person, and someone told me you like to write, and, well, I'm just the opposite. I can't write anything. So, I thought you might be able to help do something to help me out about that crappy shelter."

"I still have no idea what you are talking about," I replied with annoyance because the half-smile playing around Paula's lips told me she wasn't being entirely honest with me in whatever it was she was trying to get me to do.

"I mean when I was working over there I really didn't want to be there but I needed the job, you know? I have a daughter and my marriage broke up two years ago and now I'm a single mom with sole custody and I can't be too picky about jobs, so I stayed there longer than I wanted to. And, when this nice shelter opened, I saw an opportunity to get out of that hell hole," she said.

"Well, I'm happy you found a new job, but I still don't know what exactly you are trying to tell me," I said. Paula seemed to be enjoying dancing around me verbally.

"What I was thinking," said Paula slowly, "is that with your skills you could help me get the word out about that awful shelter and about that bastard Harrington. I thought you could write about it. Send it to the newspaper or something. Or, maybe you know a better way. But, the point is that that place is bad and most of the animals there don't make it out alive, and the people there don't give a shit. They are just in it for the money. I thought animal people around here might want to know what is going on at the place."

I didn't tell Paula what Sherri had told me about her - that she was a big part of the problem and right in the middle of it - that she was a shelter manager who enjoyed killing. I didn't care about sparing Paula's feelings because I didn't think she was a nice person. But, I always felt protective of Sherri. I felt that if Paula knew Sherri was talking about her behind her back she'd find a way to get revenge. I hardly knew this woman but I was sure she was the deeply vengeful type. If you believe in auras and that sort of thing, you'd say you could see or feel a very toxic aura emanating from Paula. I thought that the name Elvira was much more suitable to her personality.

As I was thinking about Sherri, Paula was

babbling on about all the abuses she had witnessed at the other shelter during her employment there. I reacted as I do to the sad commercials on television by animal rights organizations - the poignant faces of cute animals, the nostalgic heartrending music, the absolute oblivion of sorrow make me want to commit suicide. I plug my ears tightly and hum, like I did when I was a kid, when some bully was torturing me with a story of animal abuse. I felt the same sort of tormenting spirit existed in Paula, and that she would have laughed in my face as those childhood brats always did if I had showed any emotion at all.

Besides, the information Paula was sharing was common knowledge among local animal rescue people. It made its way through the grapevine and was always at the back of my mind. As a relative newcomer to the area I'd listened to plenty of stories about the bad shelter as animal people wanted to bring me up to speed on the local culture. Some stories seemed impossibly clouded with rumor and vitriol while others rang true. What I could never understand was why, with all the seeming passion for animals and the concern among local animal lovers, did nobody ever expose this shelter and its alleged abuses or take a meaningful stand of any kind?

Why didn't anybody ever call or write the

newspapers? Why didn't people form a committee and approach the shelter owners directly? Any approach to show concern and to expose any wrongdoing would have gone a long way to help the poor, doomed animals in that place. The faces of the cats and dogs I saw pressed desperately up against the cages on my one walk through there haunted me and always will.

I finally managed to extricate myself from the uncomfortable conversation with Paula in that claustrophobic room. When I got safely into my car I called Sherri and asked her more of what she knew about Paula.

"Pure fucking evil," was Sherri's immediate comment. "She's like the Angel of Death. She enjoys killing. Don't let her try to butter you up with stories of her compassion for animals. She was always up front and center and ready to take on death duties at that place."

"How do you know all this?" I asked. I knew that Sherri had never volunteered at any shelter. This was not so much because she didn't like to work with shelter animals, as she was great with all animals, it was that she hated to deal with people.

"My cousin Randy...well, he's really my second or third cousin, but he works there, or worked there I should say, until he got fired."

"Wow, really! He actually worked at that place. Poor guy." I remembered meeting Sherri's cousin Randy and he was a large, slow-witted, idealistic and kindly person, no match for Elvira-Paula.

"Yeah, he did for a while," said Sherri. "It really messed him up and that's part of the reason I hate that place so much."

"Well," I replied cautiously, as I wasn't in the mood to hear any more sordid and sad animal abuse tales at that moment, "Why did they fire him then?"

"He started to complain about things going on there to the owner, that asshole Louis Harrington. Got fired right away. Randy knew it would happen, I'm pretty sure. He'd had it by then anyway. They wanted him to kill the dogs and he hated it, but that Angel of Death was always willing to step in so Randy didn't have to do that too much. He just brought all the dead bodies out at the end of the day to the back yard to be cremated. And, that's where that place makes a good buck - cremation. They provide cremation services for the entire county."

"Wow." That was all I could say. I couldn't really take it all in - people killing companion animals for perverse pleasure or a feeling of sick power and absconding with donation money from well-meaning people. I don't know why I couldn't accept it, since I'd known even as a kid that such evils existed, but I still didn't want to live in a world where people could be so terrible.

"Well," I said tiredly, not really wanting to know more but feeling compelled to find out more about the mystery surrounding that shelter, "Why hasn't anybody anywhere around here done anything about this? If Harrington is telling people that he's helping animals, and taking donations for that purpose and he is really hurting them, isn't that illegal? Couldn't someone just write a letter to the editor of some of the local papers and expose the shelter so at least people won't donate any more money?"

"Nobody will do that around here," replied Sherri. "Yeah, people like you come here and think 'It's Massachusetts. It's progressive here. Nothing bad ever happens here. There's no corruption here.' Well, you all are dead wrong. This place is so corrupt you wouldn't believe it – the entire state, but especially down here. It's backwards in many, many ways."

Sherri was starting to pick up momentum now. I could hear her sucking in puffs of tobacco smoke and exhaling loudly as her voice roughened and deepened a few notes. "Yeah, the state agricultural inspectors. They are a fucking joke. Look, they come down and raid my place even though they didn't know shit about that new parvo strain – as if it is all my fault."

"They make a big deal out of it and take my dogs away. But, do they ever come down and check out Harrington's shelter? No. Because he's old money and he's connected here and that shelter pays for his big house on Rocky Neck, and his big parties with all his big friends, and some of them work in state government and nobody is going to take him down. That's what he thinks anyway."

"And, all the old ladies with their old family money - when they die they give over their wad to Harrington and his shelter. 'Dear sweet man, always trying to help the animals.' Shit, those graves here behind my house. All the old bats in Rocky Neck have their pets buried here, even their horses, and believe me, they pay a pretty penny to do it. They wouldn't set foot in Harrington's death shelter but they come out here and put flowers on the grave of their sweet Pookie or Puffy and they pay a big whopping yearly fee for the privilege."

"Wait," I had to interrupt Sherri because she was on a roll, talking and smoking, and I stated the obvious, "If Harrington is burying all these animals behind your property, and is taking donations to do it by misrepresenting what his non-profit organization actually does, why don't you speak up? Why haven't you ever told anybody this stuff? And, you have your cousin as a witness to what goes on at the shelter, too."

"Well…" said Sherri slowly, "Okay, I'll tell you why but you are not to repeat it. You already know that Harrington lent me money but he also owns the right-of-way to my property, or he did own it. I also borrowed money from him when I bought this place to pay for the easement to my driveway because it's shared with his pet cemetery. He charged me over forty grand for it. And, I paid it; I'm still paying it, because I wanted this place. It was my dream."

"I'd drive by this place as a kid and think 'Someday I'm going to have a rescue farm there.' So, when it came on the market and I could do it, I got it. I had to pay Harrington to finalize the deal because what good is buying a property if you can't drive your car on it? So, he's got me. The easement isn't paid off yet, and if I talk or say anything about what goes on at the cemetery he'll pull the easement back. I just know he will. He's that spiteful. And then I'll be screwed. We've got everything tied up in this place."

When Sherri finished venting and stopped to take a breath, I told her about my conversation with Paula and how she seemed to want me to write something about the shelter and Harrington for the newspapers.

"First off," replied Sherri, "The local papers won't

print what you write. They always protect that asshole and that shelter. They always have. They want everyone to believe the city has a wonderful little happy shelter there. There was a woman a few years ago who tried to expose that place through the papers. She did get something published, eventually, and then Harrington came down on her like a ton of bricks. He hit her with a slander suit. She moved away. I don't know if the suit ever went through."

"But, if I were you, I wouldn't think about messing with that creep. Like I told you, he's an old wharf rat lawyer. He defends fishermen down on the wharf when they want to put one over on the conservation commission. If you write something about him, you might get sued for libel, or worse, like I said before you might find yourself bobbing up and down one night in the water before you sink under the wharves with an anchor tied to your waist."

"Oh come on," I replied laughing. "That sort of stuff doesn't happen over animal shelters and non-profit organizations, does it? I mean, how much money can really be in it?" The whole story sounded like a made-for-TV movie and absurdly influenced most by Sherri's appetite for drama and gossip.

"Have you ever seen that bastard Harrington's house?" asked Sherri. "Check it out sometime. You'll have to find someone in Rocky Neck to let you in since it's a gated community with a guard, but if you go, I'll give you the address. Then you'll see how much money is in it. It's all the old bats and their millions. I'd say Harrington's place is worth at least ten-million. And, if you haven't heard yet, he's building a brand new shelter and crematorium in the next town over from here so he can up his game - bring in more animals, more cremation money, more donations - and, in my opinion, I think there's more to it than that. I think the whole thing is tied up with the fishing business somehow - maybe drugs - money laundering on a small scale, but a lot for around here.

"I bet the dead animals are just the tip of the iceberg. There is bigger money in all of it than just the donations. I'd bet you anything the shelter business is just a front and a cover up. Believe me; Harrington will do anything to defend his turf. Anything. Everyone around here is afraid of him. You were wondering why nobody ever speaks up? They are afraid. Harrington will get at you if you speak up, and all the rescue people know it, so they all go on as if nothing is happening and pretending they are doing something great for the animals when the big elephant in the room is always there staring them in the face. They pretend it's not there because they are afraid - all chicken-shit assholes."

I knew that Sherri had built up a lot of animosity over the years towards the animal rescue community but I wasn't really sure why or what had started it. I assumed it influenced much of her accusations against Harrington and his shelter and the lack of action from the rescue people. But, if even a small percentage of these stories were true - and they were coming now from three people - then the situation was very disturbing.

That night, Mark retreated to the far regions of the bed as I tossed and turned in my effort to keep my mind off the evil shelter so I could fall asleep, but I stayed hopelessly awake. I'd try to think about something banal, like buying clothes or decorating the house, but my mind always came back to the shelter situation. Should I respond to Paula's challenge and write a letter to the newspapers? It seemed such a puny, insignificant action, yet supposedly Louis Harrington had success in suing another writer for libel. He must be covering up something bad, or why on earth would a busy and powerful attorney care what some middle-aged animal lover wrote about him in an op-ed?

It was the sense of entitlement in all of it that enraged me most. My brother warned me about

Massachusetts when he left his job in Boston for California. The old money and old families and their assumption that they were above the law and first in line for favors.

My brother didn't tell me any specifics of what had actually happened to him to prompt his move. He just told me he was tired of the old school way of doing business. Was this sort of thing what he had meant? Old families - landed gentry - land-rich locals taking positions of power for themselves and laughing at any outsider that tried to interfere?

Depressingly, this awful situation had the most powerless of all beings - poor abandoned and abused companion animals - bearing the brunt of a money and power grab.

I decided that when I next went to Hidden Falls I would ask for more details from Paula. Then, I thought that I didn't want to talk with that toxic woman and hear more of her horror stories. But, I thought, as an outsider I could perhaps do something other residents with family roots could not. Maybe, I wouldn't be as susceptible to threats of Harrington as the locals who had lived here for generations and had old families, real estate, and reputations to protect. How could Harrington really touch a nobody like me?

But, on the other hand, I did want to fit in here

and be a part of a community. Mark and I were new to this place, but my family was certainly not. My grandmother loved this part of the country and often visited southeastern Massachusetts, from Hingham to Tiverton, Rhode Island, visiting second and third cousins - dozens of far-removed and closer relatives. I loved this place before I ever saw it because of my grandmother's stories. In fact, I learned from my grandmother that I was the granddaughter, twelve times back, of a Mayflower family - those tough, determined people who made the trip across the Atlantic and survived that first desperate winter to breed exponentially and fill this place with new inhabitants.

My mother scoffed at my grandmother's genealogical research. The two didn't get along well, and my mother viewed my grandmother's Mayflower aspirations as further evidence of her snobbery and narcissism. But, I loved and admired my grandmother. She was outgoing and life-loving and fun. She loved travel, antiques, old cars and houses and, most of all, her genealogical explorations that took her around the world and most often right into the territory in which we were now living.

So, this was a new home to me geographically, but in my heart it was my hometown - the place of my family's origin on this continent - and, I too had been enjoying locating and researching family sites from my grandmother's old genealogy books. I didn't want to become a local pariah for speaking up against a power player like Harrington.

I was dismayed that Harrington was tainting this special place I wanted so much to love and feel at home in. I was overwhelmed and starting to feel apathetic. In talking with Sherri, I just felt that people were hopelessly horrible. Perhaps, any possible action was futile. Why not just lay in bed and snuggle comfortably with my own dogs and do nothing? Because, nothing would ever, ever change people.

But, outrage won over apathy. What right did this creepy lawyer have to take charity money - given in memory of beloved pets by sentimental well-meaning wealthy animal-lovers - and turn around and betray their trust by killing other less fortunate animals?

Harrington was advertising that he was running a no-kill shelter, a place that should be a sanctuary and second chance for abandoned and abused animals, and then turning around full circle and just killing, burning and dumping their poor bodies as if they were so much trash in a landfill.

I felt tears starting to burn my eyes as I tossed around in the twisted, damp comforters covering our old brass and iron bed. Every time I took a turn the bed heaved a loud squeak and Mark would sigh in frustration. He knew from years of experience not to say anything when I was having a restless night, and he would never think of asking me to sleep downstairs on the sofa. But, my mind wasn't on the suffering of Mark at that moment.

How could someone do this, I thought over and over? How could people be so awful, so utterly, depressingly evil and uncaring? I felt that old howl well up inside me, the one that developed as a kid growing to learn just how terrible people could be towards other animals - a howl, a scream built up silently in my mind and my gut waiting to emerge. It was so painful holding in anger and outrage all the time, but if I started screaming, how would I ever stop? There seemed to be no end to the evilness of people.

Finally, as the sky over the neighbor's rooftop started to lighten to cold, slate gray color, I fell asleep by cuddling up with Ricky's warm body. He always knew when I was upset and had recently developed a habit of licking my feet to calm me down. I'd seen him perform this same nurturing, calming action with Maggie and Sable when they were either itchy or agitated. It seemed funny and weird at first but his gentle licking could bring relaxation into my twitchy brain too, and calm me right down, eventually sending me into a blissful sleep.

Then, Ricky would push his ninety-pound body between Mark and me and lay down with his big warm back towards me and his feet splayed out, ever so slowly pushing Mark further and further towards the opposite edge of the bed. That night, again, I found the best remedy for anger at the actions of people was in snuggling with my dogs. But then, at the end of the night, I had to get up and do something.

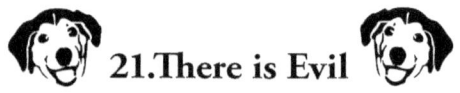 21. There is Evil

I woke up the next day determined to find out more about Louis Harrington and the disturbing stories about his city animal shelter. It was so convenient for some wealthy criminal from the waterfront enclave of Rocky Neck to bring their dirty business to the city and then go home to a commune of sheltered neighbors that were happily ignorant about the origins of all his money. Some of his neighbors never ventured out beyond their rock-walled, ocean-view homes, and very few ventured into our crowded little city just a few miles away.

All the anxiety that tormented me the night before was further purged after an hour's walk with my best buddy, Hawkins. What did I have to lose if I spoke out about Harrington and his nasty shelter? I was just a little nobody animal shelter volunteer, part-time professor and a newbie in town. I didn't own real estate that could be taken from me on the basis of a dodgy easement like Sherri. Perhaps Harrington, with his supposed fortune, had some pull at the liberal university I taught at but I doubted it. Even if he did it wouldn't matter much. My college was so left-leaning that any public social activism would be a credit to my resume. Mark's situation was similar at his university.

In the morning light, all the worries that made me toss and turn the night away seemed distant and unfounded. I thought that in all probability Sherri, her cousin Randy, Paula and everyone else were simply sharing gossip that had evolved and grown over the years into these monstrous stories. I couldn't believe that one person, Harrington, could be so powerful and have such wide reach throughout all of southeastern Massachusetts to create a culture of silence, covering up entrenched animal abuse and graft.

I still planned to hunt down Paula at the shelter that afternoon and get more details. But, there was no need to seek her out. I was leaning over the deep sink scraping the remains of the afternoon feeding out of dozens of stainless steel bowls when Paula came up behind and me and asked if I had a minute to speak with her. We went back into that little claustrophobic room, with only one small window in the door - like an insane asylum.

"Maybe you had some time to think about what I was saying yesterday after you had to take off so fast last evening? You seem like a nice person and I know you care about the animals. I've seen that. So, why don't you hear me out, and I'll tell you what I've seen while working at the hellhole."

"If you are so concerned," I asked, "Why don't you do something yourself? You are an eyewitness to everything. Why would you want to pass all this information off on to me and have me write about it? If what you say is true, why don't you go after the newspapers or television news? Let them put it out there."

"I can't do that for two reasons," replied Paula slowly, as if she thought I was stupid or had been rehearsing her answer to this question. "One - the papers won't print anything about Harrington. He's too connected. Two - if I put something out there, he'll come after me and ruin my career. You are just a volunteer here because you want to be, because you like animals and all that. Well, I went to school to learn to do this. I didn't do well enough to get into a good veterinary school, but that's okay because I'd rather manage shelters. This is what I do best. This is what I do for a living and Harrington will make sure no other shelter in the country will hire me if I rat him out."

I didn't believe her. Again, the tales about this one man seemed surreal as if he were a storybook antihero with supernatural powers. He was just a man. One man. Nobody was that connected, and even if he was, why would he care what one lowly shelter manager had to say about him? He could just deny it and the gossip would go away. Nobody would challenge him. The entire scenario seemed implausible.

But then, when I thought about it, the stories about the sex abuse scandal and cover-up by the Catholic Church was making a regular appearance in the local newspapers. If such a venerable organization could cover up such atrocities for decades, then silence everyone by intimidating any person who tried to reveal the truth, why couldn't one crooked lawyer do the same to save his little nest-egg, fancy home in a gated enclave, and whatever other treasures he had stashed away here in our corner of Massachusetts?

"Okay," announced Paula interrupting my train of

thought, "I'll list all the worst shit I saw at that place when I was there. Then afterwards, if you decide you don't want to do anything, that's fine. Just go about your business walking the dogs and cleaning the cages and feeling good about yourself for doing it. That's fine. But just hear me out. I need to get it off my chest anyway, and I'd rather tell it to someone who cares."

"Fine," I said bracing myself against the back of the metal chair, "Go ahead. I'll listen."

"Well…" began Paula slowly and obviously enjoying her starring role as supplier of secret information, "There are really only a few things they do that are really actionable."

Paula stopped and let the word actionable sink in to let me know how long she'd been thinking about the lack of ethics at the place she'd chosen to work for over five years. I didn't stop her and remind her that in all the time she'd witnessed the acts she was about to recite she'd never chosen to speak out to anyone about it. But, I'd hear her out then decide whether or not what she was telling me was credible.

"Okay here it is; the worst thing is that they don't really adopt out any animals, or very many I should say. Once in a great while the perfect animal will come in - a dog that is young, in good shape, and completely passive or a cat that is declawed, calm, and preferably a kitten or a fancy breed - those they might actually put up for adoption. The thing is, Louis being a lawyer, doesn't want to get sued for liability if a dog bites a new owner or a cat scratches a kid. So, he just doesn't adopt them out. The place is really just a crematorium. The towns pay the shelter an annual fee to cremate their unwanted animal population.

"The shelter part of the operation is just a smokescreen. The animals that come in there don't really have much chance of coming out again alive. Especially owner turn-ins. They'll say, or they told me to tell people all this bullshit - that we'd behavior test the animal, then put the animal up for adoption. Soon a nice new family would come along and everything would be so nice. No guilt for the owners that decide to dump their pet at the shelter that way. But, really, the minute the door closes that animal is dead. They never put an owner-turn-in up for adoption. They just kill them, unless maybe if the animal is young and purebred and of a very passive breed…then maybe…But, for the most part the place is all about killing.

"The cats that come in there go down right away. They're supposed to keep strays for three days according to state regulations but if there is one tiny thing wrong with the cat - nervous, not eating, anything - they're gone right away. If someone comes in looking for their cat and it's dead they just say, 'Oops, we did an assessment of your cat and it was sick or injured or had serious behavioral issues.'

"See, they have all convinced themselves - Louis and all his shelter workers - that they are doing the public a good service by protecting them from all the vicious animals out there. That's how they justify the killing. But, really, it's about the money. It costs a lot to have a good vet look at all the animals. It costs a lot to have a vet euthanize the animals, too. They never spend money to treat a sick animal. They like to turn them over as fast as possible because the shelter gets a fee from the towns for every animal they put down. They have shelter workers kill the animals because it costs too much to have a vet in to do it, plus an outsider would know what was going on then.

"The sickest part is that they spend money on some very nice advertisements - you've probably seen them in your local paper - cute puppy and kitten photos and some bullshit about how hard they all work to find them good new homes. It's all bullshit. But, the ads attract the suckers by the thousands. The board of directors for instance - they are all from Rocky Neck or very close by. They are all friends of Louis's. They may like animals and feel good about themselves for being on the board of a shelter but they are careful not to look too closely. They don't want any trouble to taint their reputations around here. They want to believe it's all nice and wonderful. They want to believe they are getting their huge tax breaks by doing something good for the animals and the community.

"And, that little pet graveyard they have going over there behind your friend Sherri's house - yeah, I know you two are buddies - those grave sites go to the biggest donors of all. Of course, some of them are Catholic and don't believe in cremation, even for their pets. So, they pony up each year to have their pet buried in that beautiful pet cemetery and they come out and they put flowers on the graves and walk their new pet around to see all the other dead pets, I mean it is really pretty out there, so why not? But, what they don't know is that their pets are not buried intact. The animals are all cremated. At best, the cremains might be buried there, but it is not their pet's body they are placing flowers on - it's ashes. They need to conserve space out there for more ashes."

"And, that's another thing. People sometimes drop by with a dead animal and want it cremated and then to have the remains placed in an urn or box they can bring home and put on the mantle, and they think those ashes are really their pets. Well, they might be -

in part. What they do is just toss all the animals in during mass cremations and mix all the ashes up. It's much cheaper that way. They say they are doing private cremations, and charging the big bucks for them, but people are getting a bunch of mixed up ashes. The shelter figures, well, who is to know? And, anyway, it's the feeling that counts. Those people feel good about paying to have their pet up there on their mantle and they are none the wiser so who gets hurt?"

Paula stopped to catch her breath and take a sip of the huge Dunkin Donuts iced coffee she'd brought into the room with her. I wished I had one, too. I felt like I was going to cry and my throat was dry and tight with anger. I'd known all this in the back of my mind already. If I thought about all the ways a shelter might cheat the public and make some dirty money these would be the logical ways. And, Sherri had already informed me of the truth about the pet cemetery. This was just corroboration of her story.

But, the cold, cynical manner in which Paula was telling me all this was infuriating and frightening. She had a little glint in her eye the entire time she was talking that told me she was mocking me or enjoyed sickening me, just as childhood bullies had enjoyed horrifying me with animal abuse stories. My main thought was that Paula didn't really care at all about the animals. She didn't want to get revenge at the shelter because of their abuses. She was telling me all this for some other reason. But before I could work out that idea Paula interrupted my thoughts and continued.

She continued with vigor, "Then there's the small stuff. Like Harrington's peons get free use of the shelter vehicles for their personal use. In fact, those cars never get used for shelter business. They are just a good perk for shelter workers like Sherri's cousin Randy so they'll keep their mouths shut about what goes on at that place."

"I don't know what Randy did recently to piss Louis off though because I heard that he's gone. It must have been something pretty big because he really is needed there. That shelter never uses volunteers. Louis says it's because of liability issues but really it's because the fewer eyes the better as far as his business goes. It makes it hard to keep up the animals, even for the few days they are there, without any volunteers, though. But, the lack of help also gives him an excuse to kill more animals, especially the pit bulls. There's just a few staff and the board never sets foot in that place, ever.

"I know you love pit bulls because you came in and got that red one out, and it's a good thing you did because he was just about to die. In fact, no pit bull ever makes it out of that shelter alive. They don't admit it to the public because they don't want any breed-advocates coming down on them, but there is actually a policy in place, drafted by Louis, to never adopt out a pit bull or a pit bull mix. He's worried about dog bite liability, of course, so that policy extends to rotties, and German shepherds, and dobermans and any other dog that winds up on an insurance breed ban list, even chihuahuas."

"Harrington is building a huge new shelter in a more rural area nearby. It's very beautiful - very pristine. They say they are doing this so they can house more animals comfortably and euthanize fewer of them, but I doubt it. I think it's just a big land grab. They'll host some huge fundraising parties in that place, no doubt. It's on some prime land that's just starting to be developed by local medical groups around here, so I'm pretty sure that later on Louis can sell the place and really cash in. He will make a killing from that property in more ways than one."

Paula laughed at her own little joke and the sound was chilling. The cocky, mocking tone of her voice told me she didn't have any compassion for the sad animals that died at that shelter, and really no regrets about whatever part she played in the mass killings and deceptions, which I guessed was a large one.

The nasty shelter sounded like a concentration camp for animals and Paula was one of the high-ranking soldiers who was now confessing, perhaps as vengeance against her superiors for some grudge, but she enjoyed the power of killing and probably would miss it at Hidden Falls. Hidden Falls would remain a true no-kill shelter despite any efforts by Paula to change it. I knew that Hector, the board and volunteers were stronger than Paula. But, at that moment she was getting a vicarious thrill by shocking me and seeing how upset I was at her recital.

Thankfully, Paula was starting to wind down as she said, "About that new shelter building - they are starting a big fundraising push for it now. All the old bats will pull out their wallets and will cough up plenty to pay for it so Louis can profit. Maybe they are all in together, but I doubt it. Most of them have so much money that they don't have to think about where it goes. They are old money and have always had it, but Louis hasn't. He's had to scrape and fight for his little chunk of the pie and he doesn't care how he gets it as long as gets to keep it."

"So, I guess you really hate the guy," I said finally, alarm bells going off in my brain. I knew Paula wanted to use me to get some sort of revenge against Louis

Harrington. I was having a hard time thinking of him as anything other than a character in a novel or movie. But, in reality, I didn't believe people were such simple black and white character studies.

Maybe Harrington really did believe he was performing some public health service by removing excess animals from the streets. Maybe he or someone in his family had been injured by a stray animal. Maybe he, like other shelter workers I'd met, believed that the peace of death was a preferable alternative to a life of struggle for an unwanted pet.

Or, most likely, he was dishonest and was abusing the trust of generous people, but was playing just within the boundaries of the law and not much could be done to stop him. Unfortunately, anyone could open a shelter and call it a humane society or any other such name and do pretty much what they wanted to as long, as they stayed within the very wide boundaries of state regulations. If I could find proof that Harrington was practicing outside of the regulations, I could report him but I didn't hear anything in Paula's recital to indicate that. He was simply operating a high-kill animal shelter and engaging in some deceptive marketing practices.

"Yeah, I do hate him," said Paula. "And, you know what I hate most? I hate that all that money going to that new shelter that those old ladies and nice people think is going to help the cute animals. That money could be coming here to Hidden Falls, a place that really deserves it, and certainly needs it."

Paula's last remark hit home. I couldn't disagree with that. It was simply infuriating. The constant fundraisers that the Hidden Falls board put on - the pornographic hypnotist party, the bake sales, the dog walks, the festival booths, the endless little events that were so much work to put together had to be undertaken just to scrape together enough funds to keep this shelter going from month to month by good people who loved animals but weren't wealthy or connected – they weren't enough to support the Hidden Falls for long if they wanted to remain no-kill.

Hector worked very hard to rehabilitate dogs with serious behavioral problems - until they could be adopted to someone perfectly suited to their temperaments. A huge portion of Hidden Fall's funds was spent on veterinary care, and while not perfect, the best efforts were made to treat and make careful decisions about the sick and injured animals that came to the shelter. Hidden Falls had dozens of volunteers to walk and entertain the animals, knowing the animals needed constant companionship to avoid kennel stress.

The first idea at Hidden Falls was always about

saving the most animals while giving them the best possible care. Everyone at Hidden Falls took that responsibility seriously, or was let go quickly, like Melissa. It was heartbreaking that a huge shelter run by greedy privileged people could rake in so much money in donations while a truly decent shelter like Hidden Falls should constantly struggle at the brink of existence.

"Okay," I said to Paula finally. "What do you think I can do?'

"Just write about this," she said. "Write to the papers, or to your friends, or just get the information out there somehow. Like I said, I can't do it. Harrington will come down on me hard. But, what have you got to lose?"

I agreed to consider writing something to try to get some concerned animal people on board to challenge Harrington. There's safety in numbers I thought. I took Ricky for a walk around the Hidden Falls grounds before I drove home and thought even more. Finally, before I went to bed, I sat at my computer and composed an email to send to the people I knew in the area who were active in animal rescue or welfare and might be concerned or outraged at what was happening to the animals at the hands of Harrington.

I listed all the key points that I found concerning

in Paula's narrative. I didn't add my own opinion or any assumptions. I just ended my appeal to those who had lived and worked in the area for a long time to make suggestions as to what could possibly be done to rectify the depressing situation and to help the animals that were unfortunate enough to fall into the care of Harrington's shelter.

When I finished the email I sent it out to a large email group. I felt a huge sense of relief seeing the words and the message sent on the screen. I felt cleansed by sending the email off. It helped wash away the taint of evil I'd felt ever since I sat in that tiny room next to Paula and listened to her sickening stories. Then I went to bed and fell asleep unburdened, listening to Mark's and Ricky's synchronous snoring.

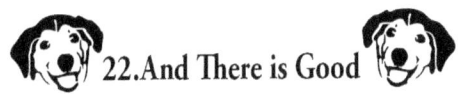

22. And There is Good

The next day I drove to work through misty back roads bathed in late fall rust and mustard yellow colors. I left the house before seven in the morning to allow at least an hour to get to my eight o'clock class and the sun was just starting to send out beams above the trees and dot the roadways with patches of light. When I was almost to the little college town of Bridgewater, I heard my phone ring. I dug it out of my bag frantically because nobody ever called that early unless it was bad news.

My first thought was that there was an emergency of some kind at home: something had happened to Mark or one of our dogs, maybe Hawkins was fighting with Ricky! Or maybe there was a crisis of some kind at school. But, that hardly seemed possible on such a brilliant fall morning. I found my phone with shaky fingers. Happily, I didn't recognize the number but I tentatively said "Hello."

A deep, throaty unfamiliar voice boomed out of the phone into the car, "What the hell do you think you are doing? Who the hell do you think you are?"

The voice shattered the tranquil state I was in after the hour-long commute on back roads, and the angry words shocked me wide awake. I sat up straight and tried to steer my truck into the campus parking lot while holding the phone on my shoulder which put the hateful voice closer to my ear. I had an idea who the owner of voice was, but my mind was still in early morning mode and not ready for a confrontation. I hoped that it was a prank call.

"This is Louis Harrington," shouted the voice, "And, you have been sending defamatory, incendiary emails out about me and I want it to stop. Now! And, I want a retraction, a written retraction, signed by you and sent out by registered mail to all of those people on your little email list this week and sent back to me by registered post, or I will sue you!"

I was horrified that Harrington was calling me only a few hours after I sent out my emailing. All of the people on my animal-rescue list were people I trusted because they cared about animals. Again I'd been stupid. I called those people my friends but I didn't know most of them very well at all. I was naïve to think that everyone who cared about animals would be sympathetic to my email. This region was one big small town. Someone on my list must have been on friendly terms with Harrington, and decided to inform him of my emailing.

"How did you get my name and number?" I asked the voice.

"Never mind how I got your information. That is my business. Your business is to make this right! I understand that you probably didn't mean for this to happen. I think you probably mean well and love animals and are just kind of stupid. But, you don't know me at all! I do know who put you up to that letter. It was that bitch Paula who now works at Hidden Falls."

The raspy voice continued, "I don't give a shit about you or what you think because you are just a volunteer. But, Paula works in this business and if she is talking about me or about my shelter I am going to sue her! She is the one I really want, and that is your way out of this problem. After you send a nice retraction letter to everyone on your list, I want you to come into my office and sign a paper stating that Paula told you everything that you wrote, and then I am going to use your letter to sue the bitch."

I can, in most situations, control my temper and not reveal much about my feelings to strangers, but the few times when I lose it, just like my father, I explode. Listening to Louis's bullying voice and thinking about all the poor animals he selfishly deprived of their lives over so many years made me feel a hot flash of rage that made me reckless.

I shouted back into the phone, "Look. Don't you ever call me again. I will never sign any kind of paper coming from you. And, I will not send out a retraction letter to anyone. Because I think everything I wrote is true! I know it is true! And, I hope someday someone finds out all about you and your sleazy shelter and that you end up in prison, you evil scumbag."

I shut off my phone and walked across the pastoral campus of classical brick buildings and autumnal trees.

I was shaking from head to toe. The brick buildings in the mist of the morning sun and the red and yellow trees were in such dramatic contrast to the violent voice on the phone I felt as if I'd dreamed up the entire conversation. I went through the motions of teaching my classes and left my phone off all day.

When I returned to my truck in the afternoon I turned on my phone again and was horrified to see dozens of messages - all from the same number - all from Harrington. He must have picked up his phone every quarter hour to leave me a nasty threatening message. I felt my nerves tingling as I clicked on the first one. It was as nasty and irrational sounding as his voice was in person. Why was I letting this guy scare me so much? He sounded truly crazy.

And, what could he possibly do to me over a simple conversational email? The situation seemed surreal, but I had brought this upon myself. I was warned by both Paula and Sherri that this man was irrational and would stop at nothing to protect his façade of respectability.

I listened to every message on my way home. Each one had basically the same content, beginning with a greeting of "You bitch!" Every message was a threat to sue me if I didn't write an immediate retraction to my email. The final two messages started to sound less like legal threats and more like promises of physical violence.

    I always bring my German shepherd, Billy, to work with me so I can walk him in the state forest on my way home. I wondered if Harrington was so demented that he'd follow me and try to hurt us if we went for a walk. Billy was good protection, but I was worried now. I was worried about my dogs and my house and my husband. Harrington sounded nastier than any person I'd encountered in my life.

    Billy was sitting up and alert to my stress in the back seat of my truck. Billy was one of those dogs that preferred to be in a truck than any other place in the world, except for romping through a forest. But that day I decided to forgo our hike and stop by Sherri's on the way home. Billy could run around in her big fenced yard while we talked.

    When we arrived at the kennel, Sherri was hosing out the dog runs in her overalls and Wellington boots. The boots were so huge that she looked like a little girl playing dress up in her father's work clothes. Tiny as she was, Sherri could get more physical labor done in one day than anyone else I knew. I thought while watching Sherri that Harrington had no excuse for claiming he was too short of staff to maintain his shelter properly. Sherri could manage her kennel fairly well all by herself.

"Hey there!" called Sherri in a knowing voice that told me she'd already heard gossip about the Harrington email.

"How are you doing?" she asked. "Has that bastard caught up with you yet?"

I told her about Harrington's phone messages, then let her listen to some of them.

"Wow! Didn't I tell you he was crazy? Pure psycho!"

"Well, do you really think he can do anything to me? I mean he can call and harass me all he likes and I'll just keep getting my number changed. But, has he actually hurt anybody? I can't even believe I'm asking this over a stupid email, but do you think he'd try to do something to my dogs or me? I don't believe he'd get anywhere suing me for writing an email, especially if everything it in is true."

"I don't know," said Sherri, "But this morning he asked you to turn over that woman Paula to him, or to sign something saying that she told you all that stuff about the shelter, right? Well, if I were you, I'd do it! She's a real piece of work anyway - a real loser. Sign whatever it is he wants you to sign and give him Paula, just so he'll leave you alone."

I badly wanted to do just that. Harrington

destroyed the serenity of my favorite season; the peaceful drive to the college, my walks with Billy in the autumn woods. I didn't want this beautiful season to be filled with stress about lawsuits and fear of being bullied by a crazy lawyer. I wanted to turn time back a day and return to my peaceful life.

But, I'd sent that email blast out for a reason. And, I felt so much peace-of-mind after sending it that I fell right into a deep sleep. I felt strongly that it had been the right thing to do. And, I couldn't take it back now. I did believe all that Paula told me was true. If I cared, if just a few of the local animal-rights advocates I'd sent it to were concerned, then we needed to take these facts and finally do something about that sham shelter. Otherwise, what were we really doing in animal rescue? Without action, we were just talking about animal rights and doing some volunteer work to make us feel good about ourselves.

"I can't do that," I replied slowly. "As much as I dislike Paula, and feel that she is up to something more than outing Harrington and his shelter, I feel we need to take a stand here. I mean this is an awful situation. It's bad for the animals, obviously, but it's bad for the entire community. If we don't do something about a place so dishonest and abusive to animals, right here in our own community, what good are we?"

"Well, I'm with you in spirit," said Sherri. "But, I can't be involved in anything you choose to do going forward. Even if Harrington knew you were here talking with me, he hates you so much now; he'd come down on me about the easement and loan. He knows how to get at people and silence them. He sizes everyone up and knows what we value, and what we have to lose, and he will threaten it.

"Everyone is always too afraid to do anything when Harrington is involved. You'll see. All those other animal-people are afraid of him, too. There are one or two others who have tried to take him on and one doesn't live here any longer and one lost her job. You'll be lucky if you get anyone to help you in this."

I felt hurt at the lack of support from Sherri. I felt angry and very alone as I rounded up Billy and drove home. I was disappointed that Sherri was more worried about her real estate issues than about all the animals that were needlessly put to death at Harrington's shelter. I started to feel a little regret about sending the email. The other animal-people probably thought I was a nut, or a troublemaker, or an outsider who was too stupid to know better than to take on an entrenched local crony.

Worst of all, people were probably going to be angry that I'd included their email addresses openly on a big list without concealing the recipients. I'd been careless. Probably some of the animal-people would also feel like suing me for bringing Harrington's attention their way. And, I wondered which one of them had ratted me out by forwarding the email to him.

When I was almost at my driveway my phone rang. I was afraid to answer it, seeing that it was another unfamiliar number. I thought maybe Harrington was trying to reach me from another phone to trick me into answering. I picked it up gingerly as if it was hot. An unfamiliar female voice spoke. She identified herself as Meg Minsky, a local dog trainer who volunteered at working with problem dogs at various shelters including Hidden Falls. She and her husband owned a beautiful Victorian bed and breakfast overlooking the ocean near to the exclusive gated community where Sherri told me Louis Harrington lived.

"Hey," said Meg cheerfully, "I got your little email last night. I bet you've had an earful already today, huh? I've talked to a bunch of animal people about it already and there are some who wish you hadn't sent it, but most of us agree that now you've done it, we need to finally do something about the situation. We all know about that awful shelter and can guess what goes on there but we've been afraid to rake up the coals. But, now your email is out there, and it all rings true, so it may be finally be time to step up and do something."

I told Meg all about the frightening phone call and messages of the morning. It was a relief to have someone sympathetic to talk with about it all, especially someone who was laughing and sounded strong and wasn't shaking in her boots at the mention of Harrington's name. I thought that maybe since Meg lived near his neighborhood she felt more at ease speaking about him; he was a known entity to her in her social circles, and his money and prestigious address didn't frighten her into submission.

"Don't worry," said Meg comfortingly. "Harrington is an old blowhard. He's all bark. I don't think he can do a thing to you for writing that email, especially if everything in it is true. It's not just your opinion, so it can't be called slander. A former employee blew the whistle on him and you are just reporting it. And, even if he tries to sue you for libel, he won't, because he knows everything you wrote is true. You can't sue for libel over telling the truth."

Meg continued, "What we need to do now is to get some proof about all the issues you listed in that email. For one, so we can protect you from getting sued, and two, so we can write the kind of letters we need to write to the state to take him down once and for all. And, I've already got some ideas."

"There are some of us that want to form a committee, an informal group, to address the issues at that shelter. So, if you'd like to join us we can meet somewhere neutral, not at a shelter like Hidden Falls, which Louis could go after if he knew we were meeting there. Actually, we may as well meet at my house. There's nothing Harrington can do to Jack and me. Besides, Jack is an attorney as well, which is good because we may all wind up needing his services. Ha ha!"

Over the next month, our little committee of shelter volunteers, private animal rescuers, dog trainers, and veterinarians met on Tuesday evenings in Meg and Jack's bow-windowed living room overlooking a rocky cliff and wild stretch of ocean. The stunning natural surroundings made the sad topic of the meetings more bearable and yet more poignant. Meg and Jack's spoiled golden retrievers snoozing on a pad in front of the fireplace were such a contrast to the animals locked in the lonely cages of Harrington's death camp shelter. Eventually, at Meg's suggestion, we were able, using the Freedom of Information Act, to acquire euthanasia records from every town

Harrington's shelter did business with over the last five years.

The records bore out the stories told to me by Paula. The shelter brought in hundreds of animals each year. Many were killed outright. Many were transferred to local high-kill shelters and were most likely killed there. A few cats and dogs - less than one percent of the total intake - were adopted to new owners. Many just disappeared and weren't accounted for in any paperwork. All the expensive, glossy newspaper advertisements put out by Louis and his cronies were deceptive or just outright lies. The non-profit was not operating as a shelter. It was just a big euthanasia facility and a for-profit crematorium.

No efforts were made to rehabilitate animals or to contact rescue organizations that might help them. None of the donor money was put towards vet expenses for the animals as stated. Clearly, the donations, which totaled millions each year, were going straight into Harrington's and his confederates' pockets. And, I wondered if Paula was ever a recipient of any of that dirty money.

We took all our facts and wrote up a document to send to the board of directors of Harrington's shelter. We stated facts about euthanasia rates, adoption rates, and expenditures that we thought they might not be aware of. We would give them a month to make changes in policy at the shelter. If no substantial changes were made in shelter policies and advertising propaganda, we would send our letter, plus the package of documents we'd compiled from local towns, to the state Attorney General's office.

All throughout the month of these meetings, Harrington had been calling me daily. Soon, I stopped answering the phone. Meetings with Meg and the others gave me an outlet to talk about Harrington's phone harassment and, instead of being a source of fear when listening alone, the crazy rants became a source of fun when I played them back for the group and we'd all laugh hysterically. Unintentionally, Harrington was bringing some much-needed humor to meetings that could have been very depressing.

The letters went out to the board. There were a few people at the meetings that had misgivings; they were frightened or felt that when the information became public people would distrust all animal shelters and donations would drop. But, in spite of the doubts, twelve letters went out and then everything was silent for a while. Even Harrington's phone calls stopped. It was eerie. We thought we might get a phone call or two from the board members, but we heard nothing at all.

We decided to discontinue the weekly meetings until we got some kind of response to the letters. If we didn't hear anything from anyone associated with the shelter within two months we'd send out our letter and packet of corroborating reports to the Attorney General and Massachusetts Department of Agriculture.

I went back to my weekly routine of teaching, walking in the woods with my own dogs and those at Hidden Falls. I missed the activist meetings. They afforded me the first opportunity I'd had to really talk with some of the other animal rescue activists around here and for the first time, I really felt a part of a strong community.

I was heading out one Saturday to walk with Billy in the fading maple and ash forest behind the university where Mark taught. On the way to the van, I saw Harrington's number pop on my phone. It had been more than two months since he'd left that torrent of ugly messages for me. As soon as I saw his number I realized that Harrington had become more than a constant uncomfortable presence always lurking in the back of my mind. He was an insidious illness like the tickling feeling in the back of my throat that warned me I was about to get my usual end-of-the-semester bout of influenza.

Harrington's guttural voice spewed out a paranoid and convoluted rant. He didn't stop once to check if I was still listening. He shouted, "You bitch. You fucking little bitch! You've really done it this time. You formed a group. A group! You formed a group with other animal people to plot against me, to talk behind my back about things that are none of your business, to look into things that are none of your business. Well, I can only think that it's all a plot among you to take my shelter down because you are jealous of our fundraising abilities, and you would like to have all that money for yourselves wouldn't you? Well, whatever your little group is planning, you all are in big trouble because you have a group looking into my shelter and writing things about it that are slanderous, do you hear? Forming a group is dissent!"

"And, I am going to sue all of you now. And, because I know you are a volunteer at Hidden Falls you must be operating as a representative for them. And, they took some of our animal control contracts away from us. That is a stable yearly fee for us and you stole it. Well, you committed slander with a profit motive and now you and your shelter and your group are all going to pay me back. You just wait. I am going to sue all of you."

I finally managed to a get few words out and said,

"Hidden Falls got good contracts because they are a good and decent animal shelter, and the citizens will get better services and the animals will get better treatment."

"You are such a self-righteous bunch, aren't you?" he replied nastily. "You should hear some of the stories I could tell you about those people in your little group. And, worst of all is that bitch you work with, Paula. She probably told you that she cares so much for the animals and that is why she quit working for me. Well, guess what? She has you duped and you are obviously very gullible. That little bitch tried to blackmail me. She told me she'd tell people all sorts of lies about my shelter if I didn't give her a higher salary. So, I fired her! And, being so stupid, you let her trick you into getting her revenge against me."

Harrington continued, "Well, everything she told you is a lie and you and your group put her lies into print and sent it to my board. When you did that you crossed the line. I am going to sue you."

Harrington's threatening diatribe sounded disconnected and incoherent, as if he'd been drinking all morning. But, I was worried. Instead of going for a nice hike in the woods with Billy, I turned around and drove over to Meg's house. On the way, I drove past the entrance gate to Harrington's Rocky Point enclave.

It was so peaceful and bucolic with weathered gray homes with white shell-strewn driveways. I wondered if Harrington was sitting in one of those expensively quaint houses right now, fuming and plotting his revenge against me and the group.

Meg listened to my recital of the one-sided phone conversation then said, "I hate to say it, but maybe it is time you found yourself a lawyer. Can I have Jack recommend one? He doesn't want to get involved himself, but he could point you to a good one. The problem here is that Paula might not have been entirely honest with you. It sounded as if she was on board with helping us and telling the truth, and she may be, but if there is one little area of untruth in all this it might just be better to be protected. Also, I don't think you, or any of us, should be talking with Harrington in person any longer. You need a professional go-between."

I considered having Jack recommend a lawyer, but when I got home I decided to find my own. I didn't want to bring more trouble to the local animal people. Also, I thought it might be better to find a lawyer that was outside of the local area in which Harrington had the most political power. I went to the computer to search for lawyers in Providence, Rhode Island. But, what sort of lawyer would take on a case like this? I didn't have any prior experience with lawyers other than to close on our house and to write our wills.

At last my Internet searches unearthed an advertisement for a lawyer that specialized in representing corporate whistleblowers. I was a stand-in whistleblower for Paula. I left a message on the lawyer's phone and tried to enjoy the rest of my weekend with Mark and the dogs.

The following Monday, I had an appointment in Providence to meet the whistleblower lawyer. His office was on the second floor of a brick building with a clothing store on the first, in a trendy area of coffee shops surrounded by schools and universities. I walked up old and very creaky stairs to an office that looked similar to my art studio in an old mill building. The ceilings were high and peeling and the floor was of roughly polished old wood. There were two lonely, worn leather sofas in the empty waiting area. I sank into one and picked up a year-old gardening magazine from a little table and waited nervously.

A middle-aged man with a head of curly gray hair emerged from a doorway and waved me inside. Sitting at a table in another high-ceiling oversized room was a blonde woman that the lawyer introduced as his daughter and law partner. The lawyer's name was Angus Kelly and he asked me to just call him Angus.

His daughter's name was Abby and she said kindly that she was available any time clients need to talk when Angus was in court and unavailable and to please call her any time I needed, then she walked out of the room. I felt comfortable in the funky old office that was more like an artist's studio than the glass and metal corporate space I had expected.

    I told Angus about the events of the last couple months and let him listen to some of Harrington's messages on my phone. He laughed but looked serious when he said, "I think the man sounds demented." Angus had never heard of Harrington in a professional capacity, which was a relief to me because it proved that he had much less influence and power than he liked to brag about. I paid Angus a five-hundred-dollar retainer and left him to write a cease-and-desist letter instructing Harrington not to call me anymore and to communicate only through Angus or Abby. Angus said he'd call as soon as he heard from Harrington, especially if it seemed likely he was going to file a defamation suit.

    A few days later I answered the phone and heard Angus' friendly voice laughing nervously, "Oh my god, what kind of enemy have you made in this guy, Harrington? He's been calling me every half-hour every day since he got my letter. He sounds really nuts.

We should probably talk about this in person."

It was clear that Harrington was going to do anything but cease-and-desist. I wondered what kind of revenge this evil lawyer had in store for me. Could he sue successfully and take our house? We didn't have much savings. Could he take our retirement accounts? I wished I'd never allowed Paula's stories to anger me so much that I sent out that group email. I felt manipulated and reckless but I knew that at the core of the stories was truth, and that innocent animals were suffering horribly because of greed and selfishness. I wanted to fight.

When I got to Providence, Angus and Abby told me that Harrington couldn't sue successfully unless anything I'd written in the original email or the letter to the board was untrue, and resulted in direct financial harm to Harrington or his shelter. As a backup to Paula, Sherri's cousin Randy had agreed to testify to his experiences at the shelter. Angus contacted Paula the day before and, as expected, she wanted nothing to do with the case going forward and would say no more. I was angry at myself for believing that Paula cared a bit for the suffering of the shelter animals. I was scared, but felt exhilarated that at last the truth was finally going to come out about that awful shelter.

I went home and waited, working half-heartedly on artwork or planning my classes and taking my dogs for long, anxiety-fueled walks. The week passed slowly and I didn't hear from Angus and, thankfully, my phone wasn't ringing with abusive messages from Harrington. I hoped that he had decided I was just a small fish and would leave me alone. The next day Angus called and told me that Harrington was going to go through with his defamation suit.

Once again, I drove past the swampy marshlands to Providence. Angus was there alone at the big table and had a stack of papers piled up in front of him.

He said, "Harrington says he really doesn't want to sue you. What he wants is to sue Paula because he thinks she is putting you up to all this. Either way, it feels a little like blackmail to me. I do think everything that Paula told you is likely the truth and I'm guessing that there is much worse that happens at that shelter that both of them want to cover up. Otherwise, how could Paula attempt to blackmail Harrington in the first place?

"But, I don't think I'm exaggerating when I say that these people are dangerous. Their behavior - their manner on these phone calls - is way over the top for the situation. I don't want to see you get hurt, and I don't mean financially. I don't know what Harrington has going on behind the scenes, but my recommendation to you is to sign these papers stating that Paula told you everything you wrote. Throw her to Harrington and get these crazy people off your back."

I wanted to do that very badly, and especially to feel the freedom of not having the constant dark threat of Harrington looming over me. I didn't care a bit about Paula, but I felt turning her over to him would be an easy way out for Harrington. After a month of empowering committee meetings, signing the papers against Paula would enable Harrington to go back to his old tricks and continue to exploit all those terrified animals in his death camp. Our group of activists hadn't worked so hard drafting those letters to just take the easy way out and agree to an enforced silence.

"No," I said to Angus. "I won't sign those papers."

"Well, I respect that. I feel bad for the animals, too. Harrington is a sad excuse for a lawyer, that's for sure! We'll do what we need to do when the time comes. Don't worry. In the unlikely case things continue on to court we'll work something out with the fees and I'll be happy to meet with your committee of animal friends."

Meg called as I was driving home and said the group was having an emergency meeting that evening.

Sherri must have told someone on the committee about what was going on with Harrington. I hadn't talked about it with anyone but Sherri and Angus and I was starting to feel worried by the silence of the group members after the Board letters went out. I badly needed their support.

My worries were relieved that evening when Meg and the group announced that they'd been talking the past week and decided to pool their money and to organize a fundraiser to help me pay for my legal expenses.

I hated the thought of going to court to face Harrington, only because the daily stress was so unbearable. But, as Meg and Jack pointed out, going to court would be the best thing for the shelter animals. The truth would come out in court in a very public forum and the exposure would force a policy change. Jack doubted that Harrington could successfully sue any of us for libel but the exposure of a court case could spell the end of Harrington's death camp.

The next day I was shocked to see Harrington's number pop up on my phone. I knew I shouldn't answer it, but I had an impulse to hear what he had to say.

"You are not supposed to be calling me," I said before he had a chance to say anything.

"Look," he said. "I don't want things to go this way. I really don't want to sue you. I just want Paula. But, I really want you to see something. I want you to come and take a tour of our beautiful new shelter building. This is what we've been working and saving for all these years - to get this building done. I don't want any trouble right before we move into our new space. We can do so much more for the animals there. You'll see what I mean when you see it. Please come and meet me there tomorrow and I'll show you around. Don't you think we should finally meet face to face anyway?"

Harrington's forced laughter was frightening. But, I was curious about the new building. We'd been talking about it during the committee meetings. And, I didn't want Harrington to think I was afraid to meet him.

When I called Sherri and told her I was going to meet with Harrington she shouted, "Don't go over there alone. Are you crazy? I told you that guy is a psycho. He's a wharf rat. He's mafia!"

I laughed. Sherri sounded so paranoid. Harrington's voice that day sounded reasonable and controlled. Maybe he was really ready to put things behind us. His offer to give me a tour of the shelter sounded like a peace offering. I'd do anything to get back to my peaceful life prior to this crisis.

Later I spoke with Meg and she too was alarmed that I was thinking about meeting Harrington alone. She offered to meet us both at the shelter. But, I had the feeling that Harrington wanted to talk alone and might be antagonized or threatened if I brought someone along with me, especially Meg.

And, I thought, what could really happen? I was going over there in the middle of the day. There would probably be construction workers around. I'd just meet with him for an hour. I hoped the meeting meant the end of the looming lawsuit and the unbearable stress.

As I pulled into the parking lot and looked at a magnificent new shelter building-in-progress, I thought about what Sherri and Meg had told me about the shelter being a real-estate grab by Harrington. If so, he certainly would be making a killing on this place. The architecture was open and airy with wide glass windows rising two stories high. The wide surroundings were lush and carefully planted with a variety of shrubs and beach grasses surrounding a pastoral rock garden and pond. The landscaping looked like the entrance to Rocky Neck. I saw a squat man in his sixties waiting in the doorway.

To my surprise Harrington was shorter than me by more than a couple of inches. Judging from his voice I expected him to be so tall he'd loom over me. He was short but his body was very wide and very muscled. He had thick gray hair and uncanny light blue eyes. He extended a hand out to me and I took it. All of a sudden, I was reminded of Sherri telling me that Harrington was a wharf lawyer. I'd expected the smooth handshake of a professional person, but Harrington's hand was huge and beefy and as rough as sandpaper, as if he'd spent his life wrangling ship's ropes, not paperwork and computers. His hand completely enclosed mine in a very powerful grip.

"Come on inside," he said.

We walked through the glass doors and I looked around, noting that there didn't seem to be anyone else in the place. Our shoes echoed on the tiled floor. I tried to laugh off my nervousness because I just couldn't believe that Harrington would risk doing me actual physical harm. We wandered through the brand new dog runs. They were much wider, lighter and cleaner than the damp, dark runs at the old shelter.

Meg told me to keep an eye out for the euthanasia rooms and to count how many I could see, but Harrington conveniently avoided those sad spaces. Finally, we walked out of the building and into a large fenced in grassy area that he told me would be used to exercise the dogs and to hold training classes.

"You see?" He said. "This place will be very different from the old place. The city would never let us expand or change. Now, we are out of the city. We can do whatever we want. Don't you think this is a beautiful place?"

"It depends on what you do with it," I replied. "Why will having a big modern shelter building change any of your policies?"

"You listen too much to Meg Minsky and the other people in your group. They have never liked me or my shelter and they'll hate me more now that I have this huge space. I have so much room here that I can take in all the cats and dogs in the area. There won't be any leftovers for the others."

I thought that was a bizarre way to talk about the unfortunate creatures that ended up in the shelter system - as if animal rescuers were fighting over deliveries of used cars. I suddenly felt trapped and panicky and I told Harrington that I needed to get home.

"Wait a minute," he said gruffly, with the familiar-sounding voice of the threatening messages. "I want you to know that I called over to Hidden Falls and had a little talk with some of the board members. I thought that they should know that using you as an agent, and then attacking me through those emails, well…that makes them liable for your actions. You are a volunteer there; you see? And you were volunteering at Hidden Falls when you wrote those terrible things about my shelter. Then Hidden Falls suddenly got my animal control contracts and that cost me money. Well, guess what? I can sue Hidden Falls just like I can sue you. Why don't you just make things easy. Go back to your lawyer and sign the papers and give me Paula."

I felt sick with anxiety at the quick turn in the conversation. How could he dare to threaten Hidden Falls? I didn't conspire with anybody there to steal any contracts. And, that money was probably just peanuts to Harrington. He didn't need it if he could afford to build this gleaming new shelter. He was just being spiteful. I looked around in a panic for a gate in the fence and found one. I started for the parking lot as fast as I could. I wanted to get far away from that beefy, corrupt wharf rat.

When I got back to my truck I was shaking and breathless. Harrington's light eyes gleamed cruelly in the distance as I shakily unlocked the door. I felt lucky to be safely locked in my truck. My phone rang and it was Andrea, the chair of the board at Hidden Falls.

"I don't want to cave to this creep Harrington," she said wearily, "but he's been calling us all day and threatening to sue us. I don't know if he can, or if he's just talking crap, but we can't take any chances right now. We just got the new contracts and we worked so hard to build our new shelter. I feel I have to do what he says. I hate to lose you because you've been a good volunteer and a good friend, but I have to let you go and get this guy off our backs. I'm so sorry but I really wish you'd never started this thing."

    I drove home in tears. I couldn't process the loss I felt at being fired from volunteering at Hidden Falls. In spite of all the hot dirty work and the sadness of the plight of some of the animals, that shelter had become an alternate family for me for many years. I couldn't imagine not stopping there on my way home from work to walk the dogs in the woods with Berta and the other volunteers. I'd miss Hector and his dog training classes. I thought back to the old Quonset hut and to Bliss and how her sarcasm and toughness had lifted me out of a deep depression. How right Sherri had been. Harrington would find a way to hurt his enemies in the most painful way possible. He'd robbed me of my family.

    The next morning Angus called and was excited with the news that Harrington called and told him that he'd decided to drop the defamation suit. I was shocked, but still too sad about Hidden Falls to feel much relief. And, I'd started to look forward to the day we could expose Harrington in court. Angus said it was probably all just a nasty bluff. Harrington was probably never planning on suing me or anyone else. He just wanted to torture me and silence our group of animal activists. He'd had his revenge and then he quickly lost interest. And, what did all the trouble amount to? Weeks and months of stress, all for nothing. That new shelter would take in even more animals only to kill them. There seemed to be nothing we could do about it.

Angus told me that in order for Harrington to drop his libel suit he'd insisted that I sign a gag order requiring that I not to write or say anything about his shelter for three years. Feeling defeated, I drove again to Providence to sign the paper.

Months later when the snow was falling and I was spending my afternoons walking my dogs around our neighborhood, I answered a phone call from Meg.

"I thought you'd want to know," she said, "I visited a friend over at Rocky Neck this morning and found out that Harrington is gone. Gone! Do you believe it? He and his wife, they just up and sold their house and left for Florida! And, you won't believe this; he gave up his board position and sold the ownership of that brand new shelter. I can't believe it! He literally didn't say a word to anyone until it was a done deal.

He just packed up and left!

"The new shelter is being taken over by a different rescue group. A good one! Isn't that amazing! I know some of the new board members and we've talked. I'm even thinking of joining them! There will be new policies, less euthanasia, active adoption advertising and training classes and they'll even adopt out pit bulls. Isn't this great? Isn't this amazing? We did it. We changed that awful place."

I was overwhelmed with happiness. It was wonderful and unexpected news. I'd resigned myself to the idea that Harrington would be a menacing presence in my life as long as we lived here. But, next I felt an overwhelming sense of exhaustion and sadness. The stress of the past year took a toll on my health. The fees to retain Angus had depleted our bank account. Worst of all, I'd lost a precious sense of community because I couldn't go back to Hidden Falls. The trust and goodwill between the board and myself had been destroyed.

But, I couldn't wait to call Sherri and tell her that Harrington was a fake - just like the Wizard of Oz - all bluff and bluster. He'd never try to tie a piece of concrete to my legs and sink me beneath a fishing boat! He'd been a master of negative public relations and had everyone running away terrified from him for all those years. He probably planted those rumors of his mafia connections so gullible people like Sherri would tremble and give in to his demands and spread more fear. But, Harrington still had a lien on Sherri's driveway, so she was especially happy that he was now living a thousand miles away.

But, why did he suddenly leave town? Maybe some of the rumors were true and someone else caught up with him. I think that the letter to the board sent out by Meg's committee may have made Harrington's neighborhood uncomfortable to live in. We'd never know for sure.

I only knew that I could go outdoors now and walk my dogs in the crisp winter weather without feeling the weight of an enemy living right around the corner. Best of all, that awful dark shelter that haunted the region for so many years was gone and torn down! And, that new beautiful shelter built by Harrington was not going to be a fancy crematorium. It was going to be run by an animal rescue group that actually cared about animals. Harrington and his shelter were gone at long last and the air in the city felt much cleaner.

23. The Cat House

The crazed feral cat leaped up to the windowsill and then somehow launched herself up even higher to the wood molding at the top of the window, dug her claws in hard and dangled there. Her tri-colored fur was sticking out and bristling, and she looked like one of the dried out puffer fish some of the beachy people around here like to dangle from their porches as decorations.

She swung back and forth and I couldn't tell if she was in pain or swinging joyously and taunting me. She had such incredible claw power that I thought she might dig her claws into the ceiling and propel herself across it.

I'd opened the top of the maternity crate barely an inch before the mother cat bashed through the small gap and on to my shoulder, using it as a launching pad while leaving a deep scratch on my shoulder down my chest. I hardly noticed the pain as I looked up and tried to figure out how to get the dangling cat down before she tore her claws out by the roots.

Just then Caroline popped her head through the closed door and let out an exclamation when she saw what had happened.

"Holy crap, I told you to put a blanket over the entire crate whenever you are opening it to feed the momma cats. They are all feral in here and they're phobic about being confined in a crate or anywhere indoors. They will do anything to get out of here, even kill themselves doing it, which would suck because we'll have a whole litter of babies to bottle feed for this momma if that happens."

"Sorry," I said a little tersely but didn't bother to mention to Caroline that she had never told to put a blanket over the crates when she asked me to come into the isolation room to feed and clean the cages housing the mom street cats and their kittens.

"Go on out and do the dishes," demanded Caroline. She'd asked me to come in to the feral room and feed the cats, which was her usual job, because she preferred to do the dishes. But, I didn't want to argue the point and left Caroline alone, armed with a blanket with which she was going to bag the crazed cat. Caroline knew how to expertly tie her up securely before she could become a thrashing ball of claws. The cat would be calmer if I left the room anyway.

I'd started volunteering at Hand-Me-Down-Cats soon after I was asked to leave Hidden Falls. I'd never planned to work at a cat-only shelter but I felt a need to distance myself from the neediness of stray dogs, and to avoid adding to the number of dogs in my pack at home. Mostly, I needed to put some distance between myself and the painful loss of my days spent at Hidden Falls.

I was less emotionally attached to cats and, at the

same time, I felt some healing from being around them since my mother had adored cats and always kept at least three in our house. Cats were her favorite companions throughout her life. When she was near death my brother and his wife worked hard to find her an assisted living apartment that would let her have her cats. They remained warmly pressed up by her side right up until the end, leaving my brother to distribute them among kindly cat-loving family members and friends.

I could volunteer here without temptation. There was no way I could bring a stray cat into a house of predatory dogs, but I could honor my mother's memory by helping the abandoned cats. Hundreds of cats filled the floors, hallways, windows, shelves, furniture and bathrooms of this old Victorian house a few blocks away from where we lived.

When I unlocked the front door at Hand-Me-Down-Cats the first thing I'd see was a big furry blanket coming at me in waves across the kitchen floor. The blanket would divide into pieces and become cats swirling around my legs, rubbing and murmuring, begging me to give them what they loved best in the world - canned cat food.

I'd go straight to the kitchen shelves and pull down some cans. At the sound of the pop tops another wave of cats would come rushing in and there would be cats covering the counters and any available surface in the kitchen, all pushing the others aside to get the best spot at the bowls.

Once in a while a spat would break out but nobody got hurt, and in general caring for cats seemed much less risky than dealing with multiple dogs, as long as I stayed in the main part of the cat shelter. The cats in the main rooms of the house were abandoned companion animals. They weren't feral like the cats in the back room. Feral cats could be nearly wild; people-hating and dangerous or just shy and looking for a place to hide.

The back room was filled with pregnant feral cats or feral mommas with litters of tiny kittens that had been trapped by volunteers. The cats came to the shelter to give birth and were kept until they weaned their babies. If the babies could be socialized they'd be adopted out. The mother cats would be spayed and inoculated, then let back outside in the same area in which they were trapped with the corner of one of their ears clipped for future identification.

Only rarely were the feral adults adopted out. Once they had returned to their wild nature most couldn't be tamed up, so they remained urban wild cats and once healthy were set free again. Shelter volunteers set out traps regularly for them so they could be inoculated for rabies and they fed the feral cats that were returned to the scraggy woods around the city dump.

The feral cats made me sad, and I tried to avoid the back room as much as possible. They also scared me to death. The new scar down my chest started to hurt in the kitchen and I saw it was bleeding through my white t-shirt. I grabbed some peroxide and braced for more pain as I poured it directly over the scratch and rubbed it into my shirt to remove the blood stain. I worried about getting scratched by the feral mommas because they were not inoculated for rabies until they had weaned their kittens.

I knew the thought of contracting rabies through this scratch would keep me awake at night even though the chances of the cat having it were slight as she'd been at the shelter for over three weeks. If she had the contagious stage of the disease she would surely be dead by now.

But, I'd still worry. There was no use in making a fuss about the scratch. Telling the shelter director might mean the death of the mother cat if she had to be tested for rabies and her kitten would be left without a nursing mother. I rubbed in some antibiotic ointment over the peroxide and tried to forget about the scratch which healed up eventually without incident.

The shelter director's name was Claire and I'd met her during the meetings we'd held at Meg Minsky's house about Harrington's shelter. She was a long-time townie and had heard horror stories about Harrington for years. She was sympathetic towards me and happy to have me working at Hand-Me-Down-Cats. I'd been uneasy about volunteering at another shelter after Hidden Falls, thinking people would worry that I'd bring politics, criticism or trouble to their shelters, but most of the animal-rescue people didn't seem to feel that way.

Claire was an aging hippie with long graying blonde hair she kept in a thick braid down her back. She was very tall and thin and walked with a perpetual stoop to her back as if she had spent her entire life trying to make herself less conspicuous by appearing shorter than she was. She had to bend her neck to move through some of the low doorways in this old house and the posture had become permanent.

I enjoyed Claire's company. She didn't have children either and these cats seemed to fulfill her need to nurture something, just as my dogs did for me. Also, she reminded me a bit of Bliss. She alternated her conversational tone between sarcastic smugness and maniacal altruism. I liked the shifts in her temper. I was used to this behavior because I grew up with it. I equated Claire's unpredictability with honesty. She wasn't holding anything back or trying to put on a show for me by changing her behavior to gain my approval. She just was who she was on any given day and she didn't much care what I thought anyway. I found her easy company.

One day when were together in the kitchen scrubbing the putty-like dried remains of wet cat food off the dishes, a knock came at the front door. I left Claire to continue with the dishes as I went to answer it. Hand-Me-Down-Cats was on a busy street, the lone residential house in an industrialized area, and we always kept the doors locked when we were cleaning or caring for the cats.

There were many straggly wanderers passing up and down this part of the road from a seedy hotel on one end to the gas station mini-marts on the other. The road between was strewn with spent lottery tickets, plastic bottles, and coffee cups. The cat shelter was a little haven of green grass with its rickety homey Victorian architecture and flowering perennial gardens in the midst of urban blight.

Behind the lacy curtains that obscured the door window, I could see three very large, burly men standing there jostling one another as they all tried to peep in at once. I thought about calling out to Claire but she would laugh at me if I was afraid to open the door without her. I felt my heart and breath race as I reached for the lock and flipped it up and turned the glass knob.

There were three large men standing on the front step of the porch and one more hidden behind them. Their clothes were filthy with grease and they smelled terrible but familiar – just like cat food.

"Hey, is Claire here right now?" one of them asked. I saw he was holding a scrawny, dirty orange striped cat in his arms. The other men reached around the man's side from time to stroke the head of the skinny orange cat.

"She's right here. I'll go get her," I said leaving the men standing at the open door but not inviting them in.

"Oh, hey Bob!" called Claire happily when she saw the men. "Come on in. Don't stand outside. What do you have with you?"

All four men pushed in through the small front door and clustered around the man holding the cat. They seemed so protective of the cat. The scene was touching and my fear disappeared. I felt silly for being so afraid of the men in the first place.

"This is Mr. Fishy," said Bob petting the cat

fondly. "We've been feeding him for the past month, but over the last few days he comes up but won't eat. We were worried he's sick so we thought we'd better bring him around here. I hope you don't mind."

"Nah. I don't mind. Here, let me see the poor guy." Claire gently lifted Mr. Fishy from the big man's arms and held him up in the air to look him over.

"He is terribly thin," commented Claire. "Has he always been this thin? He's probably got a parasite problem and also looks very dehydrated. His eyes don't look great either. It's good you brought him over. I'll keep him for a while and get some fluids into him and some antibiotics won't hurt until we can get him to the vet. Is that okay with all of you?"

The men looked sad at the thought of giving up their companion cat but they nodded as a group and turned to walk off the porch and down the road. Claire explained that the men were all garbage workers from the Durfee Landfill up the street - a vast grassy hillside dumping ground for most of the city waste.

The landfill was surrounded by an urban forest of scrappy trees and a filthy waterway filled with tires and blowing trash. Unfortunately, people also dropped off their unwanted pets, mainly cats, in the woods, foolishly thinking they were returning them to a pleasant life in nature.

Most of the cats eventually found their way to the Durfee Landfill, attracted by its distinctive fishy aroma. Some of the burly workers there, like the four who came to the door, were very fond of cats and fed and cared for the abandoned animals until their boss became upset at the daily distraction. Then the men would gather up all the cats they could hold and carry them down the road to Claire. Being a no-kill shelter, Hand-Me-Down-Cats was preferred by the men and their boss to calling city animal control, or bringing them to Harrington's city shelter where they thought in the past, as did most everyone else, the cats would just be killed.

"I didn't want to tell them, it would upset the guys so much, but I don't know if this one's going to make it," Claire said as she placed Mr. Fishy on the kitchen counter to look at him more closely.

"His eyes don't look good at all - kind of cloudy if you can see - and that's not a good sign in a younger cat. And he is young, probably only about a year old, though he looks so much older with his matted fur."

Mr. Fishy's fur was not just matted. It was encrusted with mud and something other sticky substance that looked like tar. Happily, Claire determined that it wasn't blood. Mr. Fishy did not seem to have any cuts or bites on him. The sticky stuff turned out to be oil and Claire thought Mr. Fishy had probably picked it up at one of the many mechanical shops over near the dump.

Maybe he was sleeping under the old cars. She hoped nobody had purposely dumped oil on him. We decided to wait until the next day to clean Mr. Fishy's fur so we didn't stress him out any more than we had to that day. Claire carefully placed him into a blanket-lined crate on the top of the counter and inserted a needle and line into his back leg for the intravenous fluids.

Mr. Fishy didn't struggle but lay down on his side and gave Claire that look I'd seen often in shelter cats and dogs, the direct, deep, peaceful gaze that communicated trust and gratitude, and relief to be in the hands of someone kind. Claire called the vet and made an appointment for her to come and visit the sickly cat the next day. The cost was higher for a shelter visit, but Claire preferred to have the vet make house calls if a cat was very ill to avoid the stress of a car ride.

In the days after Mr. Fishy arrived, I had meetings after work and was away from the shelter. When I returned and unlocked the kitchen door the usual flood of cats came rushing up to me but I didn't see the crate with Mr. Fishy in it on top of the counter. I looked around the house where there were plenty of crates sitting about with all sizes and colors of cat in them, but there was no sign of Mr. Fishy.

I sighed and thought the worst. It was horribly sad that people could think that dropping a cat off in the woods was a good solution to their pet-ownership problems. Poor Mr. Fishy must have contracted a pretty nasty parasite and just didn't get medical help fast enough. I was so sad. Mr. Fishy had seemed like an especially sweet cat.

I decided to get to work and deal with the feral cats first that day. My plan was to get them out of the way fast then do something more enjoyable like feeding and playing laser tag with the floor cats. That always got the entire crew exhausted. I braced myself to enter the feral cat room. The smell in there was overpowering.

This time I had a blanket with me to drop over the crates prior to opening to gates to pick up the food bowls and litter boxes. As I went from crate to crate I thought how cute each little pile of kittens looked nestled up against their wild mothers. I hoped they wouldn't inherit their mother's feral natures and that they would find nice homes.

As I was bending way over to reach a bowl at the far corner of one of the long crates I felt a hard slap on the side of my head and banged my head on the side of the metal grating as I stood up in shock. I thought the slap came from a human being who snuck in the room, possibly Caroline rudely correcting me for doing something wrong. But, strangely, nobody was in the room with me except the cats and they were all safely in cages.

Then I saw a glint of orange color in the patch of late afternoon sunshine that was warming a blanket laid on the top of a stack of crates. I looked closer and it was Mr. Fishy! He'd somehow sneaked into the room with the feral cats on an earlier shift and got locked in there. He'd had an amazing transformation with just a few days of Claire's special treatment of fluids, medications and love. He looked at me with golden eyes looking healthy and shiny. His eyes were also full of mischief.

I walked over to pet his newly clean bright rust colored fur and he reached out a big paw and smacked me on the side of the head again. All that day, Mr. Fishy trotted after me as I did my chores at Hand-Me-Down-Cats. Every time I bent over he took the opportunity to smack me on the side or back of my head.

I quickly became attached to Mr. Fishy. I never bonded with cats as quickly as I did with dogs, though my mother adopted so many cats as I was growing up. But, Mr. Fishy had a distinctly dog-like sense of mischief and fun. He was hitting me one minute and rubbing against my legs to be picked up and held the next. I started to feel sad at the thought of Mr. Fishy getting adopted and going to a new home where I wouldn't be able to visit with him every day. The shelter would seem empty without his antics, even though it was teeming with cats.

But, months passed and Mr. Fishy never seemed to find the right adopters. Many visitors came into the shelter on weekends and filled out applications for the cute kittens, the Maine coon cats, Siamese cats, mixed-breed cats, and elderly cats. Nobody wanted to adopt Mr. Fishy. Maybe his glinting yellow eyes scared people. Or, maybe people were put off by the way he'd stand perfectly still then suddenly burst into action, darting from one corner of the room to the next, smashing into furniture and legs along the way.

Whatever the reason, Claire started to sigh every time she looked at Mr. Fishy. I knew by now what that sound meant. Claire was thinking of transferring Mr. Fishy to another shelter or turning him back over to the men at the dump. At Hand-Me-Down-Cats, as at most shelters that called themselves no-kill shelters, the animals that didn't find homes quickly were transferred to other shelters to give a new group of visitors a chance to see if they might find the right match.

The drawback was that in transferring animals this way there was no guarantee that another shelter might not euthanize the animal. Claire always sought out transfer shelters that were low-kill, but sometimes the animal would then end up being transferred from shelter to shelter for years, eventually showing signs of stress or shelter fatigue. I didn't want that to be Mr. Fishy's fate.

One weekend in the late fall a couple of friends from a writer's group I'd joined wanted to come and take a look at residents of Hand-Me-Down-Cats. They had recently lost a beloved cat to old age and after a period of deep mourning were hoping to adopt another homeless cat. I knew that any cat fortunate enough to be chosen by these two women would be guaranteed comfort and love for life. Their house was strewn with cat toys, kitty condos, blanket-covered kitty nests in the corners of sofas, and the best healthy cat foods, and most of all, heaps of love and affection.

On Sunday, Jean and Beth came to the cat house and made their way through the furry, meowing masses. They picked up cats and held them. They played laser tag with the cats and tempted them with dangly feathers to gauge their energy level and playful spirits. The two women narrowed down their selection to a few cats. They couldn't come to a decision. I was about to suggest that they go home and come back later in the week when they'd had a chance to think about and consider all the cats they'd met that day.

All of a sudden I heard a shriek from Beth. She was holding the side of her face. Then I saw Mr. Fishy on the top of a cat perch next to her. Attracted by the voices of the two women talking, he'd reached out and given one of them a hard smack on the side of the face. Mr. Fishy never put his claws out when he smacked people. I'd come to realize the blows were his ultimate sign of affection and I'd never seen him hit anyone besides me and Claire.

"I think he's chosen us," said Jean as she laughed and pulled Mr. Fishy off his high perch into her lap. "And, look - I think the reason is that we have the same color hair! He's a nice Irish kitty with bright red hair."

Beth came over to pat Mr. Fishy, too. They played and cuddled with him for an hour and were sad to finally take leave of him after filling out an adoption application. They were heading right over to the pet store to get a new bed and toys for Mr. Fishy and couldn't wait to bring him home in two days after Claire had checked over their application and called their veterinary references.

"You will have no problem with Claire approving your adoption," I assured my friends. "You are the best cat moms I've ever met."

I was right. Claire was relieved that someone so responsible wanted to adopt Mr. Fishy, and she admitted that she was ready to send him off to another shelter within the week as a new group of abandoned adult cats would be coming in from the kind men at the landfill site. I was just happy that Mr. Fishy, now called Ian, a nice Irish name, was going to a place where I'd be able to see him again and sit with him and wait for him to show his affection for me with a smack on the side of my head.

24. The Sadness of Southern Dogs

Though I dreaded the inevitable heat of summer, spring was a welcome season that year, especially when volunteering at Hand-Down-Cats. We could open all the windows wide, except for the feral-room windows, as those cats could claw though a screen in a second if they escaped their cages. But the rest of the house was filled with the scent of honeysuckle, sweet pea and lilacs that pushed out the ammonia smell of the litter boxes.

The cats all came alive after their collective long winter nap and wanted to play wildly with each other. I thought about what a change it was this year caring for the indoor cats instead of walking dogs on leashes through the spring-green forest with Berta at Hidden Falls. Still, it was a joy to see the cats enjoying laser tag and catnip-baited fish poles. I felt really relaxed for the first time since Louis Harrington packed up and left town.

One lazy, warm afternoon in April the volunteers were all sitting outdoors on the front stoop when Claire came out to find us to tell us something she said was important to the shelter. I braced myself for the usual round of well-meaning nagging - cats weren't being given their medications properly, litter boxes and dishes weren't properly cleaned, or doors were left unlocked at night. But, judging from Claire's facial expression she had more on her mind than our lack of cleaning ability.

"Well, I thought you all should be the first to know," she said, "The board all approved some major changes I'd been wanting to make around this place for a long time. Don't take this the wrong way. I really,

really love cats, but relying on cat adoptions alone for a good part of our funding just isn't going to cut it. We need to expand and start taking in dogs. Dogs get adopted faster and we can charge higher fees. So, starting next week, the basement rooms will all be converted into runs for dogs."

At first, I was happy to hear the news. I'd missed meeting and walking all the new dogs that came into Hidden Falls, and there was a large, shady fenced back yard behind the Hand-Me-Down Cats' house that was going to waste and would be a perfect space in which to exercise and train dogs. Also, in spite of Hidden Falls now having the local animal control contracts for stray and abandoned dogs, there was still an overflow of dogs, especially pit bulls, in need of a good shelter.

"Wow! That sounds great," I said. "Will you be taking in dogs directly from animal control, or will they be sent over from Hidden Falls?"

"Nope," replied Claire with the familiar sharp sarcastic tone to her voice, "We aren't taking in any local dogs. I don't want a whole shelter full of hard-to-move pits. We need to increase our adoption income, not spend more money. We're going to bring in young southern dogs of breeds that people actually want to adopt."

I felt my heart sink. "Not again," I thought.

Another shelter board thinking that bringing up southern dogs and puppies was going to be the solution to all their financial problems. I knew from experience that the very opposite could be true. It was impossible to quarantine and vaccinate all of animals in the shelter for some of the unknown diseases traveling up with these dogs. At least at Hand-Me-Down-Cats, we wouldn't be mixing local and southern dogs and therefore putting local dogs at risk for infection from diseases to which they had no immunity. At least not until they were adopted out.

"Just please be careful," I begged of Claire. "Both Sherri and Hidden Falls had some serious problems with the southern dog transports, and I'd hate to see anything bad happen here, too."

"No, no. We've got it all under control," said Claire in her brusque know-it-all tone. "We've already got approval from the state. The inspector came here and says the basement will work as a quarantine area for the shelter, and just to make sure we're safe, we'll be having the dogs quarantined off-site for two weeks so they'll be sure to be clean before they ever get here."

"Well, okay. At least you have a good plan," I replied tentatively.

Quarantining the dogs off-site was a good idea and Claire did plan very well for the big change. I was already looking forward to running around with the new dogs under the big trees in the backyard. But, later that afternoon, I saw Claire hunched over her computer searching the southern dogs lists obsessively. The expression on her face looked very much like Sherri's and Melissa's when I'd seen them doing the same thing. I had a powerful sense of foreboding.

Claire must have been planning the transformation of the shelter for a long time without telling anyone because the very next week the basement was filled with ten barking, howling hounds. It turned out that Claire had a passion for hound dogs and hunting dog breeds. This was the dominant breed-type coming up from southern shelters anyway. My early doubts seemed unfounded, and I was happy to see that over the next month that adoptions of these dogs was rapid and not one of them stayed in the basement kennels long enough to develop shelter stress.

I gave Claire a lot of credit for having the marketing foresight to select breeds that were uncommon in Massachusetts and therefore desirable. Although, I felt terribly sad when local people would turn up on the doorstep with a local dog they needed to give up and we couldn't accommodate them. I'd send them off to Hidden Falls, hoping they had room for another pit bull and trying not think about what would happen to the poor dog if they didn't. I wished that Claire would make some allowances and agree to take in a few local dogs.

One warm and sunny afternoon I had a group of hound dogs out in the backyard tossing and was tossing tennis balls to tire them out. I was the one getting winded. I wasn't used to these breeds. I was used to walking the pit bulls that alternated from pokey to power pulling. They would pull my arms out of their sockets for the first five-minutes of a walk only to flop down in exhaustion after that and become mellow and malleable.

In contrast, I could toss balls for the hounds for an hour straight and they still wanted more play time. One of the Hand-Me-Down-Cats board members named Alicia stepped out on the small deck to watch me play with the dogs.

"It's kind of fun having all these dogs here," I said. "It's a lot more work, but more fun than constantly scraping up cat litter."

"Well," drawled Alicia in a sarcastic voice, "If you say so."

"What do you mean," I asked. "Claire said everyone on the board was excited about having the southern dogs here."

"Well, that depends on what you mean by

excited," laughed Alicia as she flipped piles of curly red hair off her shoulders and face.

"So, you don't like having them here?'

"Well, it doesn't matter what I want, or what any of us wants, does it? All that matters is what Claire wants. Personally, I think it's too much work having all these dogs here, and a lot of volunteers are complaining and are leaving us. They wanted to work with cats, not dogs. Plus, this place is called Hand-Me-Down-Cats. Right? Now we have to change the name, and change it legally on all the incorporation papers. It's just a big pain in the ass.

"But, everyone voted to bring the dogs here because it was pointless to fight it because they'd be here anyway. Claire can do whatever she wants. This is her house; you know? She owns it. So, nothing the board says makes any difference at all. If we truly disagree with Claire, it's the highway for us. She'll just find a new board; you see? She's done it before."

I'd didn't want to talk shelter politics. I needed a respite from shelter politics after Hidden Falls. I wanted to lay low and enjoy coming in to help out with the animals, relax and play with them for a bit, and above all return home with a peaceful mind.

"So, what are you going to call the shelter now?" I asked halfheartedly.

"It's called Rebound Hounds," laughed Alicia.

"Wow! That was fast. Who came up with that name?"

"Who do you think?" asked Alicia rhetorically as she bent down to pick up a gutted tennis ball and tossed it to the pack of brindle and white hounds. "Honestly, I like having the dogs here too. I'm just worried. Claire is fine as long as nothing goes wrong. We'll see how it goes, but I worry that something bad is going to happen, and she won't be able to handle it with all these dogs. I just have a bad feeling about this."

Alicia's bad feeling was prophetic, but when something bad happened it didn't happen to the dogs. The misfortune befell the shelter cats. One afternoon a few weeks later I stopped in and Claire was at her desk with head on her hands and holding one of the older cats in her lap while a few others were whisking around on the desk spreading paperwork all over the place. Claire didn't make a move to stop them. The cat on her lap seemed to be wheezing and had a slight cough.

"Do you hear that?" asked Claire without raising her head from hands. "I'm worried."

"It's just a little cough," I replied. "Don't you think it's probably nothing?"

"Well, it might be just a little cough if this cat was

the only one with it, but go upstairs and listen. They are all doing it."

I left Claire at the desk for a minute and walked up the curving Victorian staircase that was usually lined with cats, rubbing my legs and scrambling for attention and treats. That day, there were no cats on the stairs at all. When I got to the top I heard a sound like someone whispering loudly in a movie theater. As I moved into the hallway dividing the warren of little cat rooms, I saw that most of the animals were lying about lethargically on the floors or inside the kitty condos. Almost all of them were wheezing. I felt panic, but I tried to appear calm as I went back downstairs.

"Have you called a vet yet?" I asked tentatively.

"Of course I called our vet right away. She's on her way over now. But, even if this is nothing, and I pray that it is, it is going to cost us a fortune. There must be thirty or forty cats that sound like this right now. And, how many more will catch whatever it is? We have over a hundred cats here. If Dr. Laura has to treat all these cats, even with her very generous discount for us, we are going to go broke."

"It will be okay," I said. "It's probably just a minor cold or upper-respiratory infection going around because it's spring, just like with people." I knew I was wrong.

"Maybe," said Claire, "But, damn that stupid bitch, Holly. I told her not to bring in any cats from other shelters while we have these dogs downstairs. The dogs are in the cat quarantine rooms and we can't leave a crate of cats down there to be terrorized by all the barking dogs, but we can't mix strange cats in with the healthy ones up here, but that's exactly what Holly did. She came here in the middle of the night last week with a crate of sick cats and in the morning I came in and I noticed they were sneezing. I told Holly to get them right out of here and she did, she took them home. Now, they are all dead."

"You mean they all died within a week?" I asked with a sense of mounting horror.

"They all died during the week at her house, and it is too late for us, I feel it. Dr. Laura is coming over but it is going to be too late. Those cats of Holly's died so fucking fast. The same is going to happen to these cats, all of our poor cats. Some of these cats have been here with us for over five years."

At that point Claire put her head down on the desk and started sobbing loudly. I put my hand on her back and tried to stay upbeat until the veterinarian arrived, but I had a solid sinking feeling that Claire's negative viewpoint was the right one to have.

And, yes, sadly, all of the cats died. Every single

cat at the shelter died within the week. I was so glad my friends had adopted Mr. Fishy before the disaster happened, but the mysterious disease dealt the shelter a devastating blow. The entire place was quarantined and the Rebound Hounds basement dogs had no place to go. So, I begged Sherri to let us house the dogs at her place for a while until we could get them adopted out.

Fortunately, most of them found good new homes fast. Still, there were three sad leftovers - all of them pit bull mixes. As much as Claire wanted to avoid the breed, the southern shelters always slipped in a few pit-mixes with each batch of dogs arriving in the north.

Summer came and Sherri's kennel was not air conditioned. The remaining three dogs were miserable and restless in the heat. The former Hand-Me-Down-Cats volunteers stopped coming out to walk them after a while, and Claire was taking a much-needed rest from the animal shelter business for a few months while the old Victorian house was being disinfected and scrubbed from top to bottom.

Then, to make matters worse, towards the end of the summer Sherri shocked me by telling me that she was leaving town and moving to Florida. She and her husband George were finally divorcing, and she was putting her kennel and house on the market immediately.

"You need to get these remaining dogs out of here ASAP," she announced.

Having Sherri move out of state was another huge loss for me. I loved coming out to visit her and walk in the little pet cemetery behind her house and kennel, especially now that Harrington wasn't in control of it. But, I'd felt Sherri's restlessness and unhappiness with her life, and I knew for a long time that a change was coming. I'd miss her terribly, and worse, I just didn't know what to do with the three leftover dogs. Once again, I felt the weight of life and death decision-making inherent in animal rescue.

I sent all of the dogs out to be neutered and fully vetted, and I advertised them all over the Internet on every available adoption website. I brought them to adoption fairs and dog walks. Everyone admired them and loved their friendly natures, but nobody wanted to bring one of them home. I tried contacting other shelters, including Hidden Falls and other rescues across New England. Everyone was full. Nobody wanted any more pit bulls.

Sherri gave me an ultimatum. She was leaving town at the end of the month and she wanted the dogs gone by Independence Day. I decided to bring them all home. I'd have to test each one with my other dogs and find out which pack would be best for each. We'd have to rearrange the bedroom situation and the access to the backyard.

I was beyond panic at acquiring more dogs. But, the situation was unavoidable. I just couldn't bring those three healthy, lovable young dogs to the vet and have them put down. Mark and my other dogs would have to deal with the fact that our house was becoming an unofficial shelter and sanctuary for misfit and unwanted dogs.

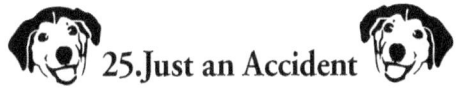25. Just an Accident

I didn't feel anything. I was aware of just a sort of non-sensation of numbness and the odd combination of a floating feeling with a surge of energy. But I looked down and my forefinger was different than it had been a second ago. It was bent backwards and the tip of it was just hanging by a tiny strip of skin. I stared at it for a moment that seemed like an hour - I just couldn't connect the sight of the hanging finger with my idea of body - long enough to see Prince lunge for my leg.

His teeth sunk deeply into the muscle of my lower leg and then, just like in the movies, I saw Mark approach in slow motion to grab the dog's collar and pull him backwards. Prince was reluctant to let go of my leg, though, and took a good chunk of flesh with him as he backed away with Mark and then stopped to look at me. I think I was screaming but I didn't hear anything. Prince looked at me without aggression but with fear and confusion, and I could see that his leg was also torn and bleeding.

My hearing and my voice came back in a rush and I hollered at Mark to shut Prince in his crate, while I grabbed Hawkins' collar with my uninjured hand and held him tightly until the crate latched safely shut. The first coherent thought I had was, "Thank goodness this happened to my left hand."

In those few moments my blood caught up with the wounds and my body started spurting blood in several directions. Mark was yelling "Oh no, oh no" over and over again. But, my normally nervous body was strangely calm - as if I'd been suddenly drugged with a heavy yet pleasant sedative. I walked up the stairs and calmly picked a towel for my leg and wrapped my hand in another. I gulped a Xanax, knowing that this altered painless state would not last for long, and grabbed my purse and keys.

"Let's go to the hospital," I said as I rounded up Mark and his set of keys. Foremost in my mind was the unreasonable dread of anesthesia I'd had since I was a kid. I knew there was no way anyone would be fixing my finger, if it could be fixed, without putting me under anesthesia. The hospital emergency room is fortunately only a mile or so from our house, but by the time we arrived the lovely feeling of serenity was slipping away and replaced by a much more familiar sensation - panic with hyperventilation.

A police officer at the desk came running towards me with a wheelchair and everyone in the waiting room was stock still and staring at my leg. I couldn't figure out why until I looked down and saw that the white towels were bright red with blood, and since I was wearing shorts, my legs were sticky and bright with blood. It oozed and wound its way out of the saturated towels and down my leg and arm as I was commanded by a nurse to hold my hand above my head.

How had such a perfectly golden early autumn afternoon turned so quickly into this horror movie? I remembered coming home with a bag of maple scones from a stop at the farmer's market on the way back from a fall drive and long walk with one of the new dogs from Sherri's kennel, Dougie, by the Slocum's River and watching the clean white sailboats heading down the river and out to the sea. The memory seemed to be from another lifetime.

I was sitting in the living room eating scones and was absorbed in reading messages on my laptop when I heard Ricky and another of the new dogs, Prince, playing a little too roughly. I reached down nonchalantly to pull them apart by the collars and saw that Ricky meant business and had Prince's leg clamped firmly in his jaws. I panicked a bit and grabbed the first liquid at hand - a cup of still warm coffee - and tossed it at Ricky's head to break his grip.

The next thing I remember is standing up looking at my severed finger with Mark yelling somewhere in the distance. The coffee worked, though. It did break Ricky's grip, freeing Prince up to bite my hand and leg.

In the emergency room, I kept the nice memory of the morning's walk by the white and blue river in my mind as various hospital personnel rushed about inserting IV lines, wheeling me around to x-ray machines, and employing a piece of dental floss to yank off my ingrown wedding ring.

Most disconcerting to me was that most of the hospital staff stopped by my gurney at some point to ask if I still had the dog that bit me. I thought, "Now, where would Prince be in the ten minutes it took to drive me to the hospital and be laid out in a gurney in the trauma unit?"

Did the nurses and doctors really think that Mark would stay back at home just for the sake of calling the police to come in and pick up the dog, take him away so we never had to see him again and quietly destroy him?

Did people think that such an action would make my wounds feel better? Make my leg heal faster? Make my finger grow back? No, it would turn this already painful day into a tragedy that would sit like a hard lump of undigested junk food in the pit of my stomach for the rest of my life.

I knew some people did things like that when their pets screwed up, lost control in a moment of panic and became the wolves or wild cats they once were. People think destroying the animal immediately - for merely succumbing to fear, or anger, or just the confusion of a moment - is the logical and correct thing to do, for the good of all of human society, of course.

I had a neighbor who had his beautiful young German shepherd euthanized. The dog tried to bite his wife during an argument. The breeder was called and said that the dog must have been upset by some violence or disturbance among the humans in the house. But, nothing the humans did wrong mattered. The death sentence was applied immediately. Animal control officers came to the house and the dog was taken away and killed. I couldn't walk by that house afterwards without feeling the weight and sadness of that event.

Thinking of the neighbors made me suddenly think of our house and I looked up at Mark to ask; "Did we close and lock the front door? Did you separate the dogs? Is Prince still in his crate? Where is everybody?" I felt the chilling sweat of panic break out all over my body as I thought about different scenarios - dogs running wild down the street and being crushed by cars, separated dogs getting together and ripping each other apart. Or, more likely, a couple of dogs left in the backyard to bark for hours until our normally tolerant neighbors lost their patience and called the police.

"You'd better go on home," I told Mark. "Go make sure the house is locked and everyone is in their places, then come back with some sweat shirts and underwear and my toothbrush, oh, and my Xanax. I don't know if they'll give me that here."

Mark glanced nervously at me lying there surrounded by nurses and surgical assistants pulling my wedding ring off my finger, setting up IV's and mopping up blood that was dripping to the floor under the gurney.

"Are you sure you'll be okay?"

"I'm as okay as I'm going to be at this point."

Honestly, I was a little glad to see Mark walk away out the little curtained room and down the hallway. His look of pure confusion and panic was making me more nervous than I already was. And, I needed more than anything to know that our house and dogs were secure. I wasn't sure how long I'd have to stay at the hospital. I thought I might wind up being there for a week.

Finally, with an extra hard yank from the nurse, the wedding ring slid over my large knuckle and off my hand. She wrapped it carefully and put it, along with my necklace, into the outside pocket of my purse, which I realized I was clinging to like a teddy bear. Then they wheeled me down the corridor to the x-ray room.

I don't remember how it got on me but I was now wearing a hospital gown. A mound of new gauze was wrapped around my leg and it was already bright red. My left hand was also a ball of bloody gauze. I must have been a real sight because an old man sitting on a bench outside another trauma unit jumped up in horror as I passed and started shouting at me in Portuguese. He started to walk along with the gurney but the nurse stopped him with a strong set of hands on his arm, although I wished she didn't. The old man seemed protective and concerned about me. It was comforting.

I've always been terrified of the hospital, since I was a kid and had to go to the hospital many times for various surgeries to fix my deformed urinary system. I hated the feeling of being out of control and strapped down with IVs stuck into my arm and into which someone could put any kind of strange chemical. I hated the drugs the most - feeling dizzy, disoriented, disembodied, and the feeling of pure terror combined with lack of control.

But, at that moment, I still was full of whatever hormone dulls the shock of a violent injury. I felt almost euphoric, and I felt no pain at all. I kept telling the nurses and attendants that I felt no pain. In radiology they kept apologizing for moving my fingers and legs around under the humming machines.

The nurse beside me kept saying, "Don't look, don't look. It will make it worse," as he positioned my torn finger on the pad below the camera. But, I wanted to see. I'm never as frightened as when I'm told I can't see something. That was usually the case when I was a kid. I always wanted to see what was going on and told I couldn't see. Then full panic would set in. This time I didn't listen, I just looked.

The top joint of my finger was separated from the middle joint and a thin strip of skin was still holding the two parts of the joint together. It wasn't as bad as it looked when the bite first happened.

"It's not as bad as we thought at first," agreed the radiologist. "It's really very clean. There must have been a lot of force right there on the joint. This is good news. The leg bite is deep but clean too. It'll heal up pretty well once we get you all stitched up."

They wheeled me back to the trauma room, which was now taken up by a man with a gunshot wound, so they kept wheeling on until they found an empty room.

"Okay," said the nurse, "Now, we can finally get you all cleaned up and give you something for the pain."

I said again that I was feeling no pain, no pain at all. I dreaded the pain medication more than pain itself. I dreaded that any morphine would slip down the IV into that little tube inserted in my arm. I remembered sitting next to my father's hospital bed, first after his heart surgery, and later in the nursing home, both times that morphine made him see dragons on the ceiling.

But, here in the emergency room everyone was speaking of morphine in glowing terms, as if it were some great consolation prize that only people lucky enough to land in the emergency room were given.

"Okay, we've got you all cleaned and wrapped up and now it's time for some happy juice," chirped a young nurse, as she reached up towards my IV tower.

"I don't want any morphine," I said.

"But what about the pain?"

"I'm not feeling any pain," I repeated.

"That will change," said the nurse.

The next second I felt the room slide sideways, my gurney seemed to flip over upside down and all the objects around me seemed to turn a pink, fleshy color. Immediately I started to vomit, first to the right side and then I turned and puked all over the floor on the left side of the gurney before the nurse came running over with a plastic pail.

"I told you I didn't want any morphine," I managed to gasp, but already I was losing my train of thought. I was losing my head. I still felt horribly nauseous but I suddenly stopped caring about anything.

Another type of nurse, or maybe she was a doctor, dressed in a dark blue uniform came running up and said, "I'm so sorry. No more happy juice for you. We'll switch you to an Ativan drip later after it wears off."

I just nodded my head weakly. I was beyond caring. I felt extremely hot, hotter than I'd ever felt before, as the smiling orderly wheeled me through corridors to the elevator. The heat didn't feel bad though, and I certainly didn't need the thin blanket that had been tossed over my legs.

I started to see real colors again. That was my last thought until later when I woke up in a pleasant room that felt familiar. Coincidentally, it was the same room my father had stayed in on one of his many trips over to the hospital from the nursing home.

I was alone in the quiet room and the sun was setting outside my window that overlooked the homey neighborhood at the backside of hospital. I still felt very warm. A distant voice in my head asked me where was Mark? What had happened with the dogs? Where was my purse? Was the house locked and secure? My awareness was returning slowly, but the warm comfortable feeling induced by the happy juice was still overriding it

What if the dogs had killed each other, or were lost on the streets? So be it, I thought. My life would be so much easier. I felt so deliciously detached and relaxed. Even if something had happened to Mark, so what? My life would only be easier still. I clicked on the ceiling TV and turned on a Brady Bunch rerun and closed my eyes, ignoring the growing chattering little voice of anxiety in my head.

A large, blond Viking-like doctor who said he'd be my surgeon came in to the room at some point and sat down in the chair across from my bed. And my nurse, Jocelyn, the one who advocated for my switch to Ativan, came in to fiddle with my IV tubes. The Viking doctor, Dr. McBride, said he needed to ask me some questions. Did I smoke? Did I drink or use illicit drugs? Was I diabetic? All of these things would disqualify me for finger reattachment surgery. If I answered "Yes" to any of his questions he wouldn't waste his time on me. The finger wouldn't mend. He might as well amputate it. I answered "No" to all his questions and he smiled.

Then he started asking me some questions I had to wonder about. Did I feel any pain yet? In my leg? In my hand? Did I have other scars on my body? Did I suffer from accidents frequently? I wondered why he asking this set of questions. Did he think Mark had hurt me? Did he think that I was a cutter or some other kind of self-abuser? "No to all," I said.

He smiled again and then pulled out his cell phone. "Good," he said, "Good." We'll go into surgery at 8:00 tomorrow morning then. And, don't worry. This really isn't as bad as it looks. It really isn't, unless you were hoping to be a hand model. Ha ha."

I saw Jocelyn roll her eyes at that comment. Dr. McBride stood up and brought his cell phone over to the side of my bed. "Check this out," he said. "This is a guy I worked on in Providence. He had an apartment full of pythons. One night a snake wrapped itself around his arm when he was sleeping and cut off his circulation. We couldn't save it."

He held his phone over and I saw a photo of what looked like a big, black blood sausage. I still felt detached but interested now. What was the doctor trying to imply by showing me that gruesome photo? Was my injury minor in comparison and this was a form of comfort? Well, the strategy was working. Or, maybe, he was trying to gauge my reaction, to ferret out whether I was a self-abuser by animal bite.

But, I really didn't want to lose the tip of my finger! This disaster wasn't anything close to the poor snake guy and his blackened sausage arm, but while my right hand was beefy from years of digging into clay and paint, my left hand, my ring hand, had been fairly decent looking in comparison - something I thought I hadn't cared about until now. And, my left index finger was almost as useful as my right in sculpting clay, in drawing and painting, in typing, in rowing a kayak, in riding my mountain bike, in walking the dogs, in doing most of the things I loved to do. I desperately wanted my finger to survive.

Finally, the doctor and nurse decided to leave me

alone and they assured me they wouldn't slip any more morphine into my IV drip unless I asked for it. I could sleep the drug out of my system for the next four hours and then the night nurse would be back in with Ativan or Xanax. I turned over on my side as best I could with my hand bandaged and trussed up above my head on the IV rack.

Where on earth was Mark? Didn't he care about me? What was going on with the dogs? I slept a bit then woke up suddenly to a darkened window with speckles of lights now glittering in the neighborhood outside. The hospital room looked a sickly green blue and felt icy cold. The morphine warmth was completely gone out of my system and I felt the dreaded ice sweat of panic congealing on my head and back. I had to go to the bathroom but I couldn't get up off the bed. I was hyperventilating and nauseous.

Everything I dreaded as a kid about being in a hospital was coming back to me all at once - the deathly feeling of panic, of being trapped, and of being entirely under the control of indifferent strangers.

I reached for the nurse call-button behind me and rang it three times. The night nurse came in and I asked if I could have my Xanax. I was desperate to get rid of the overwhelming panic. He informed me that I still had a half-hour to go before I could take a Xanax and why didn't I just have some more morphine? It was more long-lasting. I could stay in a beautiful, indifferent state of mind for days until I was released from the hospital. In spite of the temptation of that awful moment, I said "No" to the morphine again.

I wanted to be able to think. I really wanted to know where Mark was and what was going on with the dogs. Why wasn't he here with me? What had happened?

The nurse shook his head in disbelief and pulled my arm out of its sling and helped me limp to the bathroom. This was my first time looking in the mirror since the accident and I was surprised by how normal I appeared. I had somehow expected my head to look something like the snake man's bloated arms. But, no, my hair was all calm and in place and my face just looked a little puffy and pale, not at all like a woman who had buckets of acid blue panic churning through her veins.

I lay back down in bed in a cold sweat and turned on the TV to watch Bonanza. The nurse trussed up my hand again and said he'd be back in a half hour with my Xanax. I supposed it was easier for staff to deal with blissfully numb patients, but I didn't care. I wanted to stay awake. I wanted to know what was going on. And, it was clear by Mark's absence that I was the only one taking care of myself here. I needed to be able to think.

The nurse finally came in with my pill and told me that he'd be getting me ready for surgery in an hour since we were going down to the operating room in about two hours. The Xanax had just kicked in when another nurse arrived with a gurney and I was hoisted out of bed and onto it with my arm still tied up to the IV.

In the operating room I saw a rush of faces coming at me and, oddly, one of them belonged to Sandy, a former fellow volunteer from Hidden Falls! I'd forgotten that she was a surgical technician at this hospital. What a coincidence that she was working on the morning of my surgery. I felt an immense sense of relief. The presence of Sandy was a sign that everything was going turn out all right.

She came rushing over and whispered in my ear, "You have a good team here. You really do. I wouldn't lie to you on that. You are very lucky!"

The anesthesiologist was talking to me in my other ear. Did I want full anesthesia, or just a nerve block? The full black out anesthesia would require an extra day in the hospital but I wouldn't feel a thing during surgery. "Nerve block," I said. Where was Mark? He wouldn't be able to handle the dogs for very long. I needed to get home! Nerve block. "Okay, if you're sure," said the anesthesiologist.

Sandy whispered again, "Animal control is here. They are right outside wanting to know what happened yesterday. Of course the ER had to report your accident to them. I talked with them and told them it was just an accident with your own dogs. Just a stupid accident. I told them you have nice dogs. They aren't going to investigate any further."

I smiled at Sandy and held her hand tightly with my good one. "I am so glad you are here!" I said. It was wonderful to have someone as competent and strong as Sandy in the operating room with me. I'd forgotten all about animal control. How great it was to have someone knowledgeable to deal with them.

"Thank you so much," I whispered.

"No problem," said Sandy. "You know I've been through the same thing. One of my dogs bit me badly a few years ago. I've been lying right there where you are now. I know how it is."

I remembered then that, yes, Sandy had surgery herself, right here at her place of work, for a bite wound on her leg inflicted by a terrified traumatized American bulldog who had just arrived at Hidden Falls. She had begged Bliss to let the dog live in spite of the bite incident. Bliss agreed reluctantly and later

Sandy adopted the dog. His name was Jock and he'd become Sandy's constant companion. She understood.

"Okay, you guys, break it up." It was Dr. McBride smiling and walking up to the table. He elbowed Sandy out of the way. "Well, I hear we're going in with just the nerve block. Okay. Good girl. You're tough. Say, do you play golf? You look as if you might play golf. I started to get a little worried about your golf swing with that finger."

I assured the doctor that I did not play golf. Then he yelled at the staff to clear out from around the operating table and called over the anesthesiologist who grabbed my left arm by the elbow and jammed a huge hypodermic needle right into the joint. For the first time, I felt pain. Then he jammed it in again at my wrist. I saw the nurse on the other side of me reach quickly for the IV drip and say, "Okay, time for the happy juice." And, the last thing I heard was Sandy's raspy voice echoing across the operating room, "Hey, who is this new doctor anyway? He's pushy."

During surgery, I dreamed I was in a soundless sleep below tons of heavy dark earth, but I could see what looked like the stem of a huge flower right next to me. I grabbed the stem and was sucked up into it and passing through it until I burst out through the head of a sunflower and was looking straight into the blinding light of the sun right in front of my eyes.

I shut my eyes tightly and asked the air, "Am I here? Am I alive? Can we please make the sun go away?"

I heard laughter and saw Sandy leaning over me.

"You're still alive, sleeping beauty," she said and patted me gently on the shoulder before stomping away in her surgical blue overalls. An orderly came and grabbed the handles of my gurney and wheeled me back to my room. I was happy to see that the bed next to mine was still empty. I was feeling that warm enveloping relaxation as the residue of anesthesia still remained in my body. Mark still wasn't at the hospital, but again I didn't care. I just wanted to sink into the mounds of clean white pillows and fall asleep.

When I awoke a new nurse was standing there with a cup of water and a Xanax to smooth the transition out of the anesthesia. The first thing she asked me was, "So where is your dog now? That's a pretty serious bite on your leg there, and your finger...well, we'll have to see how that goes when the bandages come off."

"What do you mean where's the dog?" I asked.

"It was your dog that bit you, wasn't it? Are you going to keep it? Or, did you call animal control to come and take it away?" the nurse asked.

"Neither," I said. "He's fine as far as I know. I wish my husband would come by and let me know how the dogs are doing though. I'm worried."

"Well," said the nurse, "I'd just worry about myself right now if I were you. And, I'd think seriously about having a dog like that around the house."

Finally, the nurse left and I lay back into the pillows and turned on the television with the remote. More stupid sitcoms. But, they were just what I needed.

I was horrified by suggestions that I have Prince euthanized. How on earth could it ever make me feel better, to heal - physically, mentally or emotionally - knowing I'd executed my dog for an accident? Prince didn't mean to hurt me when he bit me. He was terrified himself, and in pain, self-protection kicked in and he bit. If I had him killed, a simple accident would become something ugly and irreparable.

I looked at my bandaged hand. Nobody had told me whether the end of my finger was still there, or whether I'd be living with a stump on my left hand. If I was left with a stump, I'd have physical therapy and learn to work with it.

Whatever happened, I thought, I'd take my bandaged finger home and, hopefully, when I got there the first thing I'd do was to curl up in bed with Ricky and Maggie and Prince and Hawkins and all my new dogs pressed up against me and fall into a blissful, warm and happy sleep.

 26. I Am So Glad You Are Here

I woke up a few hours later to the bouncy twittering sounds of more Brady Bunch sitcoms and, finally, there was Mark sitting on the side of my bed. He'd woken me up by rooting around under my mounds of pillows while looking for the TV remote.

"I hate this show so much," were his first words to me. "I have to change it. It's really not congruous with this hospital setting."

He'd parked a huge, stalky red amaryllis flower on my side table and finally located the remote on the floor. I was extremely joyful and relieved that Mark had finally turned up at the hospital, though I knew from experience that he just wasn't great company in trauma situations. His thinking, his whole being, in fact, strived to be as far away as it could get from stress at all times. Mark channel surfed until he settled on a more hospital-appropriate selection - M.A.S.H. reruns.

I was almost afraid to ask, "So, how is Prince?" Mark replied, his eyes still directed towards the television, "Oh, Prince is okay, I guess, but he doesn't want to come out of his crate at all. I think he knows he did something awful. He seems depressed. And, I could only get him out to go to the bathroom once and his front leg looks pretty swollen and painful."

"Can you please take him to the vet tomorrow if I'm going to be stuck here another day?" I pleaded.

Prince could wait one more day with a swollen leg until Tuesday. I knew that asking Mark to take Prince to the emergency vet today, on a Labor Day holiday weekend, would be too much. The several hour wait, the medical decisions needing to be made, and the payment of an exorbitant fee would be beyond Mark's capacity for stress.

Then I felt another awful wave of panic start to rise as I thought that I had no idea when I would actually be able to leave the hospital. I needed to get home to deal with the dogs.

Just then, one of my few non-animal friends, Gloria, strode through the door. Gloria was the opposite of Mark in almost every way. Gloria loved the drama of visiting people in hospitals, bossing the nurses and doctors around, and offering her two-cents worth of advice to anyone who would listen.

"Hey, I brought the coffee you asked for," she said, handing me a huge cup of steaming Dunkin' Donuts coffee with cream.

I was confused and asked, "When did I ask for coffee? I haven't talked with you for days."

"You must really be high right now," laughed Gloria. "You called me a couple of hours ago and said you had a wicked bad headache and needed caffeine. That's the worst thing about hospitals. They don't get that you can't just go off the caffeine cold turkey, but they won't give you anything but decaf."

It felt so strange to have called and talked with someone, and even requested something from them, and not be aware of it. Was Gloria just messing around with me? I grabbed my phone from the side table and looked at the record of my recent outgoing calls. Sure enough, there was Gloria's number and I'd called it a couple of hours ago.   My brain was a void. I had no recollection at all of the hours coming out of anesthesia. I had to check who else I might have called. I was hoping to the keep this incident as quiet as possible to avoid commentary from all the people who already considered me a crazy dog lady.

But, at that moment, I was glad I'd been sleep-calling. My unconscious self knew what I needed. That wonderful hot cup of coffee was more than welcome.

Without my usual caffeine, my head felt like a spike was being slowly screwed into it just over my left eye. I reached for the cup gratefully.

"Hey, hold that down low. That nurse is watching us from the hallway. We don't want her confiscating your caffeine," said Gloria, sagely.

Mark asked her, "Did you bring me one of those, too?"

"No," Gloria replied, "because I didn't think you'd be here. When I spoke with Lori she said you hadn't been back here since you left the emergency room."

Gloria didn't say this angrily, but in the teasing, bantering tone she and Mark used for all their exchanges. I realized then, as I had many times before, how grateful I was for my crazy friends. What would I do without friends who snuck me in a large Dunkin' Donuts coffee the day after emergency surgery? I'd certainly be terribly lonely, frightened and isolated - trying to soldier on through this incident without any laughter.

Mark was a kind person, really, but he needed a lot of care himself. Crazy artist friends, crazy animal people, crazy dogs and quirky husband - from the day I packed my belongings in my car and drove out of my parents' driveway, my domestic life stopped developing along traditional lines.

"Well," said Gloria to Mark, "Where the heck were you last night that you couldn't get your butt back over to the hospital?"

"I had to take care of the dogs," he replied. "Then, I was so hungry after the emergency room, I just had a huge craving for Kentucky Fried Chicken so I went and got a bucket of chicken, ate the whole thing and just crashed."

Mark must have been extremely stressed out. He rarely ate animal products and was always careful about what he put into his body. Consuming an entire bucket of Kentucky Fried Chicken must mean his anxiety was off the charts.

"You should have called me," said Gloria to Mark.

"No, I was really out of it," he replied. "I needed to lie down and calm the dogs down. They are so upset. Prince and Ricky are sad. And Sable knows something is going on. She's spinning around in circles in the kitchen. Dougie is upstairs whining and he couldn't fall asleep last night without his mama in the bed next to him. And Hawkins is barking nonstop and won't eat. I hope the neighbors didn't complain to the city about all the noise."

I knew our household would be chaotic after the

fight. Dogs fight, then five minutes later can be buddies again. Still, they are sensitive to violence and loss. Maybe they all thought that Prince had killed me and that was why I wasn't home. Knowledge of their anxiety reaction added to my sense of urgency to get out of the hospital as soon as possible.

At that moment, the doctor came in with a pair of scissors and announced that he wanted to take a look under the bandages. Finally, I could see if my finger was still attached to my hand. The nurses hadn't been able to supply me with that information. My hand looked like a soccer ball made of bandages. The doctor clipped away at the gauze and peeked under, but I couldn't see anything myself. I finally got the nerve to ask if my finger was still there.

"Oh, yes, yes," he said and ended my suspense. "It's there and everything is reattached - blood vessels, nerves, tendons - although it may be quite a while, if ever, that you'll be able to use it normally again."

I'd figured as much as soon as I saw my finger hanging by a strip of skin with the fragmented bone detached. I just didn't want a stump for a finger. I didn't want people always asking how it had happened then having to decide whether to tell the truth or make something up. If I told the truth, I'd have to answer the inevitable question of whether I'd had Prince put down or not, and be subject to judgment either way.

The doctor looked at my chart and announced, "Well, you're going to be in here for at least two more days."

"Two more days? I can't! I feel fine now. I want to go home," I whined.

"Why do you have to go home so fast?" said the doctor looking directly at Mark. "Can't your husband get a pizza to eat for a couple of nights? You're not going to be doing much cooking with that hand anyway."

I laughed and didn't bother to explain to the doctor that I rarely cooked anything at home, that Mark was the household cook, and was a very good one. I didn't explain that I needed to get home for the dogs. He'd just think I was crazy.

Gloria piped up, "I'll take care of him while you're in here," she said. "I've got enough stew and soup in the freezer to last for a few months. You just enjoy your time out here in the hospital. Relax, read and watch the tube."

"See," said the doctor, "Problem solved." He turned and walked out, frowning at Mark.

"What's his problem?" asked Mark. "Doesn't he understand what I've been through in the last couple of days?"

Gloria and I just looked at each other and laughed. Typical. I felt very relaxed now and my headache was becoming less severe as I drank the coffee. I'd stay in the hospital for a couple more days and look out the window over the houses of this little city and try not to worry so much about Prince and the other dogs. They'd be okay until I got back home.

I begged Mark to at least start Prince on some antibiotics. I always kept some on hand in the cupboard. He promised that he'd do it and bring him to the vet first thing in the morning. He and Gloria left the hospital laughing together, heading over to her place to thaw out some lentil soup. I lay back on the mounds of clean, crisp white pillows and linens. They were a welcome luxury, compared to the dog-hair covered surfaces at home. I looked past the big amaryllis to the streets and rooftops beyond. This weird little eccentric city was now my home and it suited me.

Two days later I was home and chaos hadn't ensued when I was away. Everything seemed under control and the dogs were calm - as if they sensed that I needed them to be that way. Prince's leg was very swollen but did not look infected. I took Dougie for a walk around the neighborhood, holding his leash with my one good hand. I had a brace and cast on my finger that made it stick straight out and I was always bumping into objects with it. I was very grateful to Dr. McBride that it was still there.

I lay down on the couch and turned on the TV to watch more sitcom reruns as Mark banged away in the kitchen making dinner. Sable crawled up on next to me on the couch and burrowed under the blanket and pressed her head tightly against my cheek. Prince jumped up behind my legs and rested his head on my back. After those two were settled, Poirot jumped up on top of the pile. It felt incredibly warm and secure to be lying there under two hundred pounds of dog. Hawkins couldn't fit so he lay on the other couch and started to snore. Dougie was living in the bedroom now, so I'd have to get up and share some snuggle time with him soon, but if I never had to move, to get up or to do anything but snuggle into that warm pile of dogs, I think I'd have been the happiest person in the universe.

27. Moving On

The finger incident made me think a lot about the

wisdom and the safety of living in a multi-dog, multi-pack house. But we continued to move on with our lives as they were - in service to dogs. No adopters for the three dogs from the Rebound Hounds shelter came through. As long as they had no other good home with kind owners, this would be their home, as long as they needed it.

My doctor finally pulled out the pin in my finger. It was very stiff, but it still worked in concert with the rest of my hand and could be useful again, though not to the same degree.

The fall semester was difficult as I had to teach one-handing drawing classes. The foam cast on my finger was huge and sticking straight out. Even though the injury was on my less dominant hand, it caused me to bump into the student's drawing boards, drop things, and sometimes, forgetting the finger didn't bend at all, poke someone in the back.

When the cast came off permanently, it felt like a triumph to finally have a real, though stubbier, finger to work with.

I'd received dozens of dog bites over my years of working with dogs, but this was my most serious injury. The leg bite looked more dramatic than my finger. It was large, purple and moon-shaped like a shark bite, but it didn't bother me as much in my daily activities as the stiffness in my finger. I could easily cover my leg wound and pretend it wasn't there. Fortunately, it never hurt much at all and didn't have any impact on my ability to walk.

I was back riding my bicycle in the state park on my way home from classes two weeks after leaving the hospital. I felt great, but my finger continued to attract unwanted attention and questions. Sometimes, I told people the truth. Most times I lied, saying that I'd had a violent encounter with a craft knife because often the truth prompted moral outrage and self-righteous judgment. People still asked: how could I let my dog situation get so out of control that a fight occurred that caused such a severe injury? How could I continue to live with a dog that bit and nearly severed my finger and leg? Not asked out loud but underlying were the more painful questions; what was wrong with me? Was I a dog hoarder? A self-abuser? Was I hopelessly needy and unstable?

Some people seemed to feel justified in grilling me about my mental health every time I revealed the true origin of my stubby finger, and how many dogs I had living in my home. But, while the daily tasks associated with running a dog sanctuary are time-consuming and difficult, I feel good about our odd lifestyle and house full of misfit dogs. And, when confronted by an aggressive questioner, I am tempted to ask if they would euthanize their human children for causing an accident that led to an injury?

My husband and I find more comfort in dogs and other animals than humans. Mark can't bear to poison or even trap and relocate the dozens of tiny mice that scamper through our house gathering up the dog biscuit crumbs from the floor. His compassion for animals was the source of my initial attraction to him, and is the bond that keeps our marriage together as we slowly turn into a couple of old codgers.

The finger amputation incident was just one of the random painful things that happen in life. This accident, like other calamitous events, happened arbitrarily - just like my cancer diagnosis a couple of months later. True to my mother's favorite old-fashioned negative maxim, when it rains it pours.

But, all the events of that fall were oddly coincidental. In biting my finger, Prince may have inadvertently saved my life! Every year for the last twenty, I went for a mammogram in late August like clockwork. My mother had breast cancer, and while the exams filled me with anxiety for weeks, I was determined to avoid being taken down by the same disease. This year, my regular schedule was disrupted. I taught a class at the end of the summer and forgot all about the annual mammogram ordeal. I was thinking about making the dreaded annual appointment on the week of the dog bite incident, but the traumatic hospital visit and surgery pushed routine health visits right out of my mind.

In late January, my finger was returning to its new-normal and I started worrying about skipping the yearly mammogram. Since I was due for a physical in a month, I decided to wait until then to schedule it. Fortunately, my doctor was flushed with excitement about a new piece of technology just acquired by her medical group – a 3D mammogram machine. She urged me to try it, saying with reverence, "It's a beautiful machine and a really great diagnostic tool."

She praised the new machine so highly that I couldn't refuse and return to the small clinic I usually went to for my regular digital mammogram. My doctor assured me the new machine reduces the number of the call backs for rescreening that have caused me so much anxiety over the years. If that was true, I was happy to make the change.

A reduction in my anxiety wasn't the result of my encounter with the new machine. Its extreme sensitivity and ability to image thin layers of tissue resulted in the ultimate call back - the one I'd always dreaded.

"It's early. We caught it really early, and it's really a very mild form," my doctors all assured me.

I went through a short-run of radiation and now have a daily medication to take for the next five years. Happily, I was able to skip chemotherapy. I felt very fortunate and grateful to my doctor and to my dog! It sounds bizarre, but if Prince hadn't nearly bitten my finger off, I'd have continued to have my regular mammogram, and it was not effective in detecting my tiny tumor. I would still be living in happy ignorance while a tiny cluster of cells the size of a sesame seed would still be growing inside me until it was large enough to be felt and then be a much worse problem.

I'm not such a Pollyanna that I'd say I'm glad my finger was nearly bitten off. But the timing of the dog bite and the cancer diagnosis was interesting. It was a chain of events that led to a fortunate outcome - an early and treatable detection of my tumor. I didn't have to suffer through the major surgery or the chemotherapy that wore my mother down for years.

My dogs were the best comfort through all of this, and walking them became the daily routine that led to a fast recovery, and got me through the challenges of radiation treatment. When I was depressed or nervous, Dougie could sense something was wrong, and curled up close, placing his solid hefty head on my stomach every evening as I read my dull, but comforting Agatha Christie books for the hundredth time.

The required MRI before surgery was the scariest exam because it would tell more definitively the extent of the rogue cells lurking in my body. During the days leading up to the MRI, there was nothing more comforting than seeing Dougie's orange back stretched across our bed waiting for me to curl around him and absorb his warmth, or to see Hawkins waiting on the couch to curl up and watch some reruns with me.

To my great relief the MRI came back entirely clean and I spent the day celebrating by taking Ricky and Dougie for a walk in the park and then perusing antique stores with my good human friend, Martha. A scary test day was transformed into a lovely day, through the help of good companions.

During my recovery, the local news broke horrific stories about the plight of animals at the local tenant farm from which Sable and Hawkins are refugees. I couldn't believe that so many years after they were rescued, the farm was still filled with starving farm animals and puppy mill dogs. I just couldn't believe it.

There had been so many complaints over the years that I assumed the town government had stepped in and shut the place down. But, it turned out that nothing had been done until a disgusted animal control officer finally went public with the truth. The number of animals there had even grown over the years, and the abuses were worse than ever.

Every day I'd listen to a news story and wonder why there wasn't a petition going around to encourage the state to shut down that horrible farm once and for all, and to press animal abuse charges against the owners and tenants. The situation was more horrific than Harrington's shelter.

I searched online and there was no petition. With a feeling of trepidation and exhaustion, remembering the whole Harrington saga, I decided to draft an online petition myself. I had to do it for Sable and Hawkins.

As soon as I put it out online, the petition website owners latched onto the story and began to promote it widely. I was amazed when it went viral. I thought I'd have, at best, a hundred responses. I planned to print them all out and send them on to local and state representatives, the town board of health and the Attorney General's office. But, owing to strong local media coverage of what has now become known as the Farm of Horrors, the petition zoomed to one thousand signatures in a day, and couple of weeks later it had nearly a quarter of a million signatures and over a hundred pages of outraged commentary.

The most vocal support for the petition came from

pit bull lovers worldwide who were appalled at the abusive puppy breeding practices happening at the farm. Figuring out how to print and mail dozens of copies of the hundred-page petition was much more absorbing and gratifying than thinking about cancer. And, the petition led to new friendships as I joined up with other groups of animal activists from neighboring cities and towns. I even met up with old volunteers from Hidden Falls - friends that I missed and hadn't seen in years. Even Alicia, the former board member from Hand-Me-Down-Cats, and many, many other animal-rescue friends came out to a town meeting to help confront the town board of health at their monthly meeting.

    I found myself getting teary-eyed as I stood outside the town hall on that warm evening with all the wonderful animal-lovers who came out to join forces at that meeting. People were waving signs to passing motorists and calling for the resignations of town officials who had failed to address the Farm of Horrors the first time it was discovered, six years after Sable and Hawkins came to live with me. Television stations from Boston to Providence were at that meeting. And, in spite of a fear of public speaking, I stood up and had my say.

    Nerves took a backseat as I handed the heavy

hundred-page printed copy of the petition to the health board director. In the cover, I'd inserted a photo of pathetic, hairless Sable, from when she was still living at the veterinarian's office. The small town hall was packed, and the animal people had a clear impact on policy. The members of the board of health were clearly stunned by the numbers and energy of the animal-rescue community confronting them.

As a result, the town's bylaws were changed to better protect farm animals and puppy mill dogs, while the perpetrators face criminal charges. We are continuing to work towards better animal breeding and farming practices across the state and nation. The abusive farmers are still fighting the town, but the animal-rights activists are sure we will win. The animals will win.

Some of my friends who are not directly involved with animal activism worry about me getting too stressed out and further damaging my health. But, for me, activism has become an energizer and antidote to both depression and illness. That wild night at the board of health meeting was the first time after radiation treatment that I started to feel a surge of healthy energy and renewed interest in life.

I forgot all about the tightening in my skin and the creeping exhaustion that encouraged me to crawl into bed early in the evening. I felt empowered and knew that I was healthier than I'd been in years. Now, I'm free of cancer and I am moving forward. I'm still afraid of illness, but I won't cringe in fear of it and I won't be disabled by my missing fingertip.

I am no longer afraid of speaking out publically about issues that matter to me. I no longer feel any guilt for what had happened during the Harrington ordeal. I am just relieved that, due to the actions of such a great group of animal loving friends, the dark city shelter of the past no longer exists. Speaking out then made a difference to those voiceless animals and to the people who care about them. Speaking out now about the Farm of Horrors will help more animals.

The farm petition has developed a life of its own and is getting a worldwide response. It gets forwarded regularly through email to state officials and legislators. And many other groups are launching petitions of their own and making an impact. More voices will join the chorus and voice their outrage at other animal abuse cases, until someday people will treat other animals with decency and compassion.

Mark and I decided together that our home will be a sanctuary for dogs that nobody wants, to accept it and enjoy our dog-filled lives. I plan to sit back and spend as many beautiful days as I can taking long walks and snuggling with our current sanctuary dogs; Ricky, Maggie, Sable, Hawkins, Prince, Poirot, Dougie, Billy and Rico. They each have a unique and funny personality. They are a lot of work, but are more than generous in sharing their joy, love, warmth and peace with us. Yes, as my father once predicted, I've become the proverbial crazy neighborhood dog lady. I can live with that.

DISCLAIMER

This is a work of non-fiction. The timing of some events have been changed and some conversations are paraphrased. Names of people, places and organizations have been changed to protect privacy.

ABOUT THE AUTHOR

Lori Bradley-Millstein is a writer, artist and college teacher living in southeastern Massachusetts with her husband and pack of beloved misfit dogs. She has an art studio within a community of artists in an old mill building in New Bedford, Massachusetts and exhibits her artwork nationally. She supports animal rescue and animal rights causes through her non-profit organization, iAnimal.org. She teaches art at Bridgewater State University in Bridgewater, Massachusetts.

www.ingramcontent.com/pod-product-compliance
Lightning Source LLC
Chambersburg PA
CBHW071138300426
44113CB00009B/1008